Praise for
The Worrier's Guide to the End of the World

"Torre's managed to write a witty and engrossing tale of loss, pain, and transformation that captivates the reader as magically as her first book. Like her previous work, I couldn't put it down! I highly recommend it!"

—**Matt Kepnes**, *New York Times* **bestselling author of** *How to Travel the World on $50 a Day*

"Through steps and more than a few missteps, Torre DeRoche opens up her heart on the pages of this soul-searching quest to find tranquility in this crazy and oftentimes maddening world of ours. Brave and honest, DeRoche guides us down a path of 'only having one life—so live it' with thought-provoking insights and laugh-out-loud humor, making the reader feel as if they are walking right beside her. You'll root, scream, and cheer for this lovable heroine as she conquers her world and personal demons one hesitant—and then steady—foot at a time. DeRoche's journey will leave an indelible imprint on your heart."

—**Samantha Vérant**, **author of** *Seven Letters from Paris* **and** *How to Make a French Family*

"Like so many of us, Torre DeRoche is wracked with fear, doubt, uncertainty, anxiety; unlike so many of us, DeRoche figured she might as well walk 250 miles through India. Which she does, with humor, grace, insight, and a fair amount of grit, too, in this lovely and wholly uplifting account of confronting our fears . . . Luckily (and always enviously), in *The Worrier's Guide to the End of the World* we get to tag along."

—**Carl Hoffman**, **bestselling author of** *Savage Harvest*

The Worrier's Guide
to the End of the World

The Worrier's Guide

to the

END OF THE WORLD

Love, Loss, and
Other Catastrophes—
through Italy, India,
and Beyond

Torre DeRoche

SEAL PRESS

Seal Press
Hachette Book Group
1290 Avenue of the Americas, New York, NY 10104
sealpress.com

Printed in the United States of America
First Edition: September 2017

Published by Seal Press, an imprint of Perseus Books, LLC, a subsidiary of Hachette Book Group, Inc.

The publisher is not responsible for websites (or their content) that are not owned by the publisher.

Print book interior design by Jeff Williams

Library of Congress Cataloging-in-Publication Data has been applied for.

ISBNs: 978-1-58005-685-4 (paperback), 978-1-58005-686-1 (e-book)

LSC-C

10 9 8 7 6 5 4 3 2 1

To Mum, for the feathers.

Kilgore Trout once wrote a short story which was a dialogue between two pieces of yeast. They were discussing the possible purposes of life as they ate sugar and suffocated in their own excrement. Because of their limited intelligence, they never came close to guessing that they were making champagne.

—KURT VONNEGUT, *Breakfast of Champions*

Author's Note

Somebody once told me that when two people fall in love, they create, in the overlap between them, an invisible entity made of the sum of their two beings. This third party is nameless and formless, and when the relationship ends, that entity begins to die. What gets mourned is the slow death of that unseen thing as it begins to wisp away into the realm of the forgotten. These entities exist everywhere: between siblings, friends, parent and child, between you and that stranger who stirred you with a warm smile on the train. If you were to count all these invisible entities going about unseen in the world, that would be 7.4 billion to the power of . . . I'm bad with numbers. An unquantifiable shitload.

This story is my best attempt to illuminate an entity that came into being when I met a woman who changed my life. To bring this entity to life, I've crafted dialogue to serve the telling using a combination of verbatim quotes, general recollecting, and fuzzy wine-soaked memories. I should also mention that, during particularly intense moments in life, time has a way of stopping, slowing, speeding up, morphing, or curling around in loop-the-loops, and so there may be inaccuracies with my account of timing here and there. Also, some names have been changed. Otherwise, this is a true story, and the characters and events are real. I have no desire to deceive you with lies; real life is peculiar enough on its own.

Contents

Monsters

WHEN I WAS a kid, I killed everyone I loved in a hundred creative ways. At night, in bed, I would craft tiny horror films in my imagination, casting my sisters, friends, and pets in the leading roles. I spared no gory details of squirting blood and shrill screams of agony when the monsters came. It was awful, but I couldn't help it. I'd count the dead instead of sheep until my eyelids grew heavy, often wet with tears from so much self-inflicted personal tragedy in a single night.

You don't need Sigmund Freud to unravel this psychological snafu: My dad was a horror movie film writer, and death and terror were my family's life as much as rolling hills and fresh air might be to the children of a farmer. But instead of learning to squeeze milk from a cow, we were taught to milk nightmares from our minds.

So skilled at his craft was my dad that Quentin Tarantino, master of depravity, once said: "Almost everything that Everett DeRoche has written is one of my favorite films." They were our favorite films, too, and we were proud to belong to him. Dad's professional accomplishments were displayed all over our home—props and concept sketches, awards and films posters—which meant, in order to go to the bathroom at night, my five sisters and I would have to sneak past giant images of a murderous chimpanzee (*Link*), a killer pig (*Razorback*), a monster in a lake (*Frog Dreaming*), and deranged hospital patient (*Patrick*).

I learned to hold my pee in.

We followed in our father's footsteps and developed macabre fixations of our own, making Dad proud when we'd dress up for Halloween using film biz tricks to get our makeup looking hyper-realistic. One year during my teens I went as a character from a movie I'd been haunted by since age four: Regan from *The Exorcist.* I dressed in a soiled nightgown with sheaths of lacerated skin hanging off my face, lips chapped and oozing. My youngest sister went as a woman who had given herself an abortion with a wire coat hanger, and my mother made a fabulous Lorena Bobbitt in her leopard-skin robe, knife in one hand, severed penis in the other.

We looked striking among all the sexy kittens, sexy lollypops, and sexy witches—so astounding, in fact, that all the sexy things were too scared to talk to us. It's obvious that nobody else knew how to Halloween properly.

We fit in nowhere, but that didn't matter. We were the Brady Bunch meets the Addams Family, tight-knit and lovingly bonded by our morbid interests. As a self-sufficient society of eight, we had each other. We were scared, sure, but we were scared *together,* for fear is powerfully bonding.

Despite all the fun we were having, there were side effects to our lifestyle, and not even my dad was immune to the consequences of his own creations. One time he took us camping in the Australian bush, and sometime in the evening, not long after night had fallen, a loud, guttural snort came from the inky blackness. We all knew what it was: *a giant killer pig!* Spooked by his own cult classic, Dad turned wide-eyed and rushed us inside the camper, locking the door behind us. As an American who had emigrated to Melbourne, he was unfamiliar with the sounds of Australian fauna; in the morning, we worked out that it was not a murderous Razorback but the mating call of a koala.

And so it was that fear became my innate mode of being, and scanning my immediate environment for threats was as natural as breathing. Though I was scared, I wasn't going to take it lying down. You can either run away from the monster or you can run toward it, all guns blazing, and I didn't want to wait around to get eaten. I was going to kick zombie ass or die trying.

In order to survive all the perceived threats, I became a strategist, and at all times of the day, and often into the night, my brain worked at a vast blueprint for my own survival and the protection of people I loved, with branching diagrams to troubleshoot every imaginable catastrophe. It was an epic handbook that I carried inside my brain: *The Worrier's Guide to the End of the World.*

The idea behind it was this: In order to have inner peace, all I needed to do was scan for dangers during every waking hour and then simply anticipate, well in advance, any possible disaster that might befall me, the people I loved, any human or animal in my immediate or far vicinity, and the planet as a whole—and have a complete step-by-step action plan in place ready to go. All I had to do was keep asking myself the same question—*What if? . . .*—so that I could be ready to deal with anything. That way, nobody would ever have to suffer the kinds of blood-squirting, agony-screaming deaths that took place in my imagination.

I was busy.

In cinemas I watched exits instead of films. On planes I watched engines for smoke. In bed I watched shadows for teeth, and in the woods I couldn't see the forest for all the possible murders. Social settings were fraught with dangers, too: What if a drunken person stumbled into the pool and drowned? What if a foldout couch gobbled someone up into its soft and suffocating folds? What if something as benign as a hairdryer slipped and made bath time into an electric Jacuzzi? The only time my mind stopped running through all the What Ifs was when it exhausted itself into sleep.

When I saw the documentary *An Inconvenient Truth* at age twenty-six, my daily worry levels shot up the line graph like Al Gore's carbon emissions diagrams. This was the dawning of the age of very real, very urgent cataclysmic events and the number of beings now in danger tallied up to one . . . two . . . three . . . four . . . five . . . six . . . *seven billion people!* That's not even counting the animals, plants, and bugs. Oh boy. Worry poured into the zeitgeist, and catastrophizing was the new black.

It wasn't until my late twenties that an osteopath introduced the word "anxiety" into my vocabulary to explain why my muscles were locked and causing headaches, and I realized then that perhaps not everyone woke in the morning trembling as if they'd been intravenously over-caffeinated during the night. I had assumed constant face pain from a clamped jaw was a standard symptom of being alive. Doesn't everyone keep their shoulders up around their ears from hypervigilance? Isn't it normal to walk around stiffened like a mannequin in a near-constant state of impending doom, lips pinched into a fake smile at parties, skin waxy with terror?

"No," said the osteopath. "That's not normal."

"Doesn't every thirty-year-old ask her boyfriend to accompany her to the bathroom in the night due to a debilitating fear that Regan from *The Exorcist* is crouching under the bed?"

"Uh, no, I don't believe so."

I sought out more information. Self-help books called it catastrophizing. The doctor called it "generalized anxiety disorder." The psychoanalyst called it "post-traumatic stress disorder." My friends called it "annoying." But these were just fancy names for what I called it: survival. I resented anyone who told me to stop worrying. "Just lie down and die," they might've said. "Just let the monsters eat you."

Worry wasn't a disorder. It was necessary. It kept me safe. It kept everyone safe. It kept everyone safe, until it did nothing for my dad.

Bowel cancer is a highly treatable condition if it's caught early, but Dad's greatest phobia—and the setting of his first hit film—was hospitals. It had been easier for him to ignore his symptoms for ten years than to confront his fear of the gurney, and so, by the time he was forced to address it, the disease had already metastasized throughout his sixty-five-year-old body, scattering his lungs with tumors, his liver, his brilliantly creative brain, sprinkling my dad with the black seeds of death.

As he fell into decline, he could no longer get up the stairs to his own bedroom, and so he slept downstairs in the room I'd had as a child, his six-foot-two frame poking through the wrought-iron bed end like a boy who'd awoken to find himself curiously elongated overnight.

One day, I crawled in alongside him and took his hand in mine. He had giant writer's hands that had supported the family by tapping at keys for forty years, but he'd suffered nerve damage during one of his surgeries and could no longer bend his fingers to type without great difficulty. Of all the changes he was going through, this was one he flatly refused to accept.

"My hand isn't working, and I can't write anymore," he told me, looking into my eyes as though I might be able to troubleshoot this issue in the same way that I sometimes fixed his computer when it froze. This was a problem I couldn't Ctrl+Alt+Del. I was out of ideas. All I had to offer him was a pained expression.

"I'm falling apart," he said, his chin quivering for a moment before his stoic façade came up like a steel gate, signaling the end of our conversation.

How could worry be a disorder? People *are* in danger. The earth *is* in peril. Worry kept me safe, though it couldn't stop the cancer from spreading and it couldn't save my relationship, either.

We'd been together for almost a decade, but a terminal illness in the family will test every relationship you have with a series of brand-new challenges; watching a parent grow more and more ill is a period of grasping, choking, desperate helplessness, set against a backdrop of dullness and stillness and waiting.

"I can't keep waiting," he said. "I need to live my life."

And just like that, I was alone.

✦

When you lose control of everything in your life at once, when up becomes down and down up and everything you knew before stops making sense, there's a universal explosion inside you, a big bang of sorts, and debris goes flying every which way from the core of your solar plexus. You can't see it, of course—nobody can, and so some people, in their attempts to help, might offer, "He wasn't the right one for you anyway," or "You just need lots of 'me' time," or maybe, "Everything happens for a reason." And then there are the wonderful people who bypass all practical advice and go straight for "Here's a tub of ice cream with chunks of butterscotch in it, I'll just leave the spoon right here."

These offerings, though caring, are absurdly nonsensical when the fabric of your reality begins propelling itself outward at detonation velocity from a solar plexus explosion. All the chunks of butterscotch in existence can't stop the obliteration, though it may take many tubs and a tightening of your pants before you acknowledge that fact.

Stuck inside this state of mind, maintaining friendships, working a job, and pursuing passions are not particularly interesting to you anymore, though you may become skilled at operating your body like a puppet, pretending to laugh and care, dabbing thick concealer on the hollow half-moons under your eyes so as not to raise alarm. If people become concerned, they will get on your case, and so you pretend when really you don't give even one teeny ounce of a shit about anything at all, and believe wholeheartedly that you never will again.

From that point on, you have only one task on your to-do list: You have to sit very still and attempt to stop the world from turning with your mind. But despite your efforts, the earth keeps spinning, the sun keeps rising, babies are born and birthdays come and go, the sun falls behind horizons and the climate warms and countries go to war and refugee babies wash up on shores—and there you are: a tiny, powerless speck on a giant blue marble, floating in the empty nothingness.

Another Siberian sinkhole pops off as if to celebrate the New Year: *Hooray!* And all at once it's January again and then February and then March, and this—*this*—is your life now.

And this isn't even as bad as it gets.

✦

It was April. The hospice nurse handed each member of my family a pamphlet with bold lettering that read "So Your Loved One Is Dying"—a rather overstated title, I thought, but I read it anyway.

"The last thing to go is their hearing," the pamphlet read, and so, when the nurse raised her voice to broadcast to everyone in the room, "Your father is now actively dying," I thought: *Shhhh! He can still hear you, lady! Exnay on the deathnay!*

You see, we kind of never told my Dad he was dying. I mean—we all *knew* it was coming, but in our household we didn't use phrases like "You're dying," or, "I'm dying, and I love you," or, "You're dying, and I'll miss you so much when you're gone." Instead, we preferred such sweet sentiments as "What's on TV tonight?" and "That was a really shit movie," and "Russell Crowe might be a dick, but you can't deny he's a great actor."

We'd only ever discussed death in the context of villains and protagonists, jump-scares and compelling third acts, and though death was my dad's professional specialty, dying was twelve kinds of awkward for him. Out of respect for his privacy, we all pretended like everything was normal and that gathering in palliative wards was what we did now as a family, for fun.

We bought snacks from the vending machine and ate cross-legged on the floor while watching television together in strained silence. Whenever a person in the next room would let out a pained moan that sounded like someone was dying—because someone was—one of us would be sure to *cough-cough* over the disturbance, yawn, and pick up a strand of unrelated conversation, like this: "So have they found that missing Malaysian Airlines plane yet?"

You've never experienced an elephant in the room until you've been party to a you're-not-really-dying elephant, let me tell you. Those bastards are enormous.

Weeks before that final day, my dad had been given a dose of morphine that had tackled down his apathetic guard, and in a rare moment of vulnerability, he'd said to me, "I'm afraid that when I close my eyes there will be nothing but black." Here was our one opportunity to have a serious conversation about what death means, to reassure him, to share an emotional outpouring, to talk existentially. It was a big moment. We *never* talked like this. His watery eyes searched mine.

Nervous, I began to ramble something about atoms coming and going and how we're all stardust and how our cells are constantly being regenerated, meaning we've all had particles of Einstein pass through us, and Beethoven, and, unfortunately, a pinch of Hitler, and maybe nothing goes anywhere but swirls around like dust, changing form ad infinitum inside one giant, never-ending quark storm, only we live up close to it so it seems chaotic and senseless, but when you zoom back it's a brilliant gemstone, and . . .

Crickets.

His jaw clack-clacked, which was something he did when he was annoyed. His fluffy white brows stitched with agitation. Perhaps it was too much too soon. Maybe I should've held back on the Hitler part. I always lose people on the Hitler part. The silence was painful. He tried to take a sip of water from the television remote while staring into the middle distance, and I realized he was stoned out of his mind on morphine.

"So have they found that missing Malaysian Airlines plane yet?" I said.

And then all of a sudden there I was clutching "So Your Loved One Is Dying," but there was nothing in the pamphlet pages about missed beats during final conversations. Besides, it was too late for any existential cram studying. Dad's breath rattled, and his eyes tried to flicker open, pushing hard against a cocktail of painkillers that could've knocked out the entire dinosaur epoch. He looked scared.

I held the giant paw of his writer's hand in mine and told him it was okay. But it wasn't okay. *He will never read another story of mine,* I thought. *Who will I tell stories to now? Who will tell me stories?*

"It's okay, Dad," I told him, stroking his hand as he labored for his last gulps of air. "We're all here with you." Sometimes this calmed him, sometimes his thumb stroked back, but mostly he was rigid with fear.

He closed his eyes.

For most of my thirty-three years, I'd been strategizing ways to keep myself safe, to keep loved ones safe, to survive any disaster. But the survival guide was all for nothing. I couldn't save anything: not myself, not other people, not animals or trees or bugs or the world. I too was afraid that when I closed my eyes, there would be nothing but black.

I curled my hand into Dad's paw and felt his warmth begin to evanesce.

Masha

1

WE MET IN a New York bar. It was friendship at first sight.

"You're Torre, right?" she asked. Her eyes lacked the shifty, distracted expression you see on most people at networking functions—they were piercing and alert, as though capturing every detail in the room, every bluff, every whiff of bullshit.

It was at an airline-sponsored event in a classy bar, put on for travel writers, bloggers, and photographers in the hope that free drinks might lead to some favorable hashtags for the airline. A perk of the job. Too many people were crammed into a small, dark space, and the crowd was busy shaking hands and swapping business cards with anything that wasn't bolted down to the floor. The bar was lined with glasses of anesthetizing beverages and bartenders who had been instructed to pour and keep pouring.

So I drank and kept drinking, trying to cleanse my woes with white wine in the way that one might flush out an infected wound with antiseptic.

"Yes, I'm Torre."

She offered her hand. "I'm Masha." She was wearing a pencil skirt that hugged her curves, tall black leather boots or high black heels or something elegant like that, maybe a shirt made of soft and delicate fabric: silk, I'd guess. Or maybe pants and a blouse? Don't ask me. I had a glass of white in both hands.

Knowing her as well as I do now, her caramel-colored hair would've been gathered back into a bun, red lipstick and smoky eyeliner would've made her green eyes pop against the porcelain of her heart-shaped face. Charisma would've been oozing out of her pores to shimmer across her smile. There's not a person in this world that Masha can't charm with her smile.

She'd told me she was planning to walk around the world on a series of pilgrimages, but she didn't look like an adventurer. She looked more like a glamorous New Yorker en route to a meeting with her wedding planner. The mismatch between her aspirations and her appearance was so confusing, I wondered if it was a networking stunt. I pressed her for more details. "So where are you going, exactly?"

"Well, I'll start in Canterbury in the UK and walk through France and Switzerland to reach Italy, and then down to Rome."

"All on foot?"

"Yes, on foot. And then from there my plan is to walk pilgrimages in Turkey, Israel and Palestine, Mount Kilimanjaro, India, Nepal and Tibet, Japan, Australia, Hawaii, Peru, and then the Camino de Santiago to finish it off."

"Holy shit."

She smiled.

"So I guess you're really fit and have all your gear ready?"

"Oh, sure. I'm *super*-organized. I've been working out every single day and have all my high-tech gear laid out, ready to go." Her deadpan expression made her self-deprecation barely detectible, and I eyed her for a lengthy spell before catching on.

"Maybe you should shave off your eyebrows," I said. "They'll cause aerodynamic drag."

"You already know me so well."

We laughed. I went to sip my wine but noticed it was already empty, so I started on the one in my left hand.

"Am I prepared?" she scoffed. "No, that's why I've called my blog 'Unlikely Pilgrim.' I'm not in shape. My bag will be stupidly heavy. I have very little idea of how this is all going to come together. But that's kind of the point, you know? To work it out as I go?"

My skin prickled with inspiration. "And you're doing all this on your own?"

"Mostly. Some friends and family members might come and join me for parts here and there," she said. "My husband is hiking Kilimanjaro with me, but he doesn't really like to travel much so—"

"Wait," I interrupted, "you're married?"

She nodded. "He's not much of a traveler. He runs a bar here in New York, and he's pretty happy just doing his thing."

"I had assumed you were single."

She shrugged. "I want to see the world. He doesn't. He knows it's something I have to do, and we've talked about it a lot. I'll take my year to travel, he'll hang out and do whatever, and then I'll come back to New York once the year ends." She eyed me sideways. "You know, you should come walking with me sometime. Let's keep in touch."

We didn't stay in touch. When I went home my dad died and my relationship ended, and I didn't keep in touch with anyone.

But six months later, by way of a blur of boarded planes, trains, and random left turns, I found myself in Cinque Terre, Italy, for no good reason beyond the fact that, in a series of strange cities and cheap hotels, I could watch the tick of a new clock, hoping time would heal all wounds.

Each morning I would sleep until the noon sun would flood the room with light, and then I would remind myself: *You have legs!* For what a great privilege it is to not only have legs, but arms and a torso and eyes that see things, to have a remarkable

vehicle made of exquisite flesh and sensory feeling with which
to explore the world, to have sunshine and air, to have breath
and a heartbeat, to have—

But your dad is dead . . .

Then I'd roll back over and go to sleep for several more
hours, because I couldn't stand my own asinine attempts at positive thinking.

When I woke, I walked. Along a cliff edge that traces the
Mediterranean, I climbed stairs. The terraces built on the cliff
face looked like colorful Lego blocks that could so easily top-
ple and drop off into the sea—plop, plop, behind which were
stepped green orchards of sweet nectarines, vineyards, and
fields of enormous lemons that pucker and bulge like an old
man's elbow. Their aromatic peels get zested to make limon-
cello, which is probably a deliciously sweet alcoholic beverage,
but I wouldn't know, because sorrow makes everything taste like
armpit. Pasta tasted like armpit; pizza tasted like armpit; salami
tasted like toe jam. If you think it's possible to eat your way out
of grief, I'm telling you it's not, unless you have a fetish for the
taste of damp and fetid places.

From the highest point on the cliff, I looked out over the
water toward the sailboats bobbing on twinkling refractions.
Memories flashed, lucid and sharp, of adventures had, now
lost. Once upon a time, I had lived on a small boat with the
man I loved and we didn't go a single minute without seeing
each other, but after I said goodbye to him at an airport as he
stood holding a ticket to another continent, the length of our
apartness would make up the rest of our lifetimes. All I had
to show for nine years of companionship was a few boxed personal items, half the money we'd saved together, and a published memoir called *Love with a Chance of Drowning*—the story
of our voyage across the Pacific Ocean. Each day I would get
heartfelt emails from readers: "I cried like a baby at the end
of your book," confessed one gay man from New Jersey in a

tender letter. "You've given me hope for my own relationship. I'm so pleased that your story had a happy ending." But page 352 wasn't the ending. It would've been inhumane to reply with anything resembling truth:

Dear Kyle,

Our love? It drowned. It broke apart like the *Titanic*, splitting in two and sinking into freezing waters while violins played and people screamed and fought over who gets a seat in the life raft. I'm terribly sorry.

Torre

Seventy-one percent of the world was now a salty, blue reminder of a failed relationship. It felt personal.

But you have legs!

Oh, go fuck yourself.

I snapped a photo of the blue water and Cinque Terre's cliffs and uploaded it, using social media for one of its most beneficial functions: to give the illusion to others that I had my life together. For two months I'd been floating around Europe, working from my laptop from any random location, hoping that creating the illusion of high spirits would become a reality in time if I simply Photoshopped a layer of golden joy over the top of all images. This is one of the perks of being a traveler with a communications degree, otherwise known as a Digital Nomad. A bum with a laptop. A homeless pixel artist.

As I started down the stairs, my phone pinged with a message. "Torre!" the message read. It was from the woman I vaguely remembered from the New York bar, Masha. "I'm one train stop away from you right now." She had begun her walk around the world and, by coincidence, was only four minutes away by train. "Do you want to meet up?"

My thumbs hovered over the screen.

"I'm sorry, I'm busy." *Delete.*

"Sure, that sounds great!" *Delete.*

"I'm sorry, I'm busy." *Delete.*

"Sure, that sounds great!" The cursor blinked.

I wanted to sink into the inviting depths of my aloneness and go back to bed. Oh, how I wanted to sleep, but I had legs and eyes and a fully functioning torso with which to experience the world. All I lacked was any iota of motivation for anything at all, but I hoped that once my body was in motion, the willingness might catch up.

You have legs!

In a blink, I hit send.

✦

She looked different than when I'd met her in New York: sun-kissed, lean, and radiantly present in the way that people are when they're soaring so close to the edge of danger. She was still more glamorous than your average adventurer, though, in her lipstick and elegant skirt, her blond hair plaited halfway down her back.

We sipped rosé at the edge of the sea in Monterosso al Mare and talked in the company of a blogger friend named Jimmy, who happened to be there, too. It was the day before Masha's thirty-third birthday. "My Jesus birthday," she joked.

For a month she'd been walking from Canterbury in the UK, mostly alone, and was well over the halfway mark on her 1,200-mile journey to Rome. By the slow and steady vehicle of her own two feet, she'd passed through the entire width of France to reach Italy, camping out in the wild or else sleeping in convents or hostels along the way.

"Do you ever get lost?" I asked.

"I climbed up the wrong mountain in the Alps once," she laughed. "I didn't realize until I'd reached the top that I'd taken a wrong turn at the bottom of the mountain. Eventually I found the right path once I climbed back down, so it was fine."

I was impressed. Her stories were captivating. What I found most inspiring was that she had the courage to embark on such a huge adventure alone, because in any given horror story, a woman who ventures into woods on her own is 100 percent guaranteed to get picked off by some kind of monster.

"How do you cope with all the dangers? Wild dogs? Snakes? Rapists?"

She shrugged. "They're out there, I guess, and they're terrifying."

I gave her a beat to elaborate, to end that grim declaration with some kind of cliché, like "You're more likely to get killed in a car accident on your way to work," but she didn't. She left her statement dangling in grim reality. In my early teens, a brawny boy had chased me along a wilderness trail, yelling obscene demands at me in a rumbling howl, but I escaped because I was nimble and speedy, and nobody could compete with my levels of adrenaline. If there were an Olympic sport for outrunning sexual predators, I'd be modeling for TAG Heuer billboards by now.

"One time," Masha said, "my cousin was walking with me and a wild dog came out of nowhere and lunged at her legs. In the blink of an eye, she flicked up her walking stick behind her and knocked the dog off the edge of an embankment."

I gulped. "What happened to the dog?"

She shrugged, unbothered. "It went rolling down the hill."

"That's . . . truly awful. Have you seen any snakes?"

At this, she turned chalky white, covered her mouth, and looked like she was going to retch. "Torre, I can't even talk about them. I just can't."

"I'm sorry, but you're walking around the world and I thought—"

"No," she said, through a mouth covered with both hands. "Just no."

Who walks around the world with a snake phobia? And how on earth had she made her way across the entire width of France with such a profound fear? Just as I had been on that night in New York, I was intrigued by this paradox of a woman. She really was an unlikely pilgrim.

"You should come walking with me for a day or two, Torre. It's so beautiful. The mountains, the vineyards, the people you meet along the way . . . It's just incredible. The Via Francigena is known as the 'Way of the Heart.' This pilgrimage is supposed to help you learn to follow your intuition."

"My intuition is currently saying: Walk off cliff, don't look back."

She laughed at my black humor, and I loved her for that. Perhaps the worst part about grief is not the sensation itself— the weight of sand in guts, the sluggishness of pushing against thick mud to do even the smallest tasks—but the fact that your very presence terrifies most people. "Negaphobia," says writing mentor Robert McKee, "is the fear of all things negative. People are afraid of expressing the darkness within them, of pointing out the darkness they see in society and in human nature." We live in the era of positive thinking and our culture of negaphobia isn't so great at knowing what to do with sad people. We try to make them laugh, get them to turn that frown upside down, or else tell them: Do not pass Go, do not collect $200, go straight on antidepressants. To be openly sad is to be a poop on everyone else's rainbow.

Masha showed no signs of negaphobia. "The pilgrimage goes all the way to Rome," she continued, "and will take three or four weeks, but you can just join me for a day. Or you can walk all the way to Rome with me if you like."

"Dooo eeett," said Jimmy.

"Dooo eeett," said Masha.

There were three weeks left before my return flight, which meant I had twenty-one days to prepare for starting life over from scratch on my own. All I wanted to do was sleep. How could I find the energy to walk all day with a stranger?

"You know what?" I pounded my fist on the table in triumphant non-commitment. "Maybe!"

We sipped our rosé and looked out at the Mediterranean Sea, where sailboats bobbed on sparkling refractions. My legs twitched, eager for adventure, to know their own strength and aliveness. Something odd stirred in my belly. Wanderlust? Inspiration? Hope? It had been a long time since I'd felt such light emotions.

But I had too much luggage: clothes and shoes, books and watercolor paints, a laptop and a camera. No hiking gear to speak of. Possibility morphed into worry as I began to ramble: "What if my shoes aren't appropriate? What if I can't find a place to store my luggage? What if it rains? I don't have a rain jacket. What if? . . ."

Masha's smile was gentle as she waited for me to finish my string of What Ifs, and then she shrugged and said, "I'm sure you'll work all that out. I set out again in two days. Have a think about it, DeRoche."

2

THAT EVENING I sat in bed in my tiny hotel room, listening to the rattle of trains as they roared past the station outside, staring at the glow of my laptop screen. I had formed a bad habit of waiting until the eleventh hour to decide where I was going next, booking trains and accommodation at midnight before rising early to drag my suitcase to another European country where I'd arrive, sleep-deprived and disoriented. Making plans in advance means knowing where you're going and why, and I didn't know those details. I didn't care. I just wanted to be anywhere other than *here*.

Despite what we might believe, the people we turn out to be and the lives we come to live out—good or bad—aren't reached through careful planning, but at the intersection of chance. Sometimes it comes down to where we're born, whom we're born to, and the luck of the draw, and then other times, it reaches back to one single decision you made in your past when you were too naïve to know where that choice would take you.

When I was twenty-four, an unexpected check came in the mail for overpaid taxes. It was enough money to buy something that I couldn't otherwise afford: a new sofa, an instrument, a down payment on a car . . . I sat with the fluttering stir of possibility for months until I worked out what I most wanted.

A new life. The money could buy me a flight to the opposite side of the world, and there, in San Francisco, I decided I would live for one year outside my comfort zone, and then return home as a new and improved version of myself. It was such a terrifying prospect to leave everything familiar behind to find a new job, home, and friends, but I hoped that taking on such a daring feat might shock me out of my anxiety. I was tired of living in depression and a state of chronic fear. Travel is nothing if not an opportunity to transform.

How simple it was to click "Book ticket" and then find myself standing in front of the Golden Gate Bridge. The surge of euphoria I felt once I got a job, a house, and new friends was addictive. I had done it. I'd leapt. I'd become a new person: a time-traveled, world-traveled woman, with toned muscles and wild hair full of kinks and coils. I felt beautiful and assured in a way that I hadn't before, adaptable and resourceful and ready to kick ass in a zombie apocalypse.

There was a problem, though. The same old worry would come back if I stayed in one place for too long. A rolling stone gathers no moss, and I knew that if I went home, the anxiety would come back. The only option, therefore, was to keep on moving, and so I met a man who loved to travel and together that is what we did.

"Book ticket."

Another simple click.

"Book ticket."

Another.

One passport stamp led to another, and another, until it was our entire way of life. We built our home high up in the clouds, in a delicate nest woven from adventure and shared experiences. Through writing, blogging, and design I turned travel into a paying profession, and not one day went by when I didn't marvel at how easy it all seemed.

Travel can make you feel invincible, as if you're inhabiting the off beats between everyone else's rhythm, as if you're cheating the rules of adult life. We were bypassing electricity bills and mortgages, car payments and obligations. We held a secret that few others knew: Life on the road is cheaper than life in a city. It costs half as much, or even less. We were citizens of nowhere— by design.

Throughout our years together, we explored the world in thrilling ways and weathered actual storms in actual boats, but never any major metaphorical ones. He was a strong leader and an adventurer who had what I most wanted—fearlessness—and, hoping to catch it from him by exposure to his pursuits, I'd spent the earliest two years of those nine living with him on a boat, sailing the seas despite my dizzying fear of deep water.

But among the exhilaration of our ever-changing surroundings was a single niggling memory: home. On the other side of the world, my nieces and nephews were growing taller by the day. My sisters were living out their lives without me there. Friends were getting married, having babies. My parents were aging. I worried that my dad looked unwell, though he hadn't yet been diagnosed. One time, while visiting home, my four-year-old niece said to me, "What is your name again?" and it was then that I learned the true cost of being nomadic: relationships.

"I think I want to go home," I said one day. In the past, all we'd had to worry about was making flights, finding accommodations, or keeping the boat from sinking in tropical waters, but now we were faced with a very un-exotic problem: a clash of values. He wanted to travel and keep traveling, but when my dad was diagnosed with cancer, my verb became more urgent. "I *need* to go home now."

He didn't.

And that was the fracture that broke us.

When I'd first set off traveling at age twenty-four, I'd left behind a square-shaped hole that I always assumed I could slot right back into, but after my dad died, home didn't feel the same as it had before. I wasn't sure where home was anymore. I felt more disoriented in my suburban hometown of Mount Eliza than I did on a chicken bus in Nepal.

"It's the weirdest thing," I said to my mum over the phone one day, trying to hide the tremble in my voice. "I can't remember how to get around the city anymore." On a visit to see my sister, I'd driven to the wrong house—the one my sister had lived in fifteen years beforehand. The most basic details about navigating my hometown eluded me, like what freeway exit led to where, or, sometimes, which side of the road I was meant to drive on. It's as though all the files relating to my life before travel had spilled out on the floor and slid every which way, before being stuffed haphazardly back into the cabinet of my mind.

I tried, I really tried—I put up with this rising panic for many months and told nobody, for how do you articulate the pervading feeling of homelessness to people who have never left their hometown? How do you explain to these people that, while you're terrible at regular adult responsibilities—home-making, scheduling, consistency—you're truly exceptional when it comes to hacking cheap flights, stopping a boat from sinking mid-Pacific, kick-starting a cold SR400, or compressing the entire inventory of your life into carry-on proportions?

Sometimes I'd get in my car and drive to nowhere. Behind the wheel, with a paper map on the passenger seat, I'd come back to myself. Music loud, window down, giant sunglasses on, and hair swaying like tendrils of submerged seaweed. Fit to fight zombies. But with nowhere to go in my tired old hometown, I'd only end up looping around suburban streets before finding a random stop, like a roadside fruit stand, where, just for something to do, I'd buy overpriced blueberries that would only end up swelling and weeping alongside me in the car.

You see, it always happens in a microsecond, almost without conscious effort. A mere twitch of your index finger and your life is carried off in a brand-new direction.

"Book ticket."

Click.

And then comes the flood of release, the nervous energy, the exhilaration, but also a formless guilt that feels like you're stealing something from someone you love, but you're not really sure what, or from whom.

"I'm going to Barcelona," I told my mother. It had been two months since my dad's funeral. I didn't want to leave her, but I didn't know how to stay.

"You're off traveling again?" Mum said. "When?"

"In one week."

"That's great," she said, supportive as always. "You'll have a great time, I'm sure."

"I'm sorry, Mum."

"Don't be sorry. I know you need to do this."

She was right. I needed to tap along to the familiar rhythm of a night train gliding along tracks to a new destination. At age thirty-four, it was the only tune I'd really learned. My heart held the beat. I needed to smell the warm, damp perfume of a new country or the sound of a foreign word pressing through my lips. Hola. Bonjour. Buongiorno. The language itself didn't matter one bit—Spanish, Hindi, Vietnamese—though a string of clichés off the top of my head ("Gaudí's architecture"/"The tapas"/"To learn Spanish") convinced everyone I told that Barcelona was a precise choice and not just a destination that presented near the top of the drop-down menu on a booking website.

Barcelona. A place to feel at home by way of never having belonged there before. In narrow streets with cobblestone

roads that opened out into courtyards of people smoking cigarettes, drinking cafés con leche, I could know myself once
more: fit to fight zombies.

Barcelona to Paris, Paris to Cinque Terre, Cinque Terre
to . . . what did it matter? The only place I had learned to feel
at peace was midair, leaping toward the unknown, but if I kept
this up my mother would age and my sisters would change and
nieces and nephews would turn into adults—without me.

A train roared by my room, rattling the paintings and pulling me back to my laptop. I opened a new browser window and
typed in the title of Masha's blog, "Unlikely Pilgrim." Her kind
eyes met mine through the screen as I read her words:

> A pilgrim is anyone who sees every day, every chance meet-
> ing, and every disappointment as an opportunity to be a
> better human being . . . A pilgrim is a traveler who walks
> the planet with intention and curiosity in order to gain a
> better understanding of themselves and others. Honestly,
> I think there's a little pilgrim in all of us.

I was intrigued by her story, but it was the last sentence I
read that got me:

> I really, really enjoy my life, and I will make you enjoy yours
> too, whether you like it or not.

I curled my fingers over the keyboard and wrote to Masha:
"Count me in."

3

At a tourist store in Milan's train station, I bought a white cap that said MILANO in red and green embroidery, a tube of sunscreen, and a travel-sized moisturizer and shampoo. I stuffed it all into a small rucksack along with a change of clothes, toothbrush and paste, a comb, a phone, my purse and passport, and a focaccia that tasted like oregano and sea salt–seasoned armpit. I rolled my large suitcase through the station and left it in storage for a cheap daily fee. My belongings now weighed only ten pounds, the tiny mass of a lapdog.

I stood in the middle of the train station chewing my lip, wondering if I'd forgotten anything. People usually spend months preparing for a long walking pilgrimage—making plans, writing gear lists, purchasing specialized equipment, training their bodies—and I'd thrown a plan and a backpack together in half an hour. I worried that this might be one impulsive adventure too far, but since thirty-four years of planning around every What If hadn't been able to prevent disaster after all, I decided it was time to throw out *The Worrier's Guide to the End of the World* and experiment with postponing all catastrophizing to the event of an actual catastrophe.

Though trying to dismiss each and every What If with "Don't worry!" is as ineffective as telling a cow not to moo, I could let them have their say and then gently respond with: *I'll figure that out when the time comes,* like this:

What if I don't have all the right equipment for a pilgrimage?
I'll figure that out when the time comes.

Easy. To pull this off, all you need is the trust that you'll have the composure, intuition, and resourcefulness to bail yourself out on the spot if or when something bad should happen—that you won't falter and become frazzled or catatonic.

I did not have those traits.

I planned on figuring that out later, too.

With a lightened load, I felt effervescent and springy-limbed in my denim shorts, a striped T-shirt, and cheap street shoes. "To hell with expensive hiking gear," I declared to nobody, pumping a determined fist in the air. "I have a new friend! I have legs! Two working legs! I get to explore the world with my own two feet!"

✦

Three days later, I was crippled.

As it turns out, walking long distances in flimsy street shoes is the sport of morons. A day of walking had become two, two had become three, and three had become a serious athletic undertaking worthy of decent orthopedic footwear. While I had a strong inkling of this fact after only five miles, I'd hoped the nagging ache was just a standard symptom of athletic fortitude. *Ignore it and it will go away,* I told myself, and when my foot ballooned to a deformed hoof in a shade of angry red, I tried willing myself with: *Ignore it harder!* No luck.

Forty miles later, it was time to confess the truth to Masha. "I can't walk anymore."

"Are you sure?"

"It feels like a knife twisting into bone on each step."

"That doesn't sound good."

"My tendon is really swollen, see?"

She bent down to inspect my ankle.

"I think it's tendonitis."

"Oh," she said, looking crestfallen.

We stood in the city center of Piacenza in heavy-hearted silence. Sweaty and disheveled, we looked out of place in this dot on the map between Bologna and Milan. Piacenza, a name that translates to "A pleasant abode," seemed too enchanting to be real, like a film set for an adorable fable about widowed Italians who'd find each other after colliding on their bicycles and bonding over spilled vegetables—"Oh! Mi scusi, bella!"

I looked down at the swollen flesh bulging from the side of my shoe. It was almost twice its normal size. Letting my injury get this bad was careless, but the conversation with Masha had been too good to leave, the scenery too beautiful with its flat stretches of farms, tomatoes red and ripe, the dusty pink sunsets with the blue Tuscan Apennine Mountains in the distance.

She had given me her walking poles to use, which I leaned on like crutches. "I don't want to hold you up, Masha," I said, guilty over the fact that, in order to get by, I was already stealing her equipment.

She chewed her lip. "Here's what I think we should do: Let's find a hotel, you can get some rest, and hopefully it will be healed by the morning."

I nodded and gave her a vague smile, but I knew that wasn't going to be enough time to solve this. According to a Google search, three to five weeks of bed rest is the recommended time for tendonitis, in order to avoid permanent damage.

We had a problem.

Masha was on a strict schedule—she was walking the world, after all, meaning we had only one spare day in the schedule for healing, not entire weeks. That left only one option:

1. This can't happen.

"I'll definitely be fine by tomorrow," I said, but that was just big talk. To begin with, there was my lame foot, but then there was also the issue of footwear. Flimsy fabric street shoes with flat soles and no ankle support had gotten me into this mess. I needed better shoes. Also, I needed walking poles to help ease the weight on my feet, and I had no rain jacket and nothing warm should the weather change. But where would I find hiking gear? I wasn't properly equipped for a long pilgrimage. *I'll figure that out when the time comes* was no longer an option—the time was *now*.

"Masha," I said, "you can just go on without me. I don't want to hold you up. I can stay here until I'm a bit better and then catch a train back to Milan. I'll be fine." That was a lie. I had no idea how I'd get around by myself with this injury.

She frowned and said, "Let's just sleep on it and see what happens, okay?"

We found a budget hotel within hopping distance, and I collapsed onto the bed, sinking into my disappointment. My What Ifs were right. Maybe I can't always *figure that out later*. Maybe my new mantra was a dud.

✦

Masha went on a food and medicine run and came back with gelato, wine, a baguette, prosciutto, white anchovies, ibuprofen, and two bags of frozen peas. She wrapped the peas in a white hotel towel and placed the package on my foot, and with my leg up on a chair, we sat at a table in our dingy hotel room eating, laughing, and waiting.

With one hand I held peas to my ankle, and with the other I sipped Chianti. "What would I do without you?"

"Well, for starters, you'd still be able to walk."

"A fair point, but it was worth it. You know, the last time I remember having this much fun was three years ago, before my dad was diagnosed with cancer and everything started to unravel."

"Aw, dead dad," she said. "Every time you mention your dad, I'm going to give you a hug from now on. A dead dad hug." She wrapped her arms around me and pulled me into the squish of a good hug.

Masha was a realist, and I liked that about her. Most people I know are optimists who keep on the sunny side of life, but optimists, though infectiously happy, don't always know how to handle people who are in grief. In an attempt to pull you back into the sunshine, they might try to put a positive spin on a negative situation, saying something like: "It's awful that you've lost two people, but just think of all the spare time you have now! How exciting is that!" And while their intentions are good, this approach doesn't give people any space to be sad when they need to be sad. Pessimists can make excellent companions in dark times, confirming that yes, life can suck, and yes, you've got the god-given right to be sad, but because misery loves company, the relationship can turn toxic as you feed each other's pessimism in a loop. That's where the realists come in. As lovers of truth, they acknowledge the world for what it is—a complex blend of positives and negatives—and they won't try to bullshit you with platitudes. It takes courage to be a realist. Masha had that courage.

She topped up our glasses with a generous slosh of wine, spilling red onto the tablecloth in the process. That made me laugh, which made my elbow lurch, which made a jar of oily anchovies spill, soiling the tablecloth once again. Hysterical, we clutched our stomachs and doubled over, and when Masha opened the saltshaker and poured a large white mountain of salt over the stains, only to knock the mountain onto the floor by mistake, we almost died from lack of oxygen.

"Torre, can you please get better soon?" Masha said between gasps for air. "I don't want you to go. I don't want to stop laughing like this."

"Me either."

"It feels like this is meant to be. We're like twins."

"Two terrified twins."

"All this time I thought it was a growth on my body with eyes, but it was you, my precious conjoined sister."

"Fine, I'll be the growth. The growth doesn't have to make any decisions."

We laughed, but a tiny part of my brain wondered if she was a figment of my imagination, created from thin air so that I wouldn't have to be alone anymore. An imaginary friend. Sometimes, while talking to her, it seemed as if I was talking to myself, because our viewpoints were so similar, our jokes so identically depraved. We'd known each other only days and yet we could already finish each other's sentences, like a pair of corny lovers, sans romance. The fact that this pilgrim showed up four minutes away by train to say "Come walking with me," at a time when the only function I could bring myself to do was walk, was certainly odd.

I reached out and poked Masha in the flesh of her arm. Real.

"What?" she said.

"Nothing."

"I've been thinking . . . " She thought for a beat, doing silent calculations on her fingers. "I can stay here two more nights. I don't think you're going to get better overnight. Two more nights, but if I don't get going by then, I won't be able to finish my pilgrimage on time."

"Are you sure?"

She looked unsure. "My dad is flying from New York to meet me in Turkey—we're going to do a pilgrimage there together. I'm already a bit behind schedule, and to get to Rome on time to make my flight to Turkey, I'll need to walk a few fifty-kilometer days, which I don't really want to have to do. Those days are painful. That's when I lose my toenails and when my joints start to experiment with bending the wrong way. Any extra days we spend here will mean extra miles I'll need to divvy up and tack onto the days I have left to get to Rome. But let's give it two days. I can afford two more days. Okay?"

But what if I don't heal in two days?

What if I'm only holding Masha up?

What if I get stuck here alone with an injury?

"I'll figure that out when the time comes."

"Huh?"

"I mean, yes, okay. That would be really great. Thank you."

✦

In the tiny sink of our hotel, I washed my clothes with a bar of laundry soap, greying the water with grit as I did every evening when I soaped up my hiking clothes. Finding a place to dry it all was a challenge, but we opened the window shutters and stuffed our squeeze-dried shirts, pants, and underwear between the dusty slats of wood, dripping water below onto the street. What we both lacked in grace we made up for in resourcefulness.

I peered out the window and onto the street below. The light in Italy has a yellow tone to it that I'd always thought, when looking at photographs or movies, had been added in post-production, but it really is soft and golden, and everything and everyone beamed with a summery glow.

"Masha, look!" I urged her over to the window.

She got up off her bed to peer out.

Blinking, I said, "There's a hiking shop right across the street."

I blinked two more times. Still real. Directly across from us was an outdoor store with hiking shoes propped in the window. *Buy us, Torre,* they beckoned, *let us make you more comfortable.* "Isn't that amazing?" I said. "I could throw a stone and hit a new pair of shoes from here. What a coincidence."

"There are no coincidences on a pilgrimage," Masha stated with firm conviction. "It's a sign."

I raised an eyebrow at her. This woman carried a worn copy of *The Alchemist* in her backpack and read passages to herself every day. I wondered if she'd fallen down the rabbit hole of delusional thinking, but I had too much respect for her and what she was undertaking to dismiss her ideas, naïve or not. She had no guidebook or paper maps—only her phone—and often no plan for where she'd spend her next night, and yet she'd managed to cross the entire width of France and a good portion of Italy by doing a backward tumble into a trust game with the universe.

"Treat every encounter and event like it's supposed to happen, good or bad," Masha instructed me. "Look out for signs, patterns, messages. They will guide you and show you the path you should be taking and the lessons you need to learn to get there. Everything happens for a reason."

It was then that I worked out the source of Masha's impressive resilience. According to her set of beliefs, she was being led by divine intervention, and even if the worst should occur, it was, according to her, an important part of the overarching script in the story of one's life. Her religion was alchemy. The universe was providing.

I was intrigued, but unconvinced.

Each time we'd spotted repetitions of the same number, Masha would call attention to it: "See? It's that same number again. It's a sign." And whenever people had shown up in the middle of nowhere at the precise moment we'd found ourselves lost, Masha had called that "a sign," too, like the time a random woman who didn't speak a lick of English had intuited we were lost and had beckoned us to follow her as she rolled up her pants, walked us through a river, along the banks, through someone's backyard, and out the front gate onto the street, where she pointed us down the road and back onto our path. We'd been lost for barely ten minutes.

"This always happens," Masha had said with a nonchalant shrug as the woman walked away. "It's the magic of a pilgrimage. Everything happens exactly when it needs to."

The word "magic" made me flinch, yet after days of walking through farmlands and villages and not even seeing a corner store, getting KO'd thirty feet away from a solution was certainly fortuitous. Maybe the storeowner was shrewd at estimating, down to the square inch, the miles-traveled-to-injuries-gained ratio on the Via Francigena, and had plopped his store down in a tendonitis hotspot. After all, we were on a walking path to Rome built in the Middle Ages, first documented in the year 867; there'd been plenty of time to perfect opportunistic business tactics.

The next morning I hopped over and asked for some shoes in my size. They had a single pair left—a perfect fit with proper support. I bought a rain jacket, a thermal fleece, hiking pants that could be zipped off at the knee to become the world's ugliest shorts, and walking poles to ease the load on my ankle. I pulled off all the tags and threw out the receipts, and then propped my gear in the corner of our hotel room as an incentive.

A friend of mine who worked in brain injury rehabilitation, named Tim, once told me a story about a patient of his who'd had a severe stroke. The patient, permanently bedbound by his condition, was a seventy-year-old Australian cattle farmer who was so stubborn, he flatly refused to participate in any rehab exercises. His body was atrophying. Inactivity would be a death sentence.

To charm the sedentary farmer into motion, Tim decided to call on the help of the farmer's one true passion. He bought a bottle of expensive whiskey and poured a dash into a small glass, which he placed at the opposite corner of the farmer's house. Tim was a hardened old Dutch man and a maverick in his alternative therapy techniques, and pity was not in his emotional repertoire. He was firmly unwilling to relate to anyone as a help-less victim, so instead of gentle words, Tim told the man: "Get your bloodyfucking ass out of bed and go have a sip of whiskey, you bastard!"

The farmer got crawling. Between bed and whiskey the man shimmied each day, accidently participating in exercise therapy en route to his beverage. But the crawling, once mastered, needed to progress into walking, so Tim moved the bottle of whiskey down the street to the neighbor's house, gave the farmer a cane, and yelled at him to go get a taste of the bloody-motherfucking whiskey again. On shaky legs, the old farmer would shuffle a whole mile to his neighbor's house for a nip of golden nectar, and a mile back to bed. *Oops!*—more therapy.

After months of this, the farmer got strong, but he was still dependent on the cane and refused to walk without it. And so one day, en route to the neighbor's house, Tim kicked the cane out from underneath the old man mid-stride, and when he didn't fall over, Tim said, "See? You don't need that bloody-fucking thing anymore, do you?" The cane was confiscated. The man walked on. By the end of rehab, the old cattle farmer could ride a horse again. Tim's experimental Whiskey Method was a success.

And while my circumstances were much different, and crawling out of bed toward my hiking gear would only worsen the injury, incentives are powerful motivators. I hoped that the new hiking gear propped up on display in the corner of the room would stop me from falling into defeat and charm my body into healing faster.

The following morning, my foot was no less swollen and bruised. Masha went back into the town center to buy Epsom salts from the pharmacy to help relax my tendons, but came back with a box of something for "Traspirazione eccessiva" that smelled like a heavily perfumed old lady had curled up and died in a box of talcum powder.

"I don't think these are Epsom salts," I said, but still I mixed the salts with hot water in a cooking pot and submerged my useless hoof.

"You'll never guess what I saw in town," said Masha, her eyes alight after returning from an excursion around Piacenza. "I went to the city's Duomo, the cathedral, and inside a glass box they have an old priest."

"Huh?"

"Shhh. Listen to me; listen. This is really important, Torre. There was this glass box with a body inside it, dressed to the nines. Whoever's in there is wearing gauzy gloves, and I think you can see his finger bones." She was giddy with excitement. "It's hard to tell for sure, but I think . . . I mean, I'm pretty sure that . . . Torre, I think it's an actual dead guy."

My eyes widened. "Oooooh, really?"

She nodded, beaming with delight. "When you're able to walk again, you'll have to come and see him with me."

Bang. She'd found my whiskey. I *had* to see the dead guy.

4

"How about we try meditating on this?" said Masha. "We can visualize your healing."

Her suggestions were heartwarming, but trying to fix a physical condition with good thoughts seemed a little non compos mentis. As appealing as new age fluff can be with all its quick-fix promises, I tend to err on the side of science, observation, and measurable knowledge. My dad, the hippy, occultist, and conspiracy theorist, once claimed to have meditated a nasty wart off his foot by visualizing it inside a white bubble of light, and for general health he drank milkshakes each morning containing two raw eggs and a banana so ripe it was black and oozing. Open to the possibility that he might've been onto something, I watched with curiosity as he ate spoonfuls of vitamin C as a cure for everything, including a range of symptoms he endured for ten years, later diagnosed as a blossoming cancerous tumor. Though science is a long way from perfect, there is something to be said for its repeatability.

However, you can't knock it 'til you've tried it, and visualizing my own healing could be no less pointless than treating my foot with deodorizer and herb cream, so I said, "Sure, let's do it!"

I lay down in bed, closed my eyes, and focused on the meditation music. Singing bowls hummed and a soprano voice sang a soothing tune as I did my best to suspend all preconceptions. *Let go, let go, shut your face,* I told my inner skeptic.

The yellow light of Piacenza filtered into the windows and through my eyelids, and I could hear the sounds from below: the rubbery tick of bike tires on bluestones, muffled conversations, coffee cups bumping saucers. *Let go, let go . . .*

It got weird.

I was standing in a desert oasis where the sand was corrugated by the wind. In front of me was a tall pyramid made of glass, its peak etched with an Egyptian hieroglyphic of an eye with a tear-like curlicue stemming from beneath it. A set of stairs led into the structure, and I walked up, pulling the fabric of my white gown behind me until I was standing in the middle of an airy interior made of glass as clear as crystal.

Where am I? I wondered.

The temple of healing, came the answer. *You have five chances in your lifetime to ask for restored health.*

I stirred, wanting to call bullshit on the whole vision.

Be quiet, shut up, let go . . .

Maybe it would've been wise to save up my tokens for something more serious than a case of common tendonitis, but that's why I'd come here, after all. I asked for health, and a warm wind blew in off the sand, tracing my skin and making the fabric of my skirt dance.

The music had stopped. The heat of the desert wind faded from my skin until I was back inside the hotel room. I cracked my eyes open, unable to tell if I'd been gone for minutes or hours. The clock told me it was forty minutes.

"I just had the weirdest dream," I said, describing the scene to Masha. We went online to look up the curly eye I'd seen etched in the peak of the glass pyramid.

"It's called the Eye of Horus," I said, clicking on an icon identical to the one I'd seen in the dream, and I read the description aloud. "It's an Egyptian symbol of healing, restoration, and protection. How weird, right?"

"I think the visualizing is working," Masha said, looking remarkably less baffled than me. I snorted because I still believed it was new age fluff, yet my skin was crawling with the heebie-jeebies from being caught unawares.

✦

"How's the foot?" Masha asked in the early morning of day three in the hotel. It was the final deadline: Get walking or quit. As far as injuries go, this was a pretty unimpressive one to get knocked out by. A broken femur, fine—defeat accepted—but a common case of tendonitis? Seriously? That was like dropping out of the Olympics due to an ingrown hair. No way. I couldn't go home. I needed to walk again. Especially since Masha had told me she'd heard rumors of Via Francigena pilgrims, upon reaching Rome, getting ushered into a secret room at the Vatican. There, I imagined being handed a tea-stained scroll with a better survival guide than the one I'd written myself:

Dear Torre,

I'd like to formally congratulate you for walking this epic distance for no good reason apart from a clichéd thirtysomething personal crisis. You know, people are dying of starvation and polar bears are drowning and it's really getting quite urgent, so . . . ugh, never mind, we won't go into all that right now.

Anyway, I understand you're not religious and have no intentions of buying into any "Jesus-y" answers to your concerns, and that's totally fine. You will find what you need written at the bottom of this letter in 140 characters, so that you can Tweet it later. No more worrying from now on!

Yours,

The Pope

I got up and walked around our room, bouncing on my legs to test the equipment. "I think it's healed!" I cried, dancing on the spot. "Oh, wait, no . . . " A tug of pain. "There it is. *Ouch.*" I tumbled back onto the bed and shook my head at her in despair. Our time together had run out.

She came and sat down beside me on the bed, but I couldn't look up at her; I was busy trying hard not to get upset. My chin puckered, betraying me.

There was the real world *outside*, and then there was the bubble we'd been living in together, full of over-sharing, ad hoc therapy, irreverent joking, and silly humor—and when you're walking through Italy, the opportunities for silly humor are endless, because every second sculpture has its own set of marble or bronze dick and balls. If you have the sense of humor of a twelve-year-old boy, I can assure you it's hilarious.

"You really can't walk on it at all, huh?" she said, stroking my arm.

"No, but I can hop like a total champion."

Her eyes turned pink. "Do you need more frozen peas?"

I shook my head again.

"A glass of wine?"

"It's eight in the morning."

"And your point is what, exactly? . . ."

I giggled, and then melancholy settled over the room. Outside the window shutters, bike spokes went *tick-tick* and cups tinked against saucers in cafés. Down the street, through the arteries of ancient alleyways, food sat in trattorias on checkered tablecloths, waiting for us to taste it, and behind the town, in the

Tuscan mountains, verdant forests of trees waited to enchant us. Long roads through wide-open spaces trembled to feel the pad of our shoes, and the Pope waited with his scroll of profound secrets. There was wine to be tasted. I had shoes. I had the willingness. But I no longer had two working legs with which to explore the world.

I looked around our tired hotel room. There were piles of towels in the corner soaked in pea juice, laundry hanging from shutters, hiking shoes tossed in corners, anchovy oil and wine on the tablecloth, salt all over the floor . . . My new hiking gear rested against the wall, waiting to be worn. There had to be a workable solution to this, but what was it?

"You know," Masha said, "I'm thinking . . . if I have to walk a few more fifty-kilometer days . . . "

"Yes?"

" . . . to finish the pilgrimage in time . . . "

"YES?"

"I've already lost enough toenails, so what's a few more?"

"So you're staying?"

"One more day. That's literally all I have to spare. Maybe we can work out a plan in twenty-four hours."

Out of relief, I burst into tears, surprising us both. Her eyes started to spill over too, and we wept together on the bed.

"Why are we crying?" she said, her chin shaking.

"Caffeine withdrawal?"

✦

On a sore ankle, I was able to limp from our hotel to a café two blocks away, where the locals were sitting outdoors, drinking wine. It was 10 a.m. on a Sunday morning. Clearly we'd found our people.

"Let's start with cappuccinos," Masha suggested. "Work our way up from there?"

"You read my mind."

Under the cool morning sun in the outdoor café, we looked out over the wide courtyard of the city. The town was alive. Charming citizens, young and old, flitted around in flowery skirts and heels, tweed suits and bowler hats, pumping bicycle pedals along alleyways lined with Gothic and Romanesque architecture. A woman in her seventies with coiffed silvery hair rode past, carrying flowers and fresh vegetables in the wicker basket of her bike, cruising along in her red kitten heels and an A-line dress. As she pedaled into the distance, I half expected her to rip through a backdrop and expose a concrete wall and a tangle of cords as an amplified voice yelled, "CUT! WE NEED MEDICS!" This place seemed too dreamy to be real. Oh, how I wanted to keep exploring it.

"Can I tell you something?" said Masha.

A waitress served up our cappuccinos, and I pressed the spoon into my foam and put it into my mouth. "Of course."

Masha kept her gaze on me, taking careful measure as she spoke. "I've had this weird thought. Like . . . okay, this is really weird. But I've been thinking about how, before you came along, I was kind of lonely and wanted someone to walk with, and then there you were in Cinque Terre, just a few minutes away by train. That's pretty amazing, right? I've had a thousand moments in my life that were too perfectly timed and effortless to seem anything but orchestrated, and I feel like this friendship was written in the cosmos a billion years ago. But a part of me is also thinking, what if you're just a figment of my imagination and I made you up so I don't have to be alone anymore?"

My mouth hung open. "That's weird."

"I know, it is, I'm sorry. I feel like an idiot. I shouldn't have even—"

"No, I mean it's weird because I've already thought the *exact* same thing about you: that you're a figment of my imagination."

"Really? Because sometimes when we're talking it feels like I'm talking to myself."

I reached out and poked her arm. Real.

"We have to find a way to get you walking again."

"We do."

She said, "You want to go see the dead guy in the Duomo after this?"

I nodded, slow and certain.

✦

The idea came to me out of nowhere, and I blurted it into Masha's face before she'd had a chance to yawn and stretch. "I can buy a bike!"

I sat on her bed, a tiny single pushed up against the wall near the door. When we'd arrived, she'd insisted I take the king-sized bed while she slept curled up in a ball on the child's bed with her shoulder jammed against the wall.

"A bike," she said, yawning and stretching out her arms. "That's cute."

"No, seriously. I can roll along beside you until my foot heals. Think about it. It's kind of like a makeshift wheelchair. It might work."

Her eyes lit up and she paused mid-stretch. "You know, that's actually not a bad idea."

"All the roads we've walked on have been flat. I can just scoot and roll, right? I mean, it's a solution for now, until my foot gets better."

"Yes. But . . . oh, wait . . . " Her face dropped. "No. The path is about to head into the mountains."

For days we'd been closing in on the mountain pass between the Ligurian Alps and the Apennines, an outcrop of peaks hovering in the far distance as a hazy blue notion that became greener and more defined by the step. It would mark the beginning of the rolling vineyards and medieval fortresses of Tuscany—an area so exquisite in reputation I was willing to sprout wings from my shoulder blades and fly there if only my body would cooperate with my desires.

"Let's work that out later," I proposed, testing my mantra out loud on Masha. I had no clue as to how we'd troubleshoot my monopod situation once we'd left the conveniences of town behind for the herb fields and tomato crops that lined empty roads in the countryside, and I was afraid of being a burden on her, and yet—

"That's a great idea," she said. "Let's see what happens, but first we need to try to find you a bike."

✦

The only bike store we could find in town was run by a creepy Ecuadorian fellow who had a poor understanding of personal space and who, for reasons unknown, kept trying to communicate something to us with a peculiar gesture that involved staring into our eyes up close while slowly rubbing each of his fingers base to tip.

"Is he masturbating his fingers?" said Masha from the corner of her mouth.

"I'm pretty sure he's fingerbating."

"Let's buy a bike and get out of here."

Parked on the curb outside the shop was a red vintage bike with a wicker basket lined with tartan cloth and a dink bar for my backpack. It was rusty in parts, with cracked tires, one single gear, and a feeble bell, and it rattled as though, at any given moment, it might fold in on itself like a push puppet. However, it had a seat and a frame and wheels that spun, and that was good enough.

"She looks like a Frankie," I said, and Masha nodded in fierce agreement.

"How much?" I asked Finger Guy.

He scrawled on a piece of dirty paper: 100 euros.

"For a rusty bike?" I exclaimed to Masha.

"That's expensive."

It was, but I couldn't keep limping from store to store, bargain-hunting for another bike. This was it. We were out of options. I paid the euros, and we made a quick escape with the squealing bike.

On the way back to our hotel, I noticed that a lot of Piacenzans had plastic flowers tied to their bikes, adding to the town's film-set charm. Such whimsical beauty was an aesthetic gift to any onlooker, and I wanted to be part of it. "Do you know what would be really great?" I said to Masha.

"What?

"If we could find a store that sells plastic flowers, for Frankie."

"We can make that happen."

Not a minute later, down a narrow bluestone alley, we happened upon a shop selling a shock of gaudy plastic flowers. It was a plastic florist. I didn't know there was such a thing.

"Well, that's a coincidence," I said.

"We manifested it," said Masha, and I laughed until I realized she was serious.

Once a florist in her New York life, Masha picked out a bouquet to wrap around the bike's handlebars, and the storeowner, holding a fluffy rabbit in her arms, sent us off on our journey with a lyrical "Buona fortuna!"

Outside, a bee landed in the stamen of my red gerbera, and as I pushed the bike past ancient architecture that had once been the backdrop for pilgrims and princes, artists and tradesmen, crusaders and Templars, I wondered if this whole episode in the land of Piacenza had in fact been a lengthy hallucination brought on by over-soaking my skin in foot deodorizer. In the golden glare of the sun, we were on the road again, making our way toward the next dot on the map of the Way of the Heart. We were rolling with life, challenges and all, and somewhere during all this, Italian food had stopped tasting like armpit and started tasting like Italian food. We had outsmarted a crippling injury with ingenuity, devotion, and a tiny dash of crazy.

I turned to Masha. "Do you know what would be really great?"

"What?"

"If we found a sweet elderly woman who will take us into her cozy home and make us pasta. A nonna."

"We can make that happen."

Make that a whole lot of crazy.

Masha's walking poles clanked on the pavement as Frankie's loud brakes squealed and moaned. Every few seconds, I'd squeeze the brakes to try to slow Frankie down to match Masha's walking pace, and the bike would go *squeee*. Masha would speed up to try to meet my runaway pace until she was close to skipping, and that was how we traveled from that point on to keep pace with one another: Skip, clack, *squeeeee*, skip, clack, *squeeeee* . . .

I tried to keep my focus on the road immediately in front of us and away from the steep mountains ahead. *But what if* . . .

I'll figure it out when the time comes, I told myself, stopping the fear in its tracks this time.

A doctor once told me that it's not uncommon for people with anxiety disorders to challenge themselves through dramatic means in the attempt to overcome their fears, to rip off the Band-Aid and get all the pain over with. Trapped beneath the burden of constant worry, a chronically anxious person might go to extremes to get rid of it. When I told the doctor I'd spent two years sailing across the Pacific Ocean despite a phobia of deep water because I hoped it would make me fearless, he'd laughed and said: "Textbook."

"People gradually habituate themselves to being more brave," says clinical psychologist and rock climber Dr. Sallee McLaren, who believes adventure sports can be an effective antidote to anxiety, "and when you realize you can be brave in one area of your life, you realize you can be brave in other areas too."

The only problem was, I'd already spent ten years of my life on the move, sailing across oceans, riding motorcycles through jungles, climbing mountains, daring myself, challenging my boundaries, wandering aimlessly around strange lands in the hope that I could shed my fears and become courageous. But courage wasn't enough. I wanted to wake up in the morning without a knee-jerk sense of impending doom. I wanted to be able to look up at a blue sky and think, "Oh, what a nice, sunny day," instead of, "I wonder if any planes will fall out of the sky today?" I wanted to be able to go to the bathroom at night without imagining Regan crouched in the corner of my room, cracked lips smiling. I'd been courageous in the face of my own gruesome imagination since I was a kid, and it was exhausting. I was so tired of it. I didn't want to be brave. I wanted to be fearless.

One last attempt, I told myself as I *squeeeeed* along. One last shot at finding peace from my own head, and then it's time to go home and settle down.

Magic

5

THE DAYS WERE hot, but we didn't notice. We got lost often but didn't care. Our bodies were sore, but that was irrelevant because the air smelled like basil, peaches, and humid earth, and our troubles tumbled from our mouths and onto the roads we traveled.

"Torre, why do you think your relationship ended?"

"We were homesick for different homes."

With only ears of Italian corn to hear our conversations, we traveled straight roads through fields and farmlands, past stretches of tomatoes and herbs, chatting while walking and scooting. I used my good foot to thrust my body along or else pedaled at a snail's pace. Walking pace is the perfect talking pace, and no matter how far offtrack we ambled, there was no way for us to get lost inside our bubble of two.

"Masha, why are you doing all these pilgrimages?"

"I grew up in Soviet Russia, but my parents moved to New York when I was young to work for the United Nations. I guess I've always felt like I don't really fit in. I'm not really sure where I belong. I guess I'm hoping I'll stumble across it while walking."

"You don't have a Russian accent. You sound completely American to me."

"I can assure you that I don't feel completely American."

Squeeeeeeeeeeeee, went Frankie on the steeper declines, screaming as if she'd been freshly widowed. We weren't even in the mountains yet, and already I was struggling to stop her on the steeper declines, using my good foot to help the bike slow down.

"So why walk the world and not, say, take the bus and train?"

"I did the Camino de Santiago, and it changed my life. I wanted to keep walking, keep seeing the world, keep having serendipitous encounters. I don't want to be haunted by a lifetime of what ifs, you know?"

"Oh, believe me, I know."

Long roads tapered into narrow alleyways into the woods and then into a faint line of crushed grass through meadows of wildflowers, which made me want to weave daisy headpieces and roll down hills in a fit of giggles.

"There he is!" Masha would cry every hour or so, spotting the unmistakable yellow pilgrim icon that marked out the way of the Via Francigena—a sure sign that we were on track. It's impossible to follow a pilgrimage and not train your eyes to look for signs.

"Found him!" I'd say, chuffed at this real-life game of *Where's Waldo?* Sometimes the pilgrim—walking staff in hand, bag slung over his back—would be large and obvious on roadside tourist signage; sometimes he'd be the size of a passport photo, hiding on a lone street pole and easier to miss than not. Other times he'd be spray-painted onto a tree trunk on the side of the path, a barely distinguishable blob of yellow hiding under a fringe of leafy green. Once, at an intersection in the woods, the path was marked with three sticks assembled into an arrow, left there by somebody unknown.

On the horizon, long before we got there, we'd spot our destination by the spire of its village cathedral, jutting up like a lighthouse for wayfarers, with pastel dwellings gathered around it. Such a sight had all the allure of the Emerald City at the end of the yellow brick road when we were hungry and tired after a day of walking. Nothing is more inviting than a destination reached by slow progress and hard work; its position on the planet and distance from everything else is so intimate to you because you've slowly traced the skin of the earth to reach it.

Bursting with the need for rest, we'd then scramble to find a place to sleep before the sun went down. Most often our accommodation would be a church, convent, or pilgrim hostel, paid for in donations. Heels throbbing, skin tender and blistered, we'd knock on an ancient door and a nun, friar, or caretaker would welcome us with open arms.

"Buongiorno!" they would say and, in Italian, they'd ask where we'd started walking from.

I'd tell them, "Milan."

Masha would say "Canterbury, UK."

"Canterbury?" they'd say, looking baffled, because it's such an absurdly long way by foot.

And Masha would reply in her best Italian, "Sì, Canterbury, piede, pellegrino." *Yes, Canterbury, foot, pilgrim.* She would walk her two fingers through the air to demonstrate.

"Canterbury!" they would exclaim in disbelief. Their eyes would grow wide, and their heads and chins would retreat into their necks, as if they were turtles in white coifs. "Complimenti!"

Masha would then point at my foot and say, "Lei piede male. Bicicletta." *She bad foot. Bicycle.* And then, "She Australia. Me Russia."

We had the sophisticated verbal expression of two-year-olds, but Masha—fluent in Russian, French, and English—could generally string enough words together to make up a cohesive sentence.

"Ahh, sì, sì," the nuns would say, and then they'd ramble in energetic Italian and we'd explain that we didn't understand anything they were saying and the nuns would ramble some more and we'd laugh and nod and say "Si! Si!" and pray for the conversation to end so we could privately remove our shoes from our swollen feet with an orgasmic tug.

They'd take us through the silent halls of the convent, up dark stairs with walls decorated with Jesuses, for no wall space was abandoned to unholy blankness when it was an opportunity to show the son of God on the cross, Baby Jesus in Mary's arms, Jesus shimmering with gold leaf, Jesus rendered in charcoal and looking generally disappointed in all of you people. In the narrow and echoing halls, we'd pass life-sized statues of Jesus flopped over on the cross, protruding way out into the walkway, so that if we weren't paying attention, we could easily run into him. "Oh, hey, Jesus. Sorry about, like, you know, *everything*."

Our hiking shoes would squeak on the polished floors, scattering dust and debris from their treads, and a miasma of stench from eight hours of walking would follow behind us like the inescapable ghosts of our hiking past. I'd feel deeply guilty about this and also about harboring my little secret agnosticism in the presence of so much holy devotion.

But it didn't seem to matter to anybody whether we were Catholic, Buddhist, or Generally Confused. Nobody demanded proof of religion before they showed us to clean beds, and sometimes even hot meals with red wine. Strangers in the street would offer to fill our water bottles or give us chilled mineral water from their homes; shopkeepers would load our bags with snacks and our heads with renewed confidence.

"Masha, don't you think it's amazing that people have been so generous with us?"

"It's been that way since I set out on my pilgrimages. That's why I love this form of travel so much."

After only days together, I'd fallen in sync with Masha's style of adventure, which was one of meandrous rambling, inspiration and improvisation, trial and error, mishap and misstep. The mistakes she made seemed to be part of it—the slapdash planning, the wrong turns, the errors—as though she enjoyed the challenge of finding real-time solutions. It was carelessness by design: a middle finger to the fears that might otherwise shape the journey, and because of this it seemed her mind wasn't clogged with planning, paranoia, or expectations but was free to be open to whatever she might find along the way. I wasn't yet sure if she was woo-woo or wise, but she was showing me what it meant to be a pilgrim.

Through Masha, I was starting to see that no amount of planning can prepare you for coping with the unknown space that exists between now and later, because it's a void that doesn't actually exist yet. It's a blank space until you arrive at it, where you bring the story of your life into being from nothing through a collaboration between your actions and the actions of the world around you. Not only was Masha comfortable with this blank space ahead, but she was plunging headfirst into it with her eyes closed and her hands tied behind her back. In place of fear, she had trust, and this trust in everything made her so light she was almost floating. It was a charming trait, and strangers would take a liking to her immediately, offering help in any way they could. Through her I could see trust brings back trust, which can only mean that fear yields fear.

As we wandered through wild and strange places with few possessions and Masha's enormous trust, we were being gifted with the kind of warmth and hospitality that transcends language barriers and belief systems. Nobody cared who we were, where we'd come from, or why; all that seemed to matter to anyone was that we were pilgrims who'd embarked on a long journey for the same reason that all seekers seek: so that we might come upon some kind of proof that we're something more than just ridiculous meatbags filled with warm guts, flying through black space on a giant blue ball.

✦

"Let's manifest something together," Masha said, as we rested on the side of the road. We were supine, partially buried in long grass and small flowers, faces to the sky under the shade of a birch tree on the shoulder of a straight road we'd been following for hours. Naps in the grass had become a regular part of our daily routine, a way to break up a long day in the sun. Frankie was propped up on her stand, looking regal and cocky with her bouquet at the fore.

The sun was at its hottest, but the temperature in the shade was mild enough to make our eyelids heavy, our talk tipsy. I felt drunk on endorphins. Sun filtered through the trees and fell down around us like gold coins. With my head on a soft pillow of grass, I watched the bug world up close: the comings and goings of small beings carrying out routines in their mysterious alternate world.

"What do you mean, 'manifest'?" I asked, quietly hoping she wasn't referring to the superstitious belief of having the power to bring, say, a shiny new car into being by visualizing the keys in your hand. *Oh dear, no. Please don't be that naïve, Masha.*

"I mean," she said, "let's manifest something we want into being by visualizing it."

Oh dear, yes.

"Um, sure," I said, not wanting to taint Masha's endearing naïveté with my world-weariness. The last time I believed in magic, I was eight years old and kneeling in crunchy leaves at dusk, looking for knots in trunks that might be doorways to fairylands. When I'd find the right archway, I'd leave a gift of an opalescent marble, hoping it might charm a fairy into granting a wish. At school I made a friend who looked like a brown-haired pixie, with alabaster skin, huge doe eyes, and a level of daring that expanded my worry-filled world. Like me, she had an active imagination, and together we'd go for walks along a stream near our homes to peer under spotty red mushrooms for signs of sprites.

We were children and such activities were cute, but then, overnight, they weren't. We hadn't even hit our teens before my friend became more preoccupied with heavy metal and pimply boys than with our expeditions, and while she was becoming officially cool, I got even dorkier and turned to investigating the powers of gemstones, attempting to harness the properties of rose quartz for love; tiger's eye for protection, stability, and grounding; and jade for fear and anxiety. To confirm their powers, I called on them to show me the winning horse in Australia's biggest race, the Melbourne Cup. I put ten bucks down on my pick, lost to a mare named Let's Elope, and gave up on gemstones, gambling, and eloping.

Life's a bitch and then you die, said the magnet on my family's fridge door. Absurdism was my parents' religion; black humor was the family's form of prayer.

When you have bohemian parents who give you absolute freedom to chase the rabbit of your curiosity, you wind up as a peculiar teenager who studies ancient Chinese divination practices in her spare time. For my thirteenth birthday, I asked for a Chinese *I Ching* set containing all the items necessary for tapping into the powers of this chance-based system of belief. It begins with flipping coins to determine whether or not you draw a solid line or a broken line. A solid line represents lightness, while a broken line represents darkness, and these lines, stacked on top of each other in groups of six, create a unique hexagram that can be interpreted to give answers to big questions. A gesture as simple as a flip of a coin determines your dark or light lines and, ultimately, your future, and because your stacks will almost always have pairings of both, you end up with a combination of good and bad. Light and dark pairings can never be separated, because shadow cannot exist without light, male without female—these contrary forces hold the cosmos together, it's said.

With my bedroom door closed for quiet, I'd spread a deep blue velvet cloth on the floor and cast eight hexagrams. Once finished, I'd refer to the *I Ching* book to interpret their meaning of my unique sets of lines, but the answers were always inconclusive. It was fun to play with for a while, but there was never a winning horse, so to speak.

I was a realist with the mind of a scientist, too logical to accept faith based on concept alone, too skeptical to believe in magic without proof, but that didn't stop me from also experimenting with tarot and astral projection, Ouija boards and Wicca, Buddhism and Wayne Dyer books, just to be sure. It was a process of elimination, and eventually I eliminated everything except the fridge magnet wisdom. *Life's a bitch and then you die.* Was that it? Was it all just an empty nothingness?

My oddball determination to understand the matters of the cosmos was driven by a single wish I'd prayed on from as early as I could remember. It was a life dream that meant the world to me, something that could motivate a young girl to study every kind of divination practice she could find, if only it could grant her one single wish.

That wish was for boobs.

As the only girl in school with a washboard-flat chest, who looked like a boy with a dress on, I saw boobs as the answer to all my problems. My older sisters had boobs, and they got to do fun things like stay up late and eat special diet food for curvy people. I wanted to eat those peculiar little packets of tasteless curry and rice too—they seemed so exclusive and fancy—but when my sisters caught me trying to heat up my own diet meal in the microwave, I was berated: "You can't eat Lean Cuisines, Torre, you're too skinny! You don't even have boobs!"

Joining the boob club was where it was all at, and by Jesus, Buddha, or the *I Ching*, I was going to get me a pair. Faith is nothing if not a desire to control the uncontrollable.

My search for mysticism got sidetracked when my friends started to smoke bongs, skip school, and listen to death metal. Though I was far too neurotic to do anything other than watch their tomfoolery unfold with both curiosity and concern, I longed to be accepted like any other teenager. They told me I looked and acted like a child (*Goddammit, boobs, where are you?*), so I replaced the posters on my walls of endangered animals with pictures of Guns N' Roses and Kurt Cobain. I hid my spirituality books, fortune cards, crystals, and velvet magic mat, stuffing away all that nonsense into the backs of cupboards. Magic was for children. I stopped looking for fairies and unicorns, stopped drawing pixies in sketchbooks.

As my friends tried new drugs and new boys, I watched with disquiet as they got closer and closer to danger. They'd drink, I'd watch. They'd crawl into beds with boys; I'd wait outside in the cold, saying, "You guys, I feel like this is a bad idea. Can we go home now?"

Not long after, the girl with whom I'd once looked under toadstools began to see fairies and trolls for real after she took a large handful of miscellaneous pills offered to her by a drug dealer at a party. One day she called me to explain, with genuine disbelief, that trolls were talking to her from inside the toilet bowl, encouraging her to stick her head into the water. Witches were speaking with her through the mirror, cackling at her face, telling her she was ugly and should die. It had been weeks since she'd taken the drugs.

"I can smell blood," she told me over the phone, her voice quivering. "It's everywhere in my parents' house. My dad is going to murder me, Torre. He's after me. What should I do?"

"I think you're imagining things," was all I knew to offer at age seventeen.

Shortly after, she ran away from home in the nighttime to escape the threat of her murderous father, who wasn't murderous at all but a desperately worried man who couldn't understand what had happened to his daughter. When they took her home, she was a ball of inconsolable, animalistic terror. The men in white coats came to take her away. She was checked into a psychiatric hospital shortly after.

A year later, she was unrecognizable; the experiences she'd had, along with the medications used to control her paranoid delusions, disfigured her small frame and her alabaster skin, bloating her body and roughening her skin from the inside out—an attack from the ghosts within. It's a trauma that nobody should have to know, especially not an eighteen-year-old, fresh out of school and full of promise. Her curious brown eyes became hooded and fixed somewhere into the middle distance, and they didn't come back to center. She was diagnosed with drug-induced paranoid schizophrenia—for life—and horror became something that wasn't just in movies anymore. It was real.

It was then that my boobs finally came in. They were plump and round and everything I'd wished for, and I never knew what to make of that or to whom I should send the thank-you note— Jesus, the fairies, the Wiccan spell I'd cast? No. Magical thinking was a symptom of schizophrenia.

In the end, it was the blunt and bleak absurdism on my parents' fridge that won: *Life's a bitch and then you die.* An empty nothingness.

"So," Masha said, interrupting my memories, "what do you want to manifest?"

"Um . . . " I couldn't think of anything to say. We were under the shade of a tree in Italy, bathed with endorphins and sunshine. Food definitely didn't taste like armpit anymore. I had one working leg, two working arms, one torso, one head, one bike, and two boobs. Asking for anything more felt greedy. "I don't know," I said. "I can't think of anything I want."

"Don't be a cop-out, DeRoche, think of something. There must be something you want."

"Okay, let me think. I've always wanted to forage for wild strawberries in the woods."

"Ah . . . okay . . . but—"

"What?"

"No, nothing, but maybe think of something else, too. Like, a plan B."

"An Italian nonna. I want to meet a sweet elderly Italian lady who will feed us homemade pasta. A gnocchi nonna."

"Okay, a nonna, love it. I'm going to manifest a kitten."

I rolled my eyes. "A kitten? Really? How is that magical? There are kittens everywhere around here. That's like saying you're going to manifest, I don't know, a tomato farm." I squeezed my eyes shut and said, "I want to manifest a tomato farm!" and then opened my eyes to glare at the field in front of us—one of the hundreds of farms we'd passed, bursting with plump red romas. "Whoa, look at that!" I said. "A tomato farm, from nothing into being with the power of my mind!"

"I'm going to manifest a bike," Masha said with her eyes squeezed shut. "A red bike with loud, faulty brakes and flowers on the handlebars." She opened her eyes and exclaimed, "Whoa, check it out, there it is. I just brought that bike into being from nothing."

"We're wizards."

"There's nothing we can't do."

"Let's save the world!"

"All right, asshole, shut it down," she said. "What I mean is that I want a kitten that won't run away from me. All the kittens I've seen so far in Italy are stray or shy. They run when I try to get near them. I want one that won't run this time."

Masha. Sweet Masha. So sweet, so guileless, so utterly bananas. Her blind faith in kismet was part of her charm, like a kid well into puberty who makes wishes to the boob fairy. But

I wasn't going to be the one to break the bad news about Santa and the Easter Bunny. We all start out in this world as believers, but then reality happens. Children run off instinct and intuition alone, while adults learn to navigate the world by intellect. And the intellect learns, from its years of experience, that life is hard and bad things happen and the desires we most want cannot be manifested from thin air; otherwise, we'd all be manifesting gorgeous men riding horses naked. (For example.)

"So let's recap." She counted on her fingers. "We have wild strawberries, a kitten that won't run away, a library café with endless cappuccinos, and a nonna who will take us in and feed us homemade pasta."

"So what do we do now? Close our eyes and squeeze from our loins while doing Lamaze breathing?"

"Just you wait, my deranged twin; you'll see." She leaned back into the grass and put her straw hat over her face, sinking down into a bed of wildflowers, her long blond plait hanging over her shoulder.

I scanned the tomato field for signs, harboring a fraction of hope that I'd spot something to catch me off-guard. I had nothing to lose at this point by keeping my eyes open for fairies. *Let go, let go, shut up.*

Minutes later, we were both snoring under the shuffling leaves of the birch tree.

6

WITH NOT A single car on the road, all was silent under the limpid morning sky, apart from birdsong, cicadas, and the shrill scream of Frankie's brakes as I tried to slow myself down. *Squeeeeeeeeeeeeeeeeeeeeeeee!*

We were nearing the mountain pass. It would only get harder from here. I dismounted the bike and pushed Frankie up the hump of a long hill, puffing from the weight of her. My wicker basket carried water, Masha's camera bag, and a few foraged tomatoes for snacking, and on the dink bar, my backpack was lashed down with a thread of string I'd found somewhere in the dirt. Frankie was heavy.

As I pushed her upward, my body on a sharp lean, the rotating pedal would bash the back of my leg, pummeling my skin into a mottled mess, but it didn't really matter. My ankles had already been grazed from brushing past bushes of stinging nettle, my legs had been chewed by curious insects, and my hair was stringy and plastered to my head with sweat.

I hopped up on the saddle. The downhill ahead was a long one. This was the good part—the payoff for my uphill work.

"Goodbye, my darling," I said to Masha.

"Ciao, my love," she said, and I let the brakes go. Into the muddy pinks, purples, and yellows of early morning, I soared into cool air that smelled of fruit ready for picking. It was August, almost harvest season, and the land was crisscrossed with rows of plump grapes, golden green and powdery purple. Between the vines, up curling driveways lined with pointy cypress, were stone farmhouses built from chestnut beams and terracotta tiling. We were almost at the border of Tuscany, and the land looked every bit its Renaissance cliché.

Most days we'd go to bed when the light faded and get up early with the sun, matching our rhythms with that of Italy's late summer. We'd take our time in the morning waking up, telling stories, recounting dreams, writing emails, packing bags, and then setting out for our mandatory morning croissant and cappuccino, which always became "Due cappuccini, per favore" and then "Tre?" Caffeinated to the point of sweaty eyeballs, we'd hoist our bags onto our backs and begin to count down kilometers. "Twenty-eight, twenty-three, nineteen . . . " Sometimes the sun would be way up in the sky by the time we got a good rhythm up.

The bike slowed in a dip between hills. On the side of the road, I waited, reclining with my head on a pillow of grass scattered with the feathery leaves of wild fennel, smelling the earthiness of the soil blending with scents of aniseed and licorice. Frankie was propped up on her stand, trembling at the joints from the speeds we'd just traveled together. She was a simple old pushbike, accustomed to the flat bluestone alleys of Piacenza and wholly unprepared for the sport of long-distance travel with her impaired companion, along country roads and into the mountains and beyond.

"I missed you, my deranged twin," came Masha's voice from behind. She unclipped her backpack and set it down, and curled her legs to sit cross-legged in the grass with me.

"I missed you too," I said. After spending each waking moment together for almost two weeks, it seemed like we hadn't seen each other in forever. It had been twenty minutes. We had so much to catch up on.

"That last slope was so much fun on the bike," I said. "But I'm not sure how many more of these hills Frankie is going to take. The brakes aren't good."

"I know. I have ears. How is the foot doing?"

"Better. I'm not yet sure if I can walk for long stretches."

"That's a problem for another time. For now: How gorgeous is this?"

We breathed it in.

"What's up, ladies?" came a voice from behind. A man named Guy had joined us. Masha had met him while hiking the Camino de Santiago and he'd come over from his home in Switzerland to stroll with us for a few days, a week . . . maybe all the way to Rome, he said. At first, having a third person around was a welcome addition to our pack. He was in his twenties, owned a successful business, and seemed friendly enough when I met him, but it had taken only half a day of traveling with him to notice that we had a small problem on our hands.

"Why are we stopped?" he asked.

"Just chatting."

"Let's keep going," he said, patting his thigh with his hand. "Come on, ladies, don't be lazy." And with that he trudged well ahead as the new self-appointed pack leader, whistling a merry tune to himself.

✦

There were days when we didn't find any restaurants for lunch and our stomachs would moan in protest, but it wasn't difficult for us to make a snack out of nature. We'd pluck juicy blackberries from the brambles, popping them into our mouths, or eat from trees ripe with plums, apples, figs, nectarines, or kiwis. Sometimes the trees were wild; other times they were dangling over private property fence lines.

I called it resourcefulness. Masha called it stealing. That didn't stop her from fashioning one of her walking poles into an ingenious fruit-pilfering device. By holding the pole by its tip and reaching up into the high branches, she'd mastered a technique of using the hand strap to hoop, clutch, and tug down the sweetest and most sun-kissed fruit from the high branches.

I pictured a nonna on the other side of the fence peering out her kitchen window to see a stick rising slowly up over her fence, looking around—right, left, right—and then cupping her juiciest nectarine before disappearing back behind the fence. Some sights are too weird to be made sense of, and besides, we were not in danger of being caught for our crimes because we walked swiftly and smelled awful and nobody in her sane mind would want to pursue us for the theft of a single peach.

Despite eating fruit almost as often as we could find it, we'd still be ravenous by lunchtime. Though there were days when we went hungry, almost always we'd find a trattoria on the side of the road, where we'd stop for a hearty meal of antipasto, fresh pasta, salad, and warm bread, washed down with a pitcher of local wine—sometimes homemade.

This was Italy.

We were walking through wine country.

What were we going to do?

Not taste all of it?

Drowsy from three courses of heavy food washed down with a fine drop, we'd stop under a shady tree for a midday nap, and, for an hour or maybe two, we'd fall sound asleep on the ground to the sounds of insects shuffling and the breeze bending the grass. We'd rouse on our bed of earth in a pool of our own dribble, grass embedded in our cheeks, bodies humming and sore in the satisfying way that follows athletic effort.

"All right, ladies, let's go," Guy would say, patting his thigh as if summoning a dog, tugging us up sharply from slumberland.

+

Fwheeee-fwoooo!

"What's that noise?" I asked Masha.

"Someone whistling?"

Fwheeee-fwoooo!

"Oh, it's Guy."

Guy was a fast walker with brawny legs, and he'd dash well ahead of us and wait at the crux of a turnoff. Once there, he'd remove his bag, take a seat, and begin whistling at us to hurry us along. When we'd arrive, he'd put his bag on and dash off ahead once again, giving us no time for stopping to rest. It was clear: Guy wanted to set the pace.

"What's the weight on that thing?" he said to Masha, pointing at her backpack. He was chewing the fatty meat off a stick of salami he carried, which he cut from periodically using a pocketknife he kept on his belt.

"About fifteen kilos."

"Fifteen? Your bag is too heavy."

"Actually, it's totally fine."

"Mine is seven," he said.

"Okay, um, congratulations?"

"What have you got in there, anyway? Rocks?" he said.

Bingo. She was carrying rocks. She was carrying rocks and a lot of other crap besides. Once, I'd watched her unpack her bag and line everything up on her bed for organization. Apart from all the normal clothes and hiking necessities, she was also hauling, on her year-long journey, various good-luck trinkets in fancy tins; a sack of lentils each infused with the individual wishes of her friends, to be released in Santiago de Compostela at the end of her journey; and a not-insignificant collection of heart-shaped rocks she'd found on the roadsides, as though they were kisses from God that she couldn't refuse.

She carried multiple full-sized bottles of generic-brand shampoo and conditioner that she'd gotten for free at the magazine she'd worked for in New York ("It will just be a waste of money to have to buy them again") along with sunscreens, moisturizers, and tinctures of oils to protect her skin from the elements. Her toiletries bag alone would've weighed as much as my entire bag. She had a thirteen-inch laptop, a DSLR camera with a zoom lens, a tangle of chargers, and a sewing kit for milking blisters. (Trust me, you don't want to know.) She had a pair of flip-flops, a long, elegant skirt for evenings, and a well-worn copy of *The Alchemist*.

Each time I asked her, "Do you have a [insert anything at all] I could borrow?" the answer was always, "You know, it's funny you should ask . . . " followed by mad digging in her Mary Poppins–like sack of treasures until she turned up the item, brushing off crumbs or leaked shampoo before handing it over. Her mother had pleaded with her to lighten her load, concerned for the well-being of her knees, but Masha remained attached to every item in that bag.

I, on the other hand, carried five kilos to her fifteen, having optimized my weight right down to all the itsy-bitsy bottles of essential toiletries. I used shampoo as body soap and carried no hair conditioner, moisturized my skin with a small tub of plain cream, and would've cut my toothbrush in half if I had a saw handy. A first aid kit was the most indulgent item I carried.

Masha wasn't a member of the lightweight travel brigade. You wouldn't find her huddled among a group of hikers engaged in the highly competitive sport of Ounce-Off. What she had on her back was incidental to her journey, and she carried it without complaint or signs of struggle. It was her body and her decision, so I never tried to make her a convert. No matter how strange her choices, she was a badass woman walking the world on her own, an unlikely pilgrim carrying love rocks and wish lentils and other curiosities, be they magical or mad, woo-woo or wise—or all of the above.

Masha answered Guy's question with kind patience, "Well, I have my camera and also laptop, and that's quite heavy, and—"

"What?" he cried. "You're carrying a laptop?"

"I do paid freelance work. I need it for income. And I use it to write a journal. I'm walking for a whole year, so—"

"I can't *believe* you're carrying *a laptop.*"

Masha was silent.

"Fifteen kilos! You should be carrying half of that weight. I'm only carrying seven, because—" he continued on, though his voice dropped off as I let go of Frankie's brakes and flew. *Squeeeeeeeeeeeeeeeeeeeeeeeeeeeeeee!*

I reveled in the silence of being alone on my bike, sad to have lost the whimsical, devil-may-care fun of our adventure now that Guy had elected himself into the alpha role. I noticed a vast shift between the playful journey we were on prior to his arrival, made up of a series of hilarious mishaps and hard-won triumphs, and the regimented path we were now on under the leadership of this new self-appointed top dog.

I was used to tolerating people like Guy. As a lifelong worrier, I'd never learned to trust my own intuition, because it was so hard to separate that delicate voice from a louder one yelling, *YOU'RE GOING TO DIE!* So I'd latched onto people who seemed stronger and more resolute, trusting their compass over my own, even when their direction was not good for me.

But I was starting to see how damaging it can be to delegate this leadership to someone outside yourself. Under the guise of being helpful, people like Guy stroke their own egos by telling others what to do, but this kind of patronizing superiority has precisely the opposite effect. Being controlled damages intuition, and intuition is what keeps a person safe. Intuition is a unique biome that exists inside all of us, which, if well nurtured, is the source of our creativity and dreams, questions and curiosities, values and decisions, passions and life energy. It's our very own moral compass—our life compass. By observing Masha, I could see that the ongoing feedback of good and bad experiences hones intuition over time, strengthening it through critical thinking and independent choices. It flourishes when we take responsibility for our own lives. It's fertilized by our mistakes and watered by our successes. The alphas and authoritarians can so easily sow seeds of doubt and trample intuition with their big, thuggish boots.

My maternal grandmother was eighty-eight when she passed away, just before my dad died. She had been a woman of great strength and determination, who had marched to her own drum and had always nudged me to follow my passion. Months after Grandma's death, I had a vivid dream about her, in which she was on the phone to my mother, delivering a sermon of life advice. Her voice was so loud and so self-assured that I could hear her sassy American drawl coming out of the receiver, firm and demanding.

"Honey," she told my mother, "there is nothing in this world that exists outside you that you don't already have within you."

When I woke up, her voice echoed in my head. They were such strange words, so foreign to my way of thinking. Until that day, I had been grasping at the leadership of anyone else around me, never suspecting that, as the good witch said to Dorothy: "You had the power all along, my dear."

Grandma's lesson was starting to settle in.

I parked my bike on the side of the road and stretched out in the grass until a voice emerged from the silence. "I'm just *saying* that carrying that much weight is completely *unnecessary*, and . . . "

I got back on the bike and pedaled off.

✦

The three of us stood in a silent union with our necks bent backward, faces turned upward to behold the sheer hill ahead.

"Oh no," I said.

The path swooped up into a series of sharp switchbacks to reach the top of a green peak before coiling away out of sight, no doubt to a drop down the other steep side. The road was loose scree, bad for braking. If I succeeded in climbing the hill, getting down the other side would be too treacherous. The time had come. I needed to figure this out now.

"I think I need to let the bike go."

Masha stroked Frankie's handlebars tenderly. "Are you sure?"

"There's no way I can make that hill. Look at how steep it is. I'm going to die on the other side."

"That right there is one bitch of a hill," she agreed.

"What's happening, ladies?" said Guy. "Why are we stopped?"

"It's time to say goodbye to Frankie."

"Who?"

"The bike."

"What are you going to do with it?"

"I don't know, leave it here for someone to find, I guess."

"How much did you pay for that thing?"

"100 Euros."

He gasped. "100 EUROS? Are you kidding me? For that old thing? How long have you had it?"

"Three days."

"WHAT?! What were you thinking? You paid 100 Euros for an old bike you owned for three days? And now you're just going to leave it here? How could you pay—"

"It's a long story," I interjected. "You had to be there, Guy."

Masha tore a piece of paper from her notebook and wrote on it "FREE BIKE/GRATUIT," along with a heart, and we stuck the sign onto the handlebars.

"I want to keep the flowers," I said. "Guy, do you mind if I borrow your pocketknife to cut the wire?"

"Women don't know how to use tools," he said.

Really? A misogynist named *Guy*? This was a coincidence that seemed scripted by a wordsmith with a cheeky sense of humor. I heard Masha's advice echo in my mind: *Nothing on a pilgrimage is a coincidence.*

"Guy," I said, "You may find this astounding, but I do know how to use a pocketknife. How do you think I do my manicures? Oh, and I also spent two years living on a boat. Can I borrow it, or not?"

He sighed, unclipped it from his holster, and handed it over. I pried open the cutters, snapped the wire, closed the tool, and handed it back. Once I'd untangled all the flowers from the handlebars, I tied them to our bags.

"Can I have the big one?" asked Guy.

"The red gerbera?"

"Yes, please."

I fitted it to his lime-colored pack with some twists of wire, creating a clash of red against green. It stood behind him, trembling at his shoulder.

In our sunhats and floral flourishes, we took off up the hill in the sunny early morning, looking like three pilgrims who might disappear among the wildflowers and never come back. From the top of the hill, I took one last look at Frankie and whispered a final "Thank you."

I was back on my own two feet. I had legs. Two working legs with which to explore the world.

7

*F*WHEEEE-FWOOOO! *Fwheeee-fwoooo!*

"Ugh," I said to Masha, "why does he keep whistling at us?"

"Come on, ladies, pick up the pace," he called out.

We caught up to Guy where the path ended abruptly at a river. He was leaning on a pole chewing a strand of hay. "Which way now, girls?" he said, his big red gerbera peeking up over his shoulder. "Looks like there's a river in our way." He gnashed his hay, pointing to the obvious.

The directional arrow led to the other side of the river, where we could see a vague path leading into scrublands.

"Should we cross?" I said.

"May as well," said Masha.

We jumped across the narrowest part of the river, but on the other side, the path dropped off without warning, ending in long, dry scrub. There were no more arrows or clues as to where we should go. We stood by the river scratching our heads, trying to work out a plan.

"We could backtrack?" I offered.

Masha thought for a second. "But it's weird, because I saw a yellow pilgrim not that long ago and it was pointing down this path. There were no deviations; we've followed only one single path. And now here we are."

Guy pulled the hay strand from his mouth and said, "I think you ladies are lost."

I marveled at how consistent he was at being a dick.

Masha furrowed her brow as she concentrated on the GPS on her phone. "There's a town upstream. Two miles or so, maybe a little less. We can follow the river to reach the main road. That road leads into a village. We can stop there for lunch. It's not the official path, but it will get us where we need to go and back in the right direction."

"Makes sense to me," I said. "Following the river sounds nice, anyway."

"If you say so," said Guy, and he took off ahead along the river, whistling in his chirpy vibrato.

The riverbanks were made up of smooth rocks that would shift under the weight of our shoes. On a tender ankle, I walked with care. Along the banks I noticed piles of scat, which looked like it could've belonged to wild boars. By coincidence, that morning I'd read about wild boars roaming the Italian countryside:

> The animal typically attacks by charging and pointing its tusks toward the intended victim, with most injuries occurring on the thigh region. Once the initial attack is over, the boar steps back, takes position and attacks again if the victim is still moving, only ending once the victim is completely incapacitated.

What if a boar came running at us from the scrub on the edge of the river? I didn't want to alarm anyone with my fears, even though there was scat everywhere, even though we were walking along an unmarked river far off the main route. I couldn't tell if this was unreasonable worry or intuition. I picked up my pace, risking my ankles.

The bank narrowed and then ran out completely. We needed to cross over to the other side.

"I'm going to make a rock bridge," said Guy, and he got to work combing the banks for large, flat stones to toss into the river, building a series of stepping stones in the shallow water to make a dry crossing.

While he did that, I took off my shoes and socks, rolled up my pants, and walked through the river, trying not to cry out as the rocks poked into the soft undersides of my feet. On the opposite bank, I sat, dried off my feet, and then put my shoes and socks back on. Guy caught up not long after.

But Masha had a different technique entirely: bothering with neither rock bridges nor dry feet, she walked straight into the river in her shoes and socks without so much as rolling up her pants—she just stomp-stomp-stomped straight on through it, wet to mid-calf.

Guy scoffed. "I can't believe you're not taking off your shoes. You'll get blisters if you walk in wet socks."

"I'll be fine, Guy."

Just around the bend we came to yet another river crossing. I sighed and sat down to take off my shoes and socks, Guy got to work on his bridge, and Masha stomp-stomp-stomped straight on through the river.

Around the next bend, we came to yet another crossing. Guy built his bridge, I removed my shoes and socks, Masha splashed straight through, and then we reached another crossing and another and then—

"Ah, fuck it," I said, stomping into the river with my shoes and socks on.

Guy followed right behind me, until all three of us were walking straight up the river, fully clothed and into deepening water.

We were nearing the bridge that would lead us back to the main road, but the current that ran below it was strong, the water up to our thighs. The riverbed was terracotta, slippery as ice. With every step my legs splayed out like a newborn calf's and the three of us battled to stay upright. Masha had a laptop and camera in her bag. She couldn't afford to lose her footing.

"Almost there," she said, leading the way.

Guy scoffed. "This is ridiculous."

The current pushed harder into our bodies beneath the bridge. We had only ten feet to go but the water was now up to our belts. I went sliding on the muddy river floor and recovered just in time, letting out a yip in the process.

"Okay, Torre?" said Masha.

"Okay."

"A few more steps."

We reached the bank beyond the bridge and crawled up to dry land—wet, bedraggled, and exhausted, but back on track.

"I'm going to find a guidebook in the next town," said Guy, breathing hard from the climb up the embankment. "So that you don't get us lost again. That was absurd." He marched off ahead of us, his whistling a little flat, his shoes spewing river water on each squelchy step.

I leaned over to Masha and whispered, "I'm going to manifest an asshole."

"Ta-da!" she said. "You're a wizard."

✦

By sunset, we were still walking. We'd done over nineteen miles, and every step felt like raw bones grinding concrete. We had one excruciating mile to go until we could rest and I was falling far behind.

"Let me take your bag," Masha offered, but I was determined to travel unaided. If I couldn't make thirty then I couldn't make fifty, and if I couldn't make fifty then I wouldn't make it to Rome. My bag weighed only five kilos, and offloading it wouldn't have helped much anyway. I had no idea how I was going to get out of bed and walk the next morning with this much electric pain rolling through my body.

We limped into a small village just after nightfall, and I collapsed on a park bench. "Can we sleep here?"

Masha tilted her head at me and said, "A tiny bit longer and we can rest."

I looked around at the townspeople, all dressed up in fancy clothes, eating dinner by candlelight under streetlights illuminating the stone-cobbled laneways. It looked like Van Gogh's *Café Terrace at Night*. We looked like sewer rats, but smelled worse.

How strange it was to remember this parallel world existing with ours, one in which people went to work, dressed nicely, smelled lovely, didn't have raw feet and wet socks, hadn't spent the day crotch-deep in a river . . .

Ravenous and exhausted, we stared at the diners like hungry dogs. They failed to see us at all. We were dirty vagrants standing against a backdrop of evocative Romanesque beauty and so unpleasantly discordant with the setting that we were filtered out of the view.

We were tired and hungry, with no place to sleep; our morale was low. Darkness had fallen.

"Hey, ladies," Guy cried, "come and see this. It's a soda fountain!"

As if built for the sole purpose of lifting the spirits of pilgrims, there in the center of the village square was an ornate fountain that poured carbonated water from its taps.

"And it's chilled!" said Masha, bubbling over with laugher. "Chilled!"

Had it spewed coins like a slot machine, we'd have been less excited. Manic, we filled all our drinking bottles with fizzy joy. This is the paradox of suffering and euphoria: the more you suffer, the greater the subsequent euphoria.

Masha took off to look for accommodations while we waited on the park bench, and she came back with news of having found a convent for us to stay in. "The bad news is, it's a mile away. One more mile and we can rest."

I dug deep and pulled myself up with my walking poles to stagger forward in soggy socks.

We arrived at the gates of the convent, where we were greeted by snarling dogs who eased off at the commands of tiny, stout nuns in black habits. "Buona sera!" they chorused, like we were old friends they'd been expecting, and then, after the usual niceties—"Russia! Australia! Via Francigena! Roma!"—they took us through long halls and looping stairwells until we reached the dorm: a giant, echoing space filled with perhaps a hundred bunk beds. It was lit by the sickly green glow of fluorescent lights and seemed to hold the ghosts of a hundred lost souls. We all felt it. This place was haunted. But an exhausted mind and body gives exactly no shits about ghosts.

We picked our beds at random and collapsed in them for minutes, but as always there was much to do before we could relax. First, we had to shower—the best part of the day, because peeling off sticky clothes to stand under warm water while a froth of sweat and dirt swirls into the drain hole is an ecstasy only second to removing hot shoes from swollen feet.

I changed into street clothes, which also happened to be my bedclothes, and though they were a long way from freshly laundered, the clothes were neither sweaty nor smelly and therefore felt like silk sheets on clean skin. The style of my one and only spare outfit was a cross between casual wear and pajamas: just comfortable enough to sleep in, just acceptable enough to wear in public. They were not quite, but almost, pajamas, and served both purposes.

But it wasn't over yet. We had to scrub our hiking clothes in the sink to ready them for the following day. When you do your laundry in the sink every night, an accumulation of miscellaneous funk builds up in the fabrics, and no matter how hard you scrub, there's a tang that refuses to wash out. One person's "smelly" is another's "Meh, I don't really care anymore," and so we'd wring them out and decorate the accommodation with our wet clothing like it was the worst Christmas ever: T-shirts dangled from doorknobs, pants dripped off the end of the bed, and a pair of wet underwear hooked onto the top of a walking pole gaped open as if awaiting stocking stuffers.

"Okay, who is ready for dinner now?" said Masha.

I had no energy left. None. I stretched out on my bunk with all limbs akimbo, the sensation of steel rods jammed up into the soles of my feet, through my knees, and up into my femurs. My body was trembling. Despite wearing every item of dry clothing I owned—two pairs of socks, a spare T-shirt, a fleece, and my down jacket—I was shivering. All systems were shutting down. Everything ached, like a flu.

"Torre, I think you need food," said Masha, sitting on my bed and petting my leg. "Food, a good sleep, and you'll be good to go again tomorrow. I promise."

My eyelids were closing. "I'm so hungry, but I don't feel like I can move."

Guy paced at the door. "Are we going now, or what?"

Masha ignored him. "We can try to bring you something back, but I can't guarantee we will find anything. Without food, you might not sleep and without sleep, you might not heal. Trust me, you will feel so much better."

My stomach moaned, a lone wolf to the moon. I measured the pain in my body against the pain in my gut, and decided I needed to find the motivation to keep walking from some deep, untapped reserve within me. We had no more rest days left in the schedule. If I didn't improve overnight, this was the end. I peeled myself off the bed to hobble along cobblestones, back toward Van Gogh's *Café Terrace at Night*, pink-eyed, trembling, and dressed in not quite, but almost, pajamas.

The streets were empty.

The candlelit tables were gone.

Storefront shutters were racketing down.

Quaint alleyways were now menacing, dark.

An angry stray cat moaned at an unseen threat.

Waaooowwwww.

I realized it was my stomach.

"Fuck," said Masha. "Everything is closed."

Around a corner, streetlamps illuminated a single pizza restaurant, still open, but the waiters were busy folding table-cloths, packing up.

Masha rushed up to a waiter. "Are you still open?" she asked in Italian.

"Please, please, please, please, please . . . " Guy and I chimed from behind like a chorus of small children.

The waiter nodded, yes, and I could've kissed him.

After a large pizza each with porcini mushrooms, prosciutto, and three cheeses, with wine, the tension of the day gave way to our usual silliness. Our cheeks glowed. Our stomachs were full. My body was almost back to normal, restored by sustenance and rest.

I leaned back into my chair and looked up at the night sky. The balmy late summer night was wrapped in the coziest warmth, but then—

"I seriously can't believe you're carrying a laptop, Masha," said Guy. "That's so ridiculous."

Again? Really?

"But I'm earning money with it," she explained. "I get paid to do social media work, and I also use it to write about my journey and to update my blog and social media pages. And it's only a small laptop. Thirteen-inch."

"You people with your blogs and social media sites." He rolled his eyes. "Always on the computer. Never participating in *real* life."

"This is my job, Guy. I get paid for it. This is my income. A writer has to be in front of a computer. It's an unavoidable part of the job."

He was tipsy now, full of smug hubris and on a roll. "You've always got your head down, always looking at your phone, never enjoying the view around you. I watch you walking past all these beautiful mountains, but your eyes are on a screen. What is the point of walking around the world if you're not even going to *look* at the world?"

"I'm checking the GPS for directions. I'm navigating the whole time and making sure we're on track." Masha looked irritated, but her voice remained calm. Calmer than I felt. Guy was a bully. I couldn't sit by and watch for much longer.

He went on, "You aren't even very good at navigating. You got us lost. Maybe you should think about going to buy some maps and a guidebook instead of using your phone to get from place to place. Maybe then we wouldn't end up walking pointlessly through a river."

"I'm sorry," I interjected, "but could you remind me again of exactly how long you've been walking this pilgrimage, Guy?"

"Three days," he said.

"Three. Right. What's that, forty or fifty miles?"

He nodded.

"Well, Masha has walked over a thousand miles from Canterbury in the United Kingdom so far. One thousand. She's already been doing this for two months and has passed through the entire width of France and Northern Italy. Mostly alone."

"Yes, so why not pack a guide book?"

"Guy," I continued, "you assume you know better than us, but why? Because your backpack is a little lighter? Because you walk faster than us? Because you carry a pocketknife on your belt? Because you're a guy? Why?"

He said nothing.

"If Masha is so bad at navigating, if her pack is too heavy, if she doesn't know what she's doing, how do you think she managed to get herself across THE ENTIRE WIDTH OF FRANCE ON HER OWN?"

His face and neck began to turn blotchy and pink. "I'm just saying that she got us lost today on the river and she should have a guidebook, so that—"

"Guy?" I said, interrupting him. "There's this word called 'condescending.' Do you know what it means, or shall I buy you a dictionary so you can look it up?"

He stared down at his pizza crumbs and went quiet. His face was burning red. We walked back to the hostel in the dark, in silence, Guy trotting well ahead of us as usual, but without any whistling this time. He went to bed without saying a word.

The following morning, he woke up early and packed his bags. When Masha asked him a question, he ignored her. He slung his pack onto his back and left without saying goodbye before we'd dressed, his big red gerbera betraying him by springing about in comical cheer on the back of his pack as he walked out the door.

That was the last time I saw him.

"I feel sad for him," said Masha. "He wasn't like this when we first met. I don't know why he felt the need to behave that way."

I felt sad for him too, but not regretful. That was the last time I'd let a bully go running around in the garden with big, thuggish boots.

8

We stood over the dead animal in silence, inspecting its tiny form: all downy grey fur and hot red guts spilling from a high-impact wound. It looked so wrong. Such small creatures should not be so horrifyingly still.

"Oh no," said Masha. "That's so sad. It's only a little kitten."

"Maybe it's the one you manifested," I joked. "The one that won't run away from you."

I had intended to make her laugh, but the joke ended up as a cruel twist when she took it literally, gasped, and said, "Oh my god, you're right, it *is* my kitten." She hung her head.

I tried to backtrack. "Maybe it's just a dead cat."

"Well, I did say that I wanted one that couldn't get away from me. I think you might be right, Torre. I shouldn't have phrased it that way when we were manifesting. You can manifest bad stuff if you're not careful about how you articulate your desires."

My skin crawled at the thought. I nodded respectfully but concealed my skepticism. It was a vague coincidence; that was all.

Through a centenary forest of chestnut and beech, we followed a winding trail through the woodlands. We walked a skinny path on a carpet of fallen leaves and snaking roots, past mossy trunks, dense and damp. It is in this part of Italy that porcini mushrooms are foraged from the forest floor. Lichens blossomed on finger-like tree roots that clutched at the soil, and in the shadows between twisting limbs, tiny insects caught beams of sunlight on their wings and hovered like glowing fairies of the glades. These woods shelter deer and wolves and all manner of other beasts.

We were giggling when something shuffled in the bushes to our left, startling us to a standstill.

Masha snapped her head toward the forest. "What was that?" She turned to look at me with an expression that I hadn't seen on her before: panic.

It was alarming to see this person—a woman walking very long distances on her own—stricken with fear. It made me want to panic too, but it wasn't a smart idea for the two of us to become simultaneously terrified in the middle of the woods. When it comes to pessimism and optimism within a team, you have to take it in turns, riding the highs and lows like a seesaw, or else balancing together in the middle—otherwise you become a useless duo. Too much optimism, and nobody will be on the lookout. Too much pessimism, and you'll never leave the house. We often argue these differences within relationships, trying to pull the other person over to our point of view, afraid we're being misunderstood—not realizing these opposites can be harmonious with each other.

As Masha slipped into panic, I took on a compensatory role, which is how I ended up with a steady pulse and a serene smile, drawling in the tone of a therapist performing guided meditation, "Don't worry. I'm sure it's nothing."

My role as the cool and collected one gave her permission to become even more unhinged. Her face contorted, and her body stiffened as she froze on the spot, ear cocked to listen for clues. The bushes shuffled again. She jumped, and her walking sticks came up off the ground. "Holy shit! What is that?"

"Just a rustle," I said. "A harmless animal." My therapist voice was overworked and came out like thick honey. "Noooothing to wooorry aboooout."

"Do you think . . . " she said, "do you think it could be a . . ." Her cheeks drained of color. She looked like she might throw up. Her hands sprang over her mouth as she said, "Do you think it might be a . . . "

"A snake?" I offered, believing myself to be helpful.

"Ohmygodasnake?" She began psychotically kicking and wobbling as if made of latex limbs, her walking poles stabbing the air around us madly, her eyes like pinballs. "Doyoureallythinkthatwasasnake?"

"No, I—"

"Torre! I cannot handle a snake! I CANNOT HANDLE A SNAKE!" She used both hands to firmly cover her mouth, as though something might crawl into her snakehole.

"Masha, it's not—"

"I can't." Her voice was muffled behind her hands. "I just can't." She moved toward me with the focused determination of a drowning victim, as though she might try to crawl on top of my head.

"It's okay, it's okay," I said, clutching her shoulders and looking into her shifting eyes. "There's no snake, Masha. I was just saying 'snake' because I thought *you* were going to say 'snake.'"

"Stop saying 'snake'!"

"I'm just trying to tell you it's not a snake."

"I can't. I can't do it. Oh my god. No. I feel sick. I can't even . . . I don't know how I'm going to . . . "

"Masha!" I said, putting my face up in hers. "It's nothing, okay? It's probably just a little finch bird shuffling around for worms."

She dared to crane her neck in the direction of the shuffle, but then snapped her eyes back to mine. "Could it be?"

"Yes, absolutely."

Her bottom lip trembled. "Do you promise?" Her voice came out so small that I wanted to swoop her up and swaddle her in muslin. I hesitated to make a promise, but we were stuck in the woods, frozen solid by Masha's phobia trigger. We needed to keep moving, to get ourselves out of the woods and to the safety of an accommodation, but she was nearly catatonic.

Her eyes pleaded with mine, begging me to comfort her. *Tell me lies*, said her expression. *Tell me sweet little lies.*

"I promise," I said. "It's a bird. Definitely, for sure, absolutely a bird."

"Definitely not a snake?"

"Nope, definitely not," and then I got on a roll with my lies, because if you tell one lie, it opens a floodgate of completely unnecessary fictions. "You see, Masha, Italy is like New Zealand. It's a snakeless country. There are no snakes here in Italy."

"Really? Is that true? Is that a true thing?"

I had no idea. When you've grown up in Australia—a country that's home to an eclectic range of deadly animals—a few poisonous snakes here or there are essentially the same as no snakes. Also, I figured that if there were a lot of snakes in Italy, I'd somehow have known that by thirty-four years of age, because I would've seen it in a movie or a television show or perhaps on a BuzzFeed list titled "Top Ten Snakes of Italy That Can Kill You," or maybe on a box of cereal, or I would have heard mention of it in the lyrics of a pop song that goes: "I love you more than all the snakes in Italy!" To be fair, that is a stupid line for a love song, but still I was quite adamant that Italy wasn't a snaky country due to a lack of pop culture references, which is the entire basis of my common knowledge.

"Nope, definitely no snakes."

Masha removed her hands from her mouth and released the breath she'd been holding on to. "Oh, wow, that's a relief."

"Well . . . " I tried to mitigate my lie a little, in case I was wrong . . . "there could be a few, like, little grass snakes or whatever, but they're mostly just cute and—"

She covered her mouth again and froze, eyes wide, skin pasty. "There are no *cute* snakes," she managed through the cracks of her fingers.

"Actually, no, there are only little finch birds and ladybugs and rainbows and kittens."

Her hands loosened. "Did you say kittens?"

"Yes, kittens."

She dropped her hands. "Naw, I love kittens." Color began to flood back into her cheeks, and her eyes adopted the semi-amused expression of her normal self. "How cute are kittens?" She let out a small squeak of joy. Masha was back.

"And donkeys."

"Nawww, I love donkeys. I love donkeys so much, Torre!"

"I know you do."

Her eyebrows relaxed as she beamed at her own thoughts, which no doubt looked like Vaseline-edged, overexposed 1980s footage of kittens chasing balls of string and donkeys wearing flower garlands.

And we were off again, putting one foot in front of the other, making miles in the beautiful snakeless country of Italy.

It was then that I got a flashback to a scene from the film *Under the Tuscan Sun,* when there was a giant snake in the protagonist's home. That was a film based on a book, a memoir—so, yes, there *are* snakes in Italy, I remembered. Deadly vipers. Dammit. I just hoped the bastards would keep to themselves so I could uphold my sweet little lie.

✦

"These aren't poisonous, right?" Masha asked, which is a preposterous question to ask after you've eaten twenty or thirty portions of mystery fruit and there's juice dribbling down your chin from several still in your mouth, distorting your language to sound like: "Heeh harr hoi-hen-hess, height?"

It's a well-known fact that you shouldn't eat random berries or fruit you can't identify, but they were really delicious and so we made an exception. They were tart and sweet, like very small plums, and they grew in heavy clusters on the trees that lined our path. We'd never seen them before. They tasted like sugar and lemon pancakes mixed with reckless irresponsibility.

"I believe . . . not?" ("Hi heh-hebe hot?") I said, my cheeks bulbous with fruit—squirrel-like. "They taste fine. Should we stop?"

"I don't want to stop."

"I don't want to stop either."

"How bad can they be? They're so sweet and juicy."

"Maybe that's what Christopher McCandless said before he ate the berries and fell asleep forever."

She stopped chewing.

I stopped chewing.

We froze and held each other's stares for several long moments, and then both shrugged and kept on stuffing plums into our mouths.

"Delicious things aren't deadly," I offered.

"Oh, is that official wilderness advice, DeRoche?"

"No, I just made it up right now, because they taste like normal sweet plums, so that probably means they're normal sweet plums." I stuffed a few more into my mouth and said, "At worst, we'll probably get really bad diarrhea and then die on the side of the walking path together with our pants around our knees."

"Journalists will jump to conclusions, and the headlines will report: Lesbian lovers found dead with pants down while hiking."

We doubled over laughing until we choked on plum juice and coughed like walruses, and then we carried on with bulging pockets full of lunch.

Our path cut through long grass that hummed with insects. "You know what would be really great right now?" I said. "If we could find those wild strawberries I asked for."

"Um . . . how would you feel if, instead of manifesting strawberries in the wild we manifested, like, wild strawberry jam. Or wild strawberry liqueur!" She put emphasis on her sales pitch to try to arouse excitement from me. "Mmm, yum, wild strawberry liqueur."

"You mean, like, from a regular store?"

"Exactly! At a store!"

"But . . . you can always find strawberry jam or liqueur at a store. I don't understand. That doesn't seem very magical. What will that prove?"

"Hmm, okay . . . " she said, disappearing off into her own scheming thoughts.

9

THE RAIN FELL fat and heavy, but we were sweating inside our rain jackets so we opted to get soaked instead. We wore only the hoods of our jackets over our hair and let the rest of the jacket flap behind us like capes, covering our bags. We looked like superheroes—two soggy superheroes, lost in the Italian countryside.

"This is definitely the right direction, isn't it?" I yelled.

"Maybe?"

Every footstep squelched into mud, but our bodies were already so saturated that we couldn't be any wetter if we got in a lake and swam. Dodging puddles was something I'd stopped bothering with; I just hoped that when we passed through them, the depth would be lower than my breathing apparatus.

"I saw the yellow pilgrim icon on the signs not far back. This has to be right. It's just so weird; it's like we're walking on private property. And the path is so close to the electric fence—dangerously close. This seems like a strange place for the pilgrimage path."

"Yeah, I agree. It doesn't seem right."

We kept walking. It's always easier to keep following the same path forward, even when you sense you may have made a wrong turn a ways back. It's a special kind of procrastination that comes from resisting ownership of the fact you might've wasted time and energy going the wrong way and will have to exert more time and energy doubling back. Sometimes it feels better to live out a few more sweet seconds or hours, months, or years in denial than to face up to this wasted time—to waste even more time in the process backtracking—and so onward we walked.

We traced the boxy edges of a paddock, carefully avoiding the electric fence and the larger puddles. At the back corner of the farm, the path dropped down into monotone woods, soiled from the downpour. Thunder cracked. The sky was charcoal grey with storm clouds, and under the canopy of the trees, it looked like night.

"This just doesn't seem right."

"I know."

We walked on, ducking under low-hanging branches and climbed the roots of twisted trees, hairy with moss beards, wrinkled with age. In the dark of the woods, I remembered then what I'd read about wild boars.

"Masha, what do you think our chances are of encountering wild boars around here?" My body had begun to tremble from the wet.

She froze on the spot and turned back to face me with wide eyes, and I decided then that maybe I wouldn't make the best therapist, since I'm too full of my own phobias and they just come spilling out of me at inopportune times, in a dark wood, or in front of small, terrified children.

Rain dropped off her nose. "Wild boars?"

"Yes, wild boars. They have them in Italy. They live in the woods." *Stop, Torre, stop talking.* "Apparently they can dash out of the bushes and charge at you."

"They can?"

You're going to scare her, just stop.

I nodded. "They come out of nowhere in forests just like this, small and hefty and full of strength, and attack your thighs with their tusks. They puncture your muscles and they just keep charging and charging until you're incapacitated."

"That doesn't sound like a thing. Are you sure that's a thing?"

"It's a thing. Believe me. My dad wrote a horror movie about a giant killer boar called *Razorback*. People don't give much thought to them—I mean, they're pigs—they're *bacon* for god's sake—but they're dangerous. Could you imagine being rammed by a pig? Just rammed and rammed until your leg was all bloody and mangled and—"

Her expression eased. "Okay, that's enough, DeRoche. There-there. Dead dad. Shhhh." She gave me a wet dead-dad hug. "We're not going to get rammed by giant killer pigs. That was your dad's imagination. It was a movie. A mooovieee."

She didn't believe me.

"No, boars are real. They really do have them here in Italy, and . . . and I have to tell you about something I remembered from *Under the Tuscan Sun*—"

"*Shhhhhh.* There are no boars here. Noooo booarrs." Her voice was thick and sweet, like honey.

I persisted, anxious to convince her. "But boars are here, I've been reading on Google about how—"

"No boars. No snakes. No Google. *Shhhhh.*"

Thunder cracked right overhead and tapered off into a bone-rattling rumble.

We screamed.

It cracked again and echoed into itself, doubling its power until it seemed like the entire sky would tear open and swallow us whole. The rain fell harder.

We yelled and then laughed and then yelled again, confused about which one of us was going to play the therapist this time, but nobody stepped up. We held the terror at bay with wisecracks.

I yelled into the downpour: "Are we going to die now? If so, we should make sure we're wearing clean underwear."

"I'm all out. But don't worry about that, DeRoche. Nobody will ever find our dead bodies in these woods."

Thunder cracked again, and we scream-laughed.

"There goes my last clean pair too."

The path led down an embankment, past a park bench, under a low-hanging branch, over a fallen tree, and across a small bridge until we came to a stop at a gate that was locked and covered in construction tape and Do Not Enter signs, in Italian. Somehow we'd reached the end of the path.

"Is there another way?" Masha peered back over her shoulders.

I twirled a few circles but couldn't see any other way forward. "I'm so confused."

I extended my tongue to have a drink from the waterfall coming off my nose. Rain fell on Masha's phone as she tried to read the GPS.

"We've followed all the arrows," she said.

"The arrows pointed straight ahead."

"So this has to be the right path?"

"Right?"

"Maybe we should just climb over it? My GPS says the main road is not far beyond the other side of that fence."

"I'm game if you're game."

Masha went first. I held her walking poles and bag while she climbed up on the fence and jumped over, and then she held mine while I did the same. There was a sense of disquiet as soon as my feet touched the other side. Which makes sense, given that it was thundering right overhead, we were rain-soaked and potentially lost, and we'd just climbed a fence with a Do Not Enter sign on it.

Thunder split my ears. We screamed.

"I'm glad my mother can't see me now," I joked, but we were too focused on trying to find the path to bother laughing. There was a small road and we began to follow it, but it had become so wet that it was almost a lake. The directional arrows we'd been following on the other side of the fence were gone. This was empty, flooded wilderness. With no path to follow, it was just trees and puddles and mud. And boars, maybe.

"What's that?" I said, pointing to a hut high up on stilts in between the trees.

Oblivious, Masha was checking her GPS as I walked over to inspect it. There was a sign written in Italian, and I didn't understand any of it, but I understood the picture. A wild boar. We were in a boar-hunting reserve.

"Let's go," I said.

She looked confused. "Where?"

"Back. We need to go back. Now."

She followed me without question. I rushed her toward the fence. If there's anything I'm good at after years of simulated drills from all the catastrophizing going on in my head, it's taking control during a crisis. While everyone is casually eating popcorn and enjoying the film, I'm mapping all exits and escape routes for children and the elderly, which means, if disaster strikes, I'm straight into fight-or-flight, fit to fend off zombies while everyone else is stalled by confusion.

Eyes narrowed, I was in rescuer mode. We sloshed through puddles that lapped at our ankles. The rain was still falling: torrential, relentless. My eyes searched the bushes for tusks, for angry red eyes, for fogs of breath steaming from flared nostrils.

"What's the matter?"

"Nothing. Let's just get out of here."

Rain dripped into my eyes, blurring my vision. Thunder cracked but we didn't bother to scream-laugh; this was no time for jokes.

We reached the barricaded fence and, without words, handed each other our poles and bags, and climbed over one by one. In high-speed rewind, we backtracked over the bridge, along the skinny path, back through the dark forest, over the fallen tree, beneath the low-hanging branch, past the park bench, up the embankment, out of the dark wood, beyond the canopy, and back into the cloudy daylight on the path by the electric fence around the paddock. The dense clouds had moved on. The storm had passed. Only a light rain was falling.

I breathed and looked at the wide-open sky, letting the rain spatter my teeth as I grinned up into sweet freedom. We were safe. The cape of my rain jacket waved in the wind.

"What was that about?" Masha said.

"Boars."

"Huh?"

"Did you see the sign? The hunting cabin? Beyond the fence?"

"I have absolutely no idea what you're talking about."

"There was a sign on the hunting lodge with a picture of a wild boar on it. We were in boar territory."

She looked back, confused. "Oh, no, I see those huts all the time. They're everywhere along the Via Francigena. It's nothing to worry about."

"Oh." I was no hero; I was a fool.

I searched the ground, looking for a suitable plot of soft soil to dig a hole and bury myself in, but then I noticed Masha's elbow. It was a hair's width from the electric fence. Just as she was moving to take a step back into it, I lurched and tugged her forward.

"There's an electric fence right behind you."

"Oh. Right. Shit."

We shuffled off in the direction we'd come from, drenched, shaken, but back on track after resolving the mystery of our confusion: We'd been following directional signage that had almost the same design as those marking out the Via Francigena, but that led to a secluded reserve instead of Rome. I wanted to hunt down the people who got those signs made and smack them over the ears with bushels of stinging nettle.

✦

Doubling back over our tracks was tedious and tiring, and our bellies were rumbling from hunger. Evidently, wading through rain and fearing for your life burns a great number of calories, because the morning and afternoon had left us ravenous. Instead of triggering fear, the thought of wild boars now made me think of pork belly tacos and prosciutto-wrapped melon. BLTs, extra mayonnaise.

There were no restaurants in sight. No blackberries, no peaches to steal from old ladies' gardens with our walking pole straps. Our plums were long gone.

"Pizza," I said, without explanation.

"Rocket and buffalo mozzarella salad," Masha replied.

"Calamari."

"Ohh."

"In butter."

"A prosciutto and cheese platter."

"Homemade pasta."

"Wine."

"Pho."

"Now that's just crazy talk, DeRoche. You can't get Vietnamese soup in Italy."

She was right. Hunger was making me delusional. We walked on in desperate silence.

"Masha," I said, trying to distract myself from my nagging gut, "how does your husband feel about you walking around the world?"

"He's fine with it. He's a good person . . . "

"And? . . ."

"And what?"

"I don't know, the way you drifted at the end of that. I thought you were going to say something else."

"I'm too hungry to talk about it, DeRoche."

✦

At 3 p.m., we emerged from the forest and out onto an empty road, desolate apart from a standalone restaurant that was radiating beams of shimmering gold like a holy temple of pizza, pasta, and wine. I almost dropped to my knees. We'd made it.

"Il pranzo è finito," said the man who stopped us at the door.

I looked at Masha. "What'd he just say?"

She shrugged.

"Finito." He tapped his watch. "Due, due."

I snapped my head toward Masha, hoping she might translate those words into something other than what sounded obvious: Lunch had finished at two o'clock and the restaurant was now closing. Italy goes into siesta in the middle of the day, and it can be difficult, often impossible, to find food again until dinnertime.

I looked beyond the man to see a thinning group of diners forking around the last crumbs of their desserts. I wondered if it would be wrong to ask the man if he would be so kind as to scrape the leftovers into our open jaws.

"He's saying lunch has finished," Masha confirmed with a sigh.

We stood in the door, as soggy and sad as lost dogs, our spirits exhausted. The next town was hours away. We wouldn't be eating until dinnertime. We thanked him and turned to leave, but he stopped us.

"Finito, finito," the man said, looking urgent.

"Okay, sì, sì," Masha said.

He looked even more pained as he tapped at his watch. "Due, due."

We nodded again, okay, and still he continued. "Finito!" He looked almost angry.

"Okay?" We were confused.

"Finito! Due!" he said again, almost yelling with frustration as he tugged us into the warmth of the restaurant, sat us at a table, and began to serve us lunch out of the inconvenient obligation of his own heart. He disappeared into the kitchen and came back with a basket of bread, olive oil, and vinegar, and sheer relief pulsed through me. When he returned the next time, he brought back a pitcher of wine, which, he explained in Italian basic enough for us to understand, was homemade with his own grapes.

The old man then began to point at our wet clothing. I looked at Masha for translation, and she shrugged. He pinched the fabric of my damp T-shirt and repeated his words again, and I shook my head at him. He talked more slowly, pinching my shirt, making his curious plea, and still more slowly I shook my head in confusion.

He gave up and took off, and when he came back he was carrying dry white T-shirts, one that read "Manager" and the other advertising a local marathon. Almost in tears from his kindness, we thanked him and went to the bathroom to change into dry extra-large T-shirts, and when we returned there were steaming bowls of homemade pasta with pesto waiting for us. All the other diners had left and the restaurant was closed—this was all just for us.

The kind man served up more wine, and we sipped our way into a thick fog of dreamy contentment.

Every country has its own unique smell that must come from the soil and the particular habits of the region, and that smell gets transferred into the wine as though a place has been squeezed of its essence and poured into a pitcher. The wine tasted the way the air smelled: of basil and peaches and expanses of plump tomatoes, of soil that wobbled in the heat with vapors of bitter herbs and woody decay. It tasted of naps in flowers, of long country roads where sunsets painted skin with gold, of kind strangers with lyrical language and the bone-tingling relief of good food settling inside famished bellies.

"Masha, if we hadn't got lost in that storm, we never would've had this experience."

"That's the magic of a pilgrimage, DeRoche. Everything happens exactly as it should."

10

Nutella oozed from the croissant and down my chin. I took a sip of my Spritz before bothering to wipe it off. Cocktails, pastries, and other treats kept us motivated, and we'd stop for a break every time we found a place that sold them. Masha's shoes were off, her socks splayed on the pavement beside us at the outdoor café like wet, dead crows. I took one look at her blistered feet and trembled. Her toes looked like Sloth from *The Goonies*, twisted and ragged, with peeling skin.

"So we have to make sure there is no room for misunderstanding this time," said Masha. She was chewing the flesh out of the orange in her cocktail. "The kitten has to be alive, healthy, and friendly. Do you want to make any revisions to your requests?"

"My strawberries have to be fresh. I don't want jam. I don't want strawberry liqueur. I don't want wild strawberry body wash. I want *actual* strawberries, found in the *actual* wild."

She winced. "Yeah, about your strawberries. I didn't know how to tell you this, but, um . . . strawberries aren't in season right now."

"So?"

"So I saw them ages ago in the Alps."

"And?"

"And the season is long finished, DeRoche."

"So?"

"So, there are no wild strawberries. And you're not going to be able to manifest strawberries out of season. There's, like, zero chance that we'll find strawberries right now."

"Wait, wait, waaaaait—isn't that the whole point of manifesting? To bring anything into existence magically, like Harry Potter?"

"Well . . . you kind of have to work within the laws of the universe. You're not going to be able to, say, fly, and if you try you'll just fall and splat, because that's how physics works. You can't mess with physics. And you're not going to be able to manifest strawberries when it's not strawberry season."

"Well, that's dumb."

"You're dumb."

"I want wild strawberries."

"You can't have wild strawberries. Pick something else. Anything. Anything that isn't biologically impossible or defiant of the laws of physics."

"Well, that's limiting." I pouted. "And it's not really magic, is it? It's just running an errand for a thing you want."

"Just pick something."

"Okay, fine. A book. I want something to read."

"Any particular kind of book?" she asked. "Remember to be specific. We don't want to end up with another dead kitten."

"A small book. In English. Something meaningful. Something to tell me what I should be doing with my life right now. Something to give me guidance."

"Perfect. An important book in English to guide you. Do you know what I want?"

"What?"

"Another Spritz." She held up two fingers to the waiter and said, "Ancora due?"

Minutes later, the waiter placed two more cocktails before us. "See?" she said with a grin, sipping her second cocktail, pinky out. "Magic."

✦

The forest was damp from a recent rain, hushed and heavy, as though the trunks had sucked up all they could drink and had fallen into drunken slumbers. We walked to the *ting* of birdcall, soles strumming rhythm on soil.

Trees are sentient in ways we're largely ignorant of. In Peter Wohlleben's book *The Hidden Life of Trees*, he sheds light on how trees are social beings who suckle their young, nurse sick neighbors, and send tiny electrical currents across a fungal network that scientists call the Wood Wide Web to warn each other of danger. They use this network to work together as communities, to share resources and increase their overall strength. Entire forests are connected in this way, silently talking to each other beneath the unknowing crunch of our shoes. For centuries after a tree has been felled, its surrounding community will keep the stump alive by feeding a sugar solution into its roots for reasons unknown. There are so many unknowns in nature, and yet we've arrogantly come to see it as an insentient provider for our needs—wood and oxygen or shade on a hot summer's day, not a civilization full of its own rich and meaningful activity. How condescending. Their inner worlds are far more complex and intelligent than we recognize.

Our path became more and more overgrown until it was just a skinny alleyway through bushy grass and wildflowers. You could reach down and pluck up a handful of flora and end up with a bouquet readymade for a vase. My head was full of nothing and everything at the same time.

Below my feet, as I walked at the speed of two and a half miles an hour, I imagined tiny invisible roots branching from my feet down into Mother Earth, plugging me into the Wood Wide Web. As I looked around the forest, I saw a thousand acts of love taking place: the roots and trunk of a tree drawing moisture up from the soil to feed young leaves; its young leaves, in turn, drawing warmth from the sun to feed vitality to the old trunk. Birds gathered sticks for nests, and trees held chicks in the safe crooks of their branches. Such beauty. Awe washed over me in a wave of tingles.

Some researchers call this rippling wave of tingles over skin and down the spine a "skin orgasm," but the technical name for it is "frisson." Frisson might come when you're listening to moving music, or sitting in a film, or being touched by someone you love. It might come when you're walking through the woods, watching the symbiosis of nature unfold before your eyes.

I squatted down to pick up a heart-shaped rock from the mud, and then the thought of wild strawberries came into my mind. I began to search the brambles.

Masha walked ahead, weaving her way around all the puddles, and I followed in her footsteps while searching. It was futile, I knew; the season was over, but I felt compelled to search anyway, when—

"Masha!"

She stopped, turned to face me.

I crouched down and plucked a red berry from its stem. It was a perfect raspberry, tiny and wild. I presented it to her on the palm of my hand, saying, "Look, I almost found a strawberry."

"That is so weird." Masha kept her eyes on mine. "I was literally *just* thinking about strawberries. I've been searching the scrub for the last few minutes, trying to find them, saying *Please, please, please please . . .*"

We carried on walking, now with our eyes focused more keenly into the scrub, when seconds later—

"Holy shit. Torre."

I stopped.

"It's a wild strawberry."

"Are you serious?"

"Yes. It's a freaking wild strawberry." She plucked it from the stem. It was semi-dehydrated, clearly past its prime, but a wild strawberry nonetheless. Her eyes were wide as she handed it over.

I took a bite. It tasted like floral perfume. "That's pretty amazing," I said.

"There's another one," she said, dashing left.

"And other," I said, dashing right.

They were all over the path. We zigzagged in a frenzy of picking, collecting the berries from all around us. They were sparse and small, but there nonetheless—these tiny, delicious coincidences. We picked and ate each one we found, savoring their different flavors. The dark red ones tasted like flowers, while the lighter ones were sweet and tart. It was like sampling from a box of mixed chocolates. "Try this one," I said, offering her a fraction of berry. "It tastes like roses."

"It does. Try this one." She handed me a uniquely different delicacy. "It tastes like cupcakes."

"This one tastes like—"

"Hey, what's that?"

I followed her finger to see a fork in the path. Nestled into the undergrowth was a wooden sign pointing right, down the slope of the mountain and into deeper, darker woods. In yellow lettering was the word "ostello"—"hostel," and beside it was the little yellow pilgrim icon of the Via Francigena.

"It's a sign," said Masha.

"Indeed it is. A wooden sign."

"It's not on the map." She looked at her phone up close. "To get to the next village on the pilgrimage, we take *this* path." She pointed left, away from the sign. "But this other path isn't on the map at all."

"Strange. An ostello in the middle of the woods? Why would anyone put accommodation out here? We're only three or four miles from the last pilgrim accommodation, so it's too soon for another rest stop."

Masha flicked her finger along the screen of her phone. "The Via Francigena website doesn't list it. It's not coming up at all."

I looked down into the thick curtain of forest. "What if there is no ostello?" I said. "I mean, *Hostel in the Woods* is basically a horror movie title."

"You're totally right. This situation has gory blockbuster written all over it."

I looked around. "A sign with a yellow pilgrim on it *would* be a pretty clever way to lure two walkers into the deep, dark woods. I mean, just look at this forest."

"I agree. It's a very rapey forest."

"It really is."

"But you know," she said, "generally speaking, rapists are not usually organized enough to have wooden signage professionally etched, painted, and staked into the ground before they do their raping. So, there's that."

"Good point. But serial killers sometimes plot their kills for years. So it's probably a serial killer."

"Yes, you're right," she said. And then: "Maybe we should be careful. If we keep talking about the things we fear, we might bring them into being."

"Like a serial killer with a coonskin hat made from a dead kitten, carrying a small, important book?"

"Torre! Shhhhhhh!"

"Don't be ridiculous, we're not going to—" A twig snapped in the woods, and I jumped. "Fine. I'll stop."

"This is really bizarre."

"How far away do you think it is?"

She shrugged. "No idea. The sign doesn't give a distance, which is also unusual. Could be a mile. Could be five."

"It could be really far away and then turn out to be nothing."

"Right. Or it might be fully booked and then we'll have to walk the whole way back, plus the extra twelve miles to reach the village we'd planned on, which means we might not reach our accommodation before nighttime. It's a gamble. But also, it might be something amazing."

We stood there contemplating the fork. Sure, finding strawberries out of season was special, but wild strawberries grow in wild places—was it really a big deal? It was probably just a case of confirmation bias. And yet my body was still tingling with frisson, my mind buzzing with possibilities, and I wondered what would happen if we followed the sign. "I'm curious," I blurted.

"So am I."

Masha spun on her heels and we ventured deeper into the woods.

11

The path we followed was bursting with raspberries, their fuzzy pink whorls too tempting not to pick on the fly and pop into our mouths as we walked. They were sweet and seedy, and though my stomach was growing full with blackberries, strawberries, and now raspberries, I didn't want to turn down the generous hospitality of the forest. With all the snacking stops, we were making slow progress toward wherever it was we were going.

The strawberries had baffled me. Maybe they were there all along, but because we believed they were out of season, we were blind to them. In her book *On Looking*, cognitive scientist Alexandra Horowitz studies the unreliable nature of human perception by taking eleven walks around her urban neighborhood with a range of experts—from artists to geologists, sound designers to a dog—in order to see the world through different eyes. She uncovers that we see only what we expect to see and that what we call "reality" is incomplete. She says we focus our attention on what we think will be there in order to avoid overload, saying that "while this might make us more efficient in our goal-oriented day-to-day, it also makes us inhabit a largely unlived—and unremembered—life, day in and day out."

By this logic, if we believe we're not going to see something, we probably won't see it. But if we can suspend our beliefs about what we think we know to be true, what might we find? Perhaps there are numina all around waiting to be discovered, only to notice them you must have the curiosity, whimsy, and openness of a child. Without intellect obscuring their experience, children float among motes of luminous possibility, but as adults we focus our attention so tightly on our preconceptions that we hardly see an inch ahead through our black-tinted, worry-fogged glasses. "Right now," says Horowitz, "you are missing the vast majority of what is happening around you. You are missing the events unfolding in your body, in the distance, and right in front of you."

"I didn't think it would be this far," Masha said after several miles of downhill walking. The slope through the forest was steep. Backtracking would be a grueling uphill climb, and still the path carried on downward with no hostel in sight.

"Maybe it will be around the next corner," I said.

"Maybe."

We walked in silence. The forest had become thick and enclosed. There were no more brambles of berries, just grey trunks and fallen ashy leaves. I crossed my arms over my chest, cold from the damp and feeling foolish for deciding to follow a random sign into the woods.

When the canopy opened up to a landscape of hills under a blue sky, I was flooded with relief. Having spent the morning with my eyes fixed into the deep woods, I had to adjust my depth of field to reach out into the seductive undulation of the hills of Parma, famous for its prosciutto and, of course, for its stinky and delicious cheese.

"Ostello!" Masha said, pointing at another sign. "That way."

We followed the edge of a slim country road that curled along S-bends through the hills until we came to an ostello on the side of the road with green shutters, terracotta walls, and arched doorways. I smelled coffee.

Masha eyed me for a beat as she grasped the door handle and pulled. Inside was a warm trattoria with wooden tables and checkered tablecloths. All around the edges of the café were piles of worn books, stacked up in teetering towers, spines creased. Smells of crushed basil and cashews spilled from the kitchen, and an old Italian lady popped her head out from the kitchen to smile at us. "Buongiorno," she said.

"Buongiorno," we replied.

"Due cappuccini?" said Masha.

The old lady nodded. She asked if we'd be staying for dinner; she was making testaroli with pesto—a local crepe-like version of gnocchi.

Masha was wide-eyed. "Torre. It's our nonna."

On the corner by the bar, several old pilgrim walking sticks, whittled from wood, hung against a lemon-yellow wall. A little boy ran past and disappeared into the kitchen.

Masha turned to me and said: "Torre. Endless cappuccinos. Rows of books. Nonna. This is the café I asked for."

"A coincidence?" I offered, though the word was feeble off my tongue this time.

"You should look for the important book you asked for, to tell you what you should be doing with your life. There must be a hundred books here. Surely you'll find it."

We split ways and began searching the piles. They were stacked high, but none were in English. Stephen King, J. K. Rowling, John Grisham, Clive Barker . . . all the popular airport books were there, only they were in German, Italian, French, Dutch. Oh no, E. L. James . . . *Phew*, it was in German. Not my book.

Masha pointed across the room. "What's that?"

Following her finger, I spotted a small pot of plastic strawberries perched on top of a stack of books. Wavelets of energy rippled up from my toes to the flesh of my neck. I walked over, heart thumping.

There it was. A single book in English. I plucked it from the pile. My head was spinning. It was as if we'd walked into a set for a film we had written ourselves. Is this what happens to the mind when you burn too many carbs? If so, it would make a great diet book: *Weight Loss Through Delusions of Enchantment.*

"What is it?" Masha asked.

"It's a guidebook."

"For what?"

"The pilgrimage we're walking."

Tingles broke out all over my body, crawling along my skin. The noise of the café dimmed until all I could hear was the pulse of my heart in my ears. Masha took my hands in hers, and we stood face-to-face in a soundless bubble of two. I held up my arm to show her my skin, and she gestured to her own gooseflesh. Her eyes were open, bemused, bewildered, as if she would soon burst into either laughter or tears or a rain of celebratory confetti. My heart went *badoom, badoom,* and I could feel Masha's pulse through her hands. *Badoom, badoom.* We were trembling.

The noise in the café turned up slowly until I could hear Masha saying, "Are you totally freaking the fuck out right now?"

I nodded.

"Me too."

"Due cappuccini," said our nonna, placing two cups on a checkered tablecloth.

✦

Our bedroom in the ostello had vibrant walls with window shutters that opened out to a grassy lawn. Outside, a group of young men were kicking a football, and behind them was a ripple of hills rising up toward the dense forest we'd come from. We were spending the night inside a Tuscan postcard.

It was still early, not even noon, so we decided to go for a hike to find a quiet place in nature to have a nap. Off the side of the windy country road, we found a tall hill to climb where we could see out over the whole valley. We lay down side by side in a meadow, burying ourselves into a pillow of long grass and flowers, hidden from view.

"I can't believe this place," Masha breathed. "It's so beautiful."

"Like a dream."

"The strawberries."

"The book."

"Nonna."

My head was swimming with endorphins. Nothing was what it seemed anymore. I held a hand up to the sun and watched the way the honey-colored light melted between my fingers. Thirty-four years of age on my hands, the lines and grooves a map to my history—a history of fear and worry. Psychotherapy and self-help books, extreme adventure and meditation: a history of failed attempts to overcome. It didn't matter how many worries I placed on imagined leaves that I floated down meditation rivers while sitting for hours on end—eyes closed, legs crossed—I still woke every morning braced for the end of the world. All the while, there was another place coexisting behind the constant chatter of obsessive catastrophizing, a place sparkling with alchemy.

This new world was unusually silent. *Astoundingly* silent. Without my busy brain chatter, I could hear the click of insects in the grass and the sound a forest makes when the breeze is still. I realized the intricate song of birds had been there all along— the music of the forest. I had forgotten to listen. I hadn't been paying attention. I felt the friction of my clothing brushing the sensitive hairs on my skin, the chill of air as it rushed in through my nose.

Was this meditation? Whenever I'd tried to meditate in the past, it hadn't gone particularly well. My mind could access only two states of being: high anxiety, or sleep. I once did a ten-day meditation retreat and, sitting cross-legged in a room full of silent students, grew baffled when I noticed that somebody had let dozens of cats into the meditation room. They were curled up on everyone's meditation cushions, purring and licking themselves. But that wasn't the only anomaly going on: there was also a performing artist at the front of the room who had appeared out of nowhere to sing us a song, and then came the time for us to applaud. The jerking movement of my hands swinging together to clap woke me up. I'd fallen asleep sitting upright. There were no cats or performers, only a room full of meditators and me with my hands an inch shy of clapping into the silent room.

While the retreat was valuable, I lacked the ability to let go while awake, because being awake meant being hypervigilant, ready for disaster, and it had obscured my ability to see. What a waste, I thought, to have spent so many years of my life powering the pointless machine of worry. It's like tying an old engine to the trunk of a tree in the hope that it might become a vehicle that will take you somewhere better than here and now, yet all it really does is chug out smoke and noise, taking you nowhere while polluting the brilliant incandescence of Now.

Something smarted on my back. Prickly weeds in the grass below were poking through my shirt and into my skin, but shifting position would've woken Masha. I stayed motionless, trusting that I was right where I needed to be, prickly weeds and all. Without the chug of my worry engine running, even the pain on my back was different. My former impulse was to gasp, brace, or complain to anyone within earshot, but no longer was it something to resist; it was something that was just *so*. A part of the experience. Now I could see that pain, either physical or emotional, is just another fact among facts: sky, grass, flowers,

birds . . . pain. What compounds it into unmanageable proportions is the resistance—the Should'ves and Could'ves; the
Why-Me's and This-Shouldn't-Be's; the What Ifs, and the Fuck-
This-Shits. But if you let it exist, because it eventually will for all
of us, it doesn't have the same power over you. It's just a crawling, radiating, electric buzz rolling along your back, down your
hips, and into your underwear.

My underwear?

Oh well.

Trust.

In this state of surrender, I dozed off.

✦

We both roused and sat up, rubbing our eyes. Though I was no
longer lying on the prickly grass, strangely the pain on my back
continued to radiate with electric shocks, and so I inspected the
flattened grass below me.

It was alive with hundreds of ants.

"Oh no, Masha! I fell asleep on an ant's nest!" I sat up and
started slapping at my back.

"Let me see."

I pulled up my shirt to show her the damage. "Are there any
bites?"

"HOLY SHIT, DEROCHE!"

"Is it bad?"

"Your entire back is one giant ant bite!"

"It is?" I tried to twist my body around to see the damage,
but I couldn't flex that far.

"Here, let me take a picture." She took a photo and showed
me the image. My entire lower back was covered in an overlapping pattern of red golf-ball-sized welts. Apparently the entire
colony of furious ants had gone to war on my back.

"They've bitten your butt, too. Dude, didn't you realize you
were getting bitten?"

"I was surrendering. Backward. Into the universe."

"Ah . . . hmm . . . okay? So you just lay there for forty minutes letting ants bite you? And you actually fell asleep through it?"

"I didn't know it was ants. I thought it was a prickly shrub. I was going with it."

"Torre . . . " she said, tilting her head and stroking my arm, "it's impressive that you endured that so gracefully. Really. You deserve an award of some kind. But, my dear deranged twin, you just let yourself get chewed up by about three . . . maybe four hundred ants. That's a special kind of insanity."

I looked down at the nest. Ants were scrambling around in the war zone, dashing around maimed bodies and surveying the damage to their colony.

I clawed at my back. It was on fire. I rubbed a finger along the inside of my waistband and pulled out three ants. "Can we go home now?" I whispered. "I have ants in my butt."

I had no idea what this meant for my recent epiphanies. The strawberries, the nonna, the guidebook . . . had I gotten wrapped up in a fantasy and completely lost my mind? During periods of grief or high distress, people can lapse into magical thinking, becoming superstitious about the events taking place around them, drawing patterns from their environment to give divine meanings to events. Humans are wired for noticing patterns: grey clouds mean rain is coming; unfurling buds tell us food will soon be growing; a certain look in a man's eyes tells us women we should cross the street and pick up the pace. We observe these causative relationships in order to stay alive. But since profound losses like death and breakup throw off our sense of security for survival, this pattern making can go into overdrive—and so the grieving mind cannot always be trusted for accuracy of perception.

We climbed down the hill and went back to the ostello, so that I could excavate a family of ants from my crotch in privacy.

Were we manifesting goddesses? Were we women who ran with wolves? I wasn't sure, but what I did know was that I was still clumsy as shit.

✦

We were eating around a big table with a small group of travelers when we heard about the viper. I saw the terror on Masha's face before I caught wind of the story, could read what was happening by her body language alone: her ashen complexion, her goggly-eyes, the way her hands sprang up to cover her snakehole.

Two cyclists from Milan were chatting in Italian with the owner of the ostello, and Masha had leaned in close with one ear to eavesdrop.

"What's happening?" I asked.

Her eyes remained fixed on the conversation. "Oh, god, Torre," she said. "Oh, this is bad. This is really bad."

"What?"

She listened for a while longer and then began to translate to me from the crack between her hand and her mouth. "There was a viper . . . out the front . . . on the road . . . just outside the ostello. Recently. Very recently."

Never mind the snake story. I was dumbfounded by Masha's sudden ability to understand quick, conversational Italian. "You speak Italian now?"

"Shhh," she said. "A woman . . . got out of her car and . . . oh god . . . oh . . . oh my god, Torre!"

"You're translating Italian now. I can't believe it."

"Shhh. She . . . oh . . . ugh . . . she got out of the car and . . . the viper . . . it was on the road and . . . on the shoulder of the road and . . . near the water fountain." She froze. Her eyes were saucers. "I can't."

"What happened?"

"She stepped out of the car and . . . I can't even . . . say . . . The woman put her foot . . . on the snake and . . . " She paused to dry-retch. "Oh, Torre!"

"And?"

" . . . it bit her."

"Okay, well, um . . . " I struggled to know how to handle our ad hoc therapy sessions with this new piece of overly truthful information. If snakes were biting people on the road, what hope did we have in the woods? "We . . . can . . . just . . . simply . . . um . . . " I stalled my speech, hoping I might find a way to comfort her somewhere in between all my long pauses. "Well, what if we just . . . um . . . "

But while I was busy stalling, Masha had retrieved her phone from her pocket and began to Google pictures of Italian snakes, flicking through page after page of horrendous images of scaly, fanged creatures, her scrolling finger stiff, eyes glassy with panic.

"You probably shouldn't do that. Google is not your friend right now. If ignorance is bliss, then information is the enemy of bliss. Put down the Google."

Her eyes were moving fast down the page. She clutched her phone, refusing to part with it. "There are four kinds of vipers here. Four, Torre. The *Vipera aspis* is responsible for 90 percent of all cases of snakebite in Italy, and it's the only snake in the Italian mountains that can kill you." Her eyes dashed down the page while her thumbs scrolled madly.

I gave up trying to play therapist and succumbed to my own curiosity, giving myself over to Google. *During mating season, the females sometimes hang in trees and can be very territorial if you get too close.*

Okay, this was all very bad news. I switched my phone off. "It's okay, we'll just . . . um . . . we can use our walking poles to um . . . " I scanned my brain files for a smart survival action plan, and all I could come up with was: *To avoid snakebite, don't walk through the woods all day, dickhead.*

Masha spoke. "You know what that means, right? We're never going outside again. Never." She'd drawn the same conclusion as I had. "And obviously cars aren't safe either, because that's how the lady outside got bitten, so we're living here now, in this ostello with the old man and our nonna and the books and the library café. This is our home. This is where we retire. This is the end of the line. Get cozy. I hope you like it."

I sighed and buried my head in my hands. In a last-ditch effort, I said: "There are only four types of poisonous snakes here. That's not too bad, right? I mean, it's not nearly as bad as Australia, and I almost never see snakes at home. Plus, you have to remember that snakes are more scared of us than we are of them. When they hear us coming, they take off. The reason that lady got bitten is because she accidently snuck up on one in a car and put her foot right on it. That won't happen to us. We make lots of noise. Don't worry."

To which she said, "Screw you and your freakish, hardcore Australian resilience, DeRoche. I know you were birthed out into a giant pit of writhing snakes or whatever, so you can do whatever you want, but this is where I live now and I'm not going anywhere and you can't make me."

12

"Okay," I said to Masha. "Just focus on the road." It had taken a great deal of effort to coax her back outside, luring her with the promise of cappuccinos and another Spritz once we got through the next stretch of forest.

To make matters worse, two additional Italian pilgrims we'd seen in the ostello had also warned us of snakes in these parts. The woman had pulled thick snake socks up to her knees before leaving the ostello, saying "Buona fortuna" on the way out.

"Good luck to you too," we replied. It looked like we'd all be needing it.

The woods now appeared a little less like a source of glittery, unicorned magic and a lot more like the perfect habitat for coiled, scaly death. We dared not put our hands in brambles to pick anything on this morning. Our lives had been sectioned off into two distinct epochs:

Life *before* Googling snakes in Italy.

Life *after* Googling snakes in Italy.

The good old days of yore were all laughter and golden sunshine and twirls in green hills, alive with the sound of music. But now the hills were alive with the sound of serpents.

"What was that?" A shuffle in the bushes would jolt Masha into wide-eyed alarm, and she'd begin keenly searching the scrub along the side of the road. She'd fix her sights on the most vaguely snaky object and shriek, "What is that? Is that a snake?"

"It's a stick."

"Oh, yeah." She'd relax. Ten minutes later, she would come to a mulish standstill once again. "What is that? Is that a snake?"

"It's a piece of old rope."

"Oh. Right."

She'd relax her legs back into a walk, albeit a slow one.

Conversation was strained. Our normal banter was stiff and jolted, our laughter nonexistent. Long, lazy naps in the grass were now out of the question, belonging to the distant era of our former younger, stupider selves. That we'd ever fallen hard asleep in long grass was now a baffling prospect.

Time passed slowly. Miles ticked by sluggishly. There was no joy in this experience. Exactly why were we walking all day, every day on end? Our surroundings were ominous and rife with threats, and the Masha I knew and loved no longer inhabited the body that was shuffling along the road beside me, jumping at every bird chirp. When we passed a quarter-inch-thick cable on the side of the path, she almost climbed onto my head. "What is that? Is that a snake?"

"It's a USB cable."

"Oh. Yeah."

"Watch out, it might jump out and charge your phone."

She wasn't in the mood for laughing; she wasn't even listening. She was too busy scanning the grass, ears cocked for dangers. My jokes fell on deaf ears.

When there was an actual snake on the road, however, she wasn't the first of us to notice it. I spotted it squashed on the road, well ahead. "Okaaaay," I said, talking in my most thickly honeyed voice. "I'm going to let you know that we are

approoaaaaaching a very much deaaaaad, very much car-flatten-
nnned animal that is in no waaaaay dangerous, and—"

"A snake?!"

"Yes, it's a snake, but—"

Her limbs became floppy latex. "Oh no. I can't. I can't do it.
I can't do . . . I can't—"

"It's a snake, yes, but here's what I'd like you to do. It's dead.
Harmless. I'm right here and you're safe. I want you to try something with me." I thought of the advice I'd once been given by a
psychoanalyst in dealing with phobias. Perhaps it was irrespon-
sible to begin meddling with the cogs and wheels in Masha's
head, but when you're on an adventure in the wild, you need
to become a versatile survivalist, and a survivalist has to wear a
lot of hats, like Bear Grylls. On this day I decided it was time
for me to wear the hat of a revered psychoanalyst and university
professor with a PhD and forty years of professional experience.
"I want you to get near it and have a look at it," I said. "Like, up
close."

"Are you crazy, DeRoche? No way. No. No fucking way."

"The closer you can get to it, the less power it will have over
you."

"You're insane."

Coincidentally, the psychoanalyst had explained to me
through metaphor that to have anxiety is like having a snake
somewhere in the room, but you don't know where that snake is.
Is it under the couch? In the cupboard? Hiding in a hole in the
wall? Coiled up in your boot? If you knew, you could do something productive about it, like walk away, kill it, or befriend it and
call it Barry—if you're into that kind of thing. But because you
don't know where it is, or even if it's there at all, you have the
adrenaline response of fearful anticipation without the release
that follows after you've fought or fled. That nervous energy gets
trapped in the body as unresolved tension. Anxiety. And so, to
find the snake in the room is better than not, because then you

run, kill it, or befriend it and call it Barry. That's why it's important to face fears: to exorcize anxiety.

But that was a metaphorical snake with a qualified therapist.

And this was an *actual* snake with an unqualified *me*.

I had no idea if it would work.

"I'll go first," I said, approaching the snake. It was a scaly
ribbon of dry skin, as intimidating as any strip of jerky might be,
which is to say not at all. Its little jaw was wide open, compressed
into a permanent scream of fright at the car barreling toward
it—now weeks gone. "Come over. I'll stand here and make sure
you're okay."

She began to inch her legs closer. Toe by toe. She stopped
and looked up at me, watery-eyed.

"It's okay, come. It's harmless. Dead. Powerless. Jerky. Come
and see it."

She scooted a little closer, a timid shuffle, holding both
hands over her mouth, her walking poles dangling from her
hands and poking out to either side of her as she moved within
four feet of it. She peered over the snake as if looking over a
cliff's edge, her face twisted up in disgust.

"I'm right here. You're safe, Masha."

Her tiny voice quivered as she said: "Can we go now?"

"Yes, let's go. You've done really well."

A little ways down the road, conversation eased as Masha
began to inhabit her own body once again, and the sound of
our laugher drowned out the slithers of any serpents.

✦

The climb up toward the pass between the Ligurian and Apennine mountain ranges was grueling and relentless. Beyond the
climb, Tuscany awaited. I took the lead so that I could be on
snake watch.

"Torre, please don't leave me and go back to Australia in a
week. I need you to be my personal snake wrangler. Like, forever."

I laughed. "What *will* you do once I leave? Aren't you planning to go to India? Doesn't India have, like, really poisonous . . . "

"Shhhh!"

"Would you quit walking if it got too scary?"

"I'll never quit. I said I would do this, and so I'm going to do it."

We fell into silence, and the sounds of the forest took over.

Left foot, right, left, right—as my limbs moved on autopilot, warmed by the flow of blood, the endorphins kicked in and every cell in my body eased into contentment until it felt disembodied. Back in the forest on my feet and safe from any nests of angry ants, I practiced surrendering into the mind space I'd found the day before on the hill. With my body floating in an ethereal realm, my mind became a radio station tuned into stunning clarity. Birdsong, leaves crunching, the sigh of trees, the touch of fabric on skin . . . Once again, there I was inside the present, free of all rumination.

You can call it meditation, or you can call it *flow*. I had only ever read about this state of being before, but it seemed as elusive as Bigfoot. Coined by Professor of Psychology Mihaly Csikszentmihalyi, flow is the experience of being fully immersed in an activity and wanting to be nowhere else apart from where you are, even with all the pains, sorrows, and imperfections of that place. It can happen during an entirely pointless exercise, like doodling or surfing or walking for weeks on end. No matter how you do it, when you surrender yourself fully to what is taking place in the here and now, instead of the ruminative *if only* or the anxious *I should*, you begin to inhabit the three-second window of now.

Three seconds. Apparently, that is the duration of a single present moment. Researchers did a frame-by-frame analysis to measure the length of post-competition hugs given and received by eighty-nine male and ninety-six female Olympic athletes and found that, on average, each hug was 3.2 seconds long. But what is odd about this phenomenon is that this same pattern of three seconds appears repeatedly throughout cross-cultural studies in everything from music to speech, movement to poetry. Poets often write three-second lines. Spoken language follows a three-second rhythmic structure. Infants have been observed to babble and gesture in three-second patterns. On average, the length of time we can keep something in mind without writing it down is . . . yep, you guessed it: three seconds. Psychologists call this window of alert perception "the feeling of nowness." And incredibly, it's not just humans who have been shown to experience this beat. Animals also display patterns three seconds in length—from chewing to defecating. Giraffes, pandas, kangaroos, roe deer, and raccoons living in zoos all show signs of moving to the same tango beat of the universe.

Life, when imagined in full, is so overwhelmingly complex and long and short and slow and fast and frightening, but when you break it down into simple beats, you get a series of tiny, manageable windows through which to peer and observe, to know the sensations of being alive, to smell and feel, to love and be loved. Three seconds. That's all there is to surrender to: the magic of a single moment.

When I came out of my daze, I realized we'd reached the peak of the mountain. My muscles were trembling, but I'd hardly been aware of the climb up, because I'd been so absorbed in the feeling of nowness. A branch could've fallen off a tree and smacked me in the head, and all I would've thought was: *Wow, that trickle of blood running down my skull feels so deliciously warm, like melted chocolate, and that shock of tingles from the impact site is so electric and excitingly painful! How lucky I am to know this feeling!*

Or (*cough, cough*) dead.

13

THE SUN BEAT down on the fawn-colored grass that lined each side of the walking path. Yellow sprigs of Spanish broom were dotted into the landscape as if by the sable of an impressionist's brush. The warm breeze bent the grass sideways and combed the hairs on the nape of my neck. Our path was rocky. We both kept our eyes down to avoid falling.

Our feet crunched gravel, and wind brushed off the grass, cooling my sweat-soaked back. "Masha, I have to go back to Australia in a few days. I won't make it to Rome. I'm so sorry that I have to leave you. I would happily walk with you forever, but I have work to get through, so I'll have to catch the train back to Milan once we reach Lucca to make my flight."

She hung her bottom lip. "You should come walking in India with me in a few months. I mean, think about it: If this is what a pilgrimage together in Italy is like, imagine what it'll be like in one of the world's most spiritual countries."

"Unbearably self-involved and overemotional?"

"Always. But with a lot more diarrhea."

"We can paint the sidewalks like Jackson Pollock's canvases."

"Most definitely. And don't forget the constant fear of rape."

"And snakes."

"We don't talk about snakes."

"There are no snakes in India."

She smiled and then went quiet. "I'm terrified. Seriously."

"What's your plan?"

"I want to follow in the footsteps of Gandhi, along his Salt March protest from Ahmadabad to Dandi, only I have no idea how to make that happen, because it's not a common pilgrimage and I've found zero information about it online. Tourism companies aren't replying to emails. I have no idea where to sleep. So I can guarantee nothing apart from this . . . " She turned and looked at me, pointing to her toothy and charming smile.

I waited.

That was it, the sum of her offering.

Our feet strummed in rhythm as I thought about India.

It was one thing to walk through Tuscany together, picking fruit, drinking wine, and twirling on hillsides, but another pursuit entirely to trace the route of a political protest along exposed roads in a notoriously harsh, male-dominated country. Seeking answers to personal questions by following in the steps of a man who devoted his life to improving human rights seemed a little incongruent. But for the atheists and agnostics among us, the anxious and depressed, the spiritually lost and the existentially confused, who are our modern-day mentors? Whose steps should we walk in? The Kardashians'? Politicians'? CEOs'? Medical doctors'?

"Take one per day," said my doctor, sliding an antidepressant prescription across his oak table, "in the morning with some food."

All hail the MD. When several parts of your life break at once, it becomes hard to tell the difference between one bout of grief and the next. That is perhaps what I resented most about the timing of the breakup: that I could no longer tell where the pain from losing my dad ended and the heartbreak began. It was all-encompassing and widespread, and I didn't know how to locate the source of it in order to start healing.

The doctor did. "You're suffering from severe depression after the breakup and your father's passing. But if you take these, you should start to feel better in about two weeks."

I was in a nose dive and wanted a quick way to level out the plane again.

"Thank you," I said, wiping the tears from the corners of my eyes and tucking the prescription into my bag. Behind the doctor, in a backlit frame, was an advertisement for Botox featuring a fortysomething woman showcasing her smooth, poisoned skin. I patted my own puffy eyes. Life is so terribly aging.

In order for the doctor to obtain a diagnosis, I'd filled in a form that analyzed my emotional well-being with a series of questions, which I had to answer by circling either *Yes, Sometimes, Don't know, Hardly ever,* or *Never.* For the question "I sometimes fantasize about not living anymore," I had circled *Sometimes.* The thought of closing my eyes and having it all go away was a refuge, and I had answered the question honestly. Strangely, though, there was no follow-up question such as, "But *would* you ever kill yourself?" because the answer to that would've been a firm "No fucking way." Out of an unbreakable loyalty and love for the people in my life, suicide is—and can never be—an escape option, but, still, he put the words "Suicidal ideation" in my diagnosis. Seeing those words next to my name made me feel like a stranger to myself.

But now I had a solution on a piece of paper in my handbag, and the knowledge that I would feel better in only two weeks was, in itself, enough to make me start feeling better. The prescription gave me a sense of control over the uncontrollable. My wings were already leveling out.

The next morning, I took a pill with food, as prescribed, but then later that day, I spoke with a friend about my decision to start taking antidepressants. "Torre!" he said, shouting into the phone. "You're supposed to feel sad! You've lost two people! You're in a state of grief! This is a completely normal reaction!" Because he's a hematologist and a man of science, his words packed weight. I tossed the pills the next morning, making a firm commitment to figure it out the good old-fashioned way: by holding my breath and taking a deep dive into the depths of my own psyche.

Of course, SSRIs are a vital option for some, and I don't want to dismiss their importance, but medication has become such a common go-to solution that we don't stop to think that, in the history of humankind—no matter the race or country—we are not the only generation of people to experience negative feelings. It's part of the human condition. Learning to crawl out of the holes we fall into is part of our personal evolution. "Depression can kill you," says author Krista Tippett. "It can also be a spiritually enriching experience." In that case, it can be a lot like adventure.

But whom can we turn to for guidance if we're not religious? Even those who start out as inspirational thought-leaders are so often packaged up and mass-produced into a merchandised brand, diluting the core message into a string of agreeable sound bites. Nothing is left sacred. No profound insight goes un-meme'd. No self-development program is safe from morphing into a cult. Even meditation is mined for money, with watered-down programs popping up all over the place, promising to make easy, bite-sized work of an otherwise intensely dedicated practice. Ain't nobody got time for intensely dedicated practices. We want our wisdom and well-being served up quick, fast, and five-star reviewed. It's just capitalism, baby.

Perhaps, then, it's no wonder that forty million people in the world's wealthiest, most productive economy—the United States—have anxiety disorders. "Few people today would dispute that chronic stress is a hallmark of our times or that anxiety has become a kind of cultural condition of modernity," says

Scott Stossel in his book *My Age of Anxiety.* Abundance brings us endless choice, but "Anxiety is the dizziness of freedom," as Søren Kierkegaard said.

So accustomed are we to pill-popping solutions and quick fixes that we are poorly equipped to confront enormous—and deeply anxiety-producing—challenges like climate change. Humanity has entered the Anthropocene, a geological age in which—according to 97 percent of climate scientists—humans are responsible for catastrophic climate change. If predictions are accurate, we will drive ourselves toward the end of organized human life as we know it. It's terrifying. So terrifying, in fact, that the critical mass would prefer to live in denial while governments, corporations, and other self-interested parties continue to push the planet toward its end. In our hunger for quick fixes and hedonistic hits, we're continuing to generate an enormous ecological debt. It seems that our shortcuts have cut short our ability to introspect and self-actualize, and we're soul-sick. Paralyzed by fear. "The enemy is fear," said Gandhi. "We think it is hate, but it is fear."

I wondered if this kind of existential fear was something that could be overcome. Though I'd come closer to finding relief from anxiety during the Italian pilgrimage, I still hadn't found a cure. *Perhaps one more adventure will do it,* I thought. *Just one more.* But then in poured the guilt of going against the promise I'd made to myself. For how much longer would I be away from home, from family, from growing up and settling down as I sought a cure for anxiety? Was it even an achievable goal? Gandhi is famous for his fearlessness, and this seemed like an opportunity to glean wisdom from his life. *Perhaps Gandhi has the answers?*

"So what are you thinking?" said Masha.

"I'm thinking: India will be pretty much exactly like this, but with more danger, snakes, men, dust, pollution, shit, and general fearing for our lives, right?"

"Exactly, DeRoche. And more dead things. A lot more dead things."

She knew my whiskey. I *had* to see the dead things.

"Can you promise me something, Masha? Can you promise we won't become those kinds of people who profess to have found enlightenment from a holy man in an orange *dhoti?*"

"And start every conversation from that point on with, 'My guru says'? . . ."

"Exactly."

"That won't be us."

"Do you promise?"

"No. We're very impressionable. I make no promises about anything. So does this mean you're coming?"

Just as I'd coaxed Masha toward the snake in order to help her face her phobia, she was drawing me to this adventure. Perhaps if I could face the worst horrors up close, I could get rid of my anxiety forever.

"Count me in," I said.

Masha wrapped a sweaty arm around my shoulder and said, "I love you so much, my deranged twin."

Madness

14

THE HOLY MAN had a long black beard with a cascade of white rippling through it, and his soft, well-fed belly pushed at his shirt buttons.

"Would you like your fortune read, ma'am?" he said.

He was a charlatan—of that I was sure, a con artist with a warm smile peddling spiritual sound bites to tourists, alongside the carts of bootleg DVDs and deep-fried insects on Khao San Road.

"No, thank you," I said.

I was waiting in Bangkok for my Indian visa to process while Masha waited for hers in Turkey, where she'd just completed a pilgrimage with her dad. But getting visas for India was proving to be a lengthy and complicated process, so I sat it out in a cheap accommodation, doing freelance work from my laptop or wandering the streets to watch the spectacle of the city.

Bangkok is everything you don't want and everything you do, crammed together into space that grows outward and upward at the speed of a tropical vine, that smells like the freshest flowers and the stalest farts whisked together. It's simmering spices and exhaust fumes, foul egg and frangipani, clean laundry and somebody's quick piss down Soi 20. It's a charlatan standing in the street, looking to get money, saying, "Excuse me, ma'am? Your fortune?"

Hawkers prey on naïve travelers, but I was no first timer in the city of tumult and temptation. I knew all the tricks and charms of the charlatans, knew how to sidestep them with speedy grace, so that not even the best salesperson could sell me a cheap umbrella in a rainstorm; I'd sooner get soaked than be fooled by the ol' sell-very-affordable-umbrellas-when-it's-pouring-rain scam. Oh no sir, not me.

I dared not look at him. I had my standard line locked and loaded on my tongue—"Nothankyou"—so that I wouldn't have to stop walking for even a moment.

He said: "You're searching for something," and I thought, *Everyone is, pal,* and I kept moving, head down.

He called out, "You travel a lot. Not to see, but to understand. You're a seeker."

And I thought: *Dude, your shtick is so late 2000s.* This "guru" was clearly capitalizing on the demand for spiritual awakenings from melancholic drifters with a surplus of money and time, for only the privileged can afford these self-indulgent episodes of metaphysical disenchantment. He was selling faith to fools. I didn't want any cheap knockoffs—not his advice, not the Prada bags for sale in the stall beside him.

"You're a worrier," he yelled after me. "Always thinking. But you need not worry."

Damn, he was good, but anyone need only look at the → || ← between my eyes to know this detail about me. *You will not trick me with your clever techniques. Nothankyou. No way. Nohow.* "Okay," said my mouth.

Down a narrow alley, he offered me a small plastic stool, and we sat. His eyes found mine and held them in a deep gaze. People don't look deep into your eyes like that very often; when they do, it's usually because they're about to say either "I love you" or "You have cancer." I shifted in my seat.

He lit a stick of incense, and it wafted a coil of smoke up into his eyes, which were yellowed, with copper-brown irises. He didn't blink. The space between us filled with sandalwood, masking the odors of the alleyway: fish sauce and stale beer, garlic simmering in a wok. It smelled mildly of bullshit, too, which is why I was suppressing a snigger. Still, he didn't blink.

"Magical Negro" is a Hollywood trope used to describe the stock exotic character who often shows up as a device in stories to further the quest of the white hero with his wisdom and mystical powers. This man would not be my plot device.

"You're very spiritual, ma'am," he told me, his voice a deep purr, eyes boring into mine. "You have a snake right here." He prodded at the flesh at his brow and held my gaze. "A prominent third eye."

I arched an eyebrow. "I bet you say that to all the ladies."

"No, I don't say it to all the ladies." He was on to me. "You think this is all a joke, ma'am, but it is not a joke." Incense smoke coiled into his eyeballs as he let that sit with me for a moment. Didn't this man ever blink? My eyelids fluttered empathetically.

Someone opened the backdoor of a restaurant and sloshed a bucket of dirty water into the drain, while a homeless dog trotted past us, nails clicking on pavement to scavenge what he could from the edible mush.

"You're very observant," he continued. "Very spiritual. You have a bright light inside you and that light draws people in. People want that light. But you must be very careful, ma'am, about giving away all your energy. You're very good at taking care of others, but, I'm very sorry to tell you, ma'am, not so good with yourself." His head bobbled around in agreement with himself.

Wasn't he merely describing the traits of a typical nurturer? Clearly he was using the standard fortuneteller's trick of being so inclusive that almost anyone could identify with his descriptions. That's how horoscopes work, too, using ambiguous information that we then match with entrenched beliefs through confirmation bias. You hear whatever you want to hear to validate whatever it is you want to believe.

"You think too much," he said. "Always analyzing, picking apart. And while you have a very open heart, a very happy heart, I'm sorry to tell you that you are concealing sadness. I'm very sorry, ma'am, but I have some very bad news."

My stomach fell. Bad news? My dad dead. My relationship finished. Seriously? More bad news? Cancer. Was it cancer? It was cancer. Oh shit. I caught myself believing his hocus-pocus and straightened up.

He tilted his head with sympathy. "Your chakras, ma'am . . . they are not aligned."

I fought the urge to make a big, wet, lip-flapping farting noise with my mouth. "Right, okay."

"Something has happened. Something painful. There is a man. Two men, actually. Do you know who these men are?"

I paused, needing a little time to work out this particular hat trick. I had it: Every woman has a man or two misaligning her chakras. As a teen, I worked part-time in a fast food restaurant, and on two separate shifts two different men went through my drive-through without pants on. I can tell you that serving an otherwise normal-looking man who is nonchalantly saying, "One cheeseburger and a small Coke, please," while a flaccid penis rests in his lap like a shriveled newborn puppy, will certainly misalign your chakras. Whatever a "chakra" is.

Once again, his predictions were vague and designed to be all-inclusive. This con man would not con me.

"You know who these men are," said the yogi. "You know who I mean. And now you must put the past behind you now. Do you promise?"

I was lost in my own thoughts about why those men had no pants on. It's like they'd forgotten to dress their bottom halves before going for a fast food run. Shriveled puppies. *Heh heh heh.*

The yogi snapped. "This is serious! I am being perfectly serious with you, ma'am. You think it is all a big joke. It is not a joke. You must promise. Do you promise?"

I shrugged and nodded weakly.

"Say it," he said. "Say 'I promise.' Be serious. This is serious. Do not be laughing." His patience was wearing thin.

"I promise," I said, choking down one last chortle.

"And stop doing *that,*" he said, pointing to my left hand. Without realizing it, I'd been jabbing at the skin behind my thumbnail with my pinky nail—a subtle anxious tick that brings a small thrill of pain when the nail bed separates from my thumb. I do it subconsciously now and then. "It's not a good habit, ma'am. Stop doing it." I was surprised he had noticed this without taking his eyes off mine. I stopped picking my nail, sat upright, and wiped the schoolgirl's smirk off my face.

He pulled out a pen and scribbled some words down on a small piece of paper, which he folded into a tight square and handed to me. "Place it into your left fist. Squeeze it shut. Do not open."

I closed it in my left fist.

"You're going to be traveling to India soon," he said.

Wait, had I told him that? I couldn't remember. Perhaps when he'd first tried to solicit me, I'd said: "I'm dropping off my Indian visa application at the consulate today, so *Nothankyou.*" Yes, that happened. I'm pretty sure that happened.

"India is a very spiritual country. It's impossible to go to India and not have spiritual experiences."

Now he seemed to be reading excerpts from a travel guide-book, and it took a great deal of willpower not to press my lips together and go *Phhhhhrrrpphhhhp.* What had started out as a novelty was now becoming tiresome, and I was regretting my decision to sit down with him in his alleyway office, concerned that he was going to ask for a lot of money for this nonsense.

He handed me a piece of paper and a pencil. "Write one word on it. Write something you want for yourself. But just one word. One single thing you want more than anything. Write it so that I can't see it, then fold it up and put it in your right hand."

I held pencil to paper and chewed my lip, and he said, "Don't overthink." I covered my writing with my hand and wrote P-E-A-C-E. Peace from my own ceaseless mind.

"Okay, now pick a bird," he said. "A strong bird."

"Eagle," I replied.

"Pick a color," he said.

"Blue."

"And now a number."

"Nine."

"Open the paper in your hand," he said, tapping his hand onto my left fist, the one with his handwriting on it. I did as he said, folding the paper open.

"Tell me what it says."

My head spun. "It says 'eagle,' 'blue,' 'nine.'" I raced to work out his trick. Maybe he had set me up to write those answers with the power of suggestion. "A strong bird" is clearly an eagle. Anyone would pick an eagle. He must've done the same with the color and the number, perhaps it was a trick of—

"Soon you will write another book," he said, moving too quickly for me to complete thoughts.

Had I told him that I write? I was losing track of what I had and hadn't told him; he was talking so fast, jumping around from topic to topic to distract me from catching onto his—

"You write books . . . " he interrupted.

"Well, that's not true. Because technically I've written only *one* book and—"

"But you also help people. You're a teacher. Not a school-teacher, but a teacher of life."

"Well, memoir is probably more in the realm of gratuitous public over-sharing than 'life teachings' but—"

"Don't give blow jobs until you're married."

I gagged on my in-breath. "What?"

"Don't do it. Until you're married. It's not good for spiritual people like you to be very intimate like this unless you have absolute trust with another person."

"Uh, well I, um . . . that's very specific." I blushed and sank into my embarrassment, going quiet.

"Fifty days from now, you will get very lucky. This is when the planets will align in your favor. Something will happen. You will get very lucky, ma'am. The date is December 25th of this year."

Christmas? Are you kidding me? Most middle-class Western gutbuckets like me get lucky on Christmas day. Presents, food, family . . . I'd be home in Australia shoveling potato salad and ham into my face and singing Dixie Chicks songs in bad nasal harmonies with my sisters until three in the morning. *I'll fly away on a sin wagon . . .*

"Show me that piece of paper again," he said, tapping my left hand. "Read it."

"Eagle, blue, nine," I said.

"Blue," he said. "You picked blue. Blue is the color of the ocean and the sky. The ocean and the sky represent freedom. Freedom represents peace. *Peace.* You want peace. Am I right? Open your hand." He tapped my right hand.

I unfolded the paper to my own handwriting: P-E-A-C-E.

But everyone wants peace. Every single person writes down "peace," every single time. Don't they?

He looked amused as he watched my face searching for logic. "What do you think, ma'am? Am I a good yogi?" He leaned back and bobbled his head with a self-satisfied smile.

I looked back down at the paper. Was there a camera on me? A little all-seeing GoPro lodged in his turban? Was he wearing a tiny headset in his ear and being informed by someone off-site from a windowless van? Maybe this was a high-tech, multi-man, yogi sting. I looked up to search for a drone. No drone. What was happening? My brain was tangling up in itself trying to work this out. There had been a lot of paper shuffling between us, all fast-paced questions and statements firing off without pause, and then that deeply disorienting statement about blow jobs. What on earth was that about? Maybe it was all designed to confuse so that he could switch out papers without me noticing, but I hadn't opened my fist at any point, so . . .

He laughed. "You still don't believe!" he exclaimed, astonished. "Even though I guessed each of your answers correctly, you still do not believe. You wrote it privately on the paper, ma'am, and it was tucked into your hand the whole time. How could I see? And yet you do not believe."

I shrugged.

"Always questioning," he said, tapping his temple with a pencil. "Thinking too much. Worrying too much. Picking everything apart, trying to understand. But I will tell you, ma'am, there is no need to worry anymore. You are very lucky." Without taking his eyes off mine, he said, "I told you to stop doing that thing to your thumb. It's not a good habit." I looked down to see that I was very discreetly pulling at the skin on my thumb again, prodding at the pain of my self-inflicted wound. I stopped.

"You have the snake between your eyes." He poked his brow. "It is very prominent. You don't believe me, but I can see it. So do not worry anymore. What did you write on the paper?"

"I wrote 'peace.'"

"Then you shall have it," he repeated, eyes warm and certain.

"Now say this with me: 'Om Namo Shiva.'"

I mumbled the chant below my breath, hoping nobody had spotted me sitting in front of this Indian yogi, looking like a gullible dimwit, but he wouldn't accept my barely inaudible mumble.

"Om louder," he said. "Like this: *Ommmmmmmm.* So that you can feel it travel up your nasal cavity."

I *ommm*'ed under my breath.

He lit fire to some paper and circled it all around my body. Smoke rose up and around us, and fragments of cold ash dropped down at our sides and onto the dusty pavement.

"You promise to put the past behind you?"

"I promise."

"You will have peace. You will be a peaceful old lady and will die while meditating."

His words touched a nerve. The thought of my dad's fearful passing made my eyes sting. I thought of the way his last few breaths were panicked gasps, even though he was surrounded by the love of his whole family. He seemed so terrified to let go and travel into the ether.

The yogi put his hands into Namaste position and closed his eyes, going silent, and I waited for a long beat, wondering what he'd say next, hoping it would be something undeniably transparent that would convince me without a shadow of a doubt that he was not a trickster at all but a psychic who saw my future as a happy octogenarian slipping off during meditation, grey-haired and coiled in lotus.

My eyes bored into his closed eyelids, and with my mind I asked him, *Wise yogi man, street charlatan, whoever you are: If you can read my thoughts, give me something else. Give me something I cannot deny. Give me a single piece of irrefutable evidence that can convince a longtime skeptic like me that this is not a trick.*

He shot open his eyes and looked into the depths of my soul.

He held out his palm.

And then he said four words containing the most essential human truth of our time: "Now I need money."

15

Masha got out of the airport taxi wearing a hot-pink scarf draped over her shoulders, her pale face enshrouded in a rose of magenta. We hugged for the first time in three months on a Delhi street.

"We're in India," I noted, pointing to our scenery, which was thrilling and terrifying and gorgeous and awful and every other adjective squished together to make up the world's longest portmanteau.

Her body was rigid to the touch. "Torre . . . I . . . this place is . . . " was all she could manage. After only an hour in the country, she looked like a cat that had been tossed into a bath. "This place is . . . "

It was the home of the past, the future, and every other place in between. With so many people and such limited space, the new had to take residence upon the old in order to exist: buildings stacked upon buildings, adverts pasted over adverts, shops spilling into shops, men sitting on one another's laps in rickshaws . . . My eyes made their way from a scabby dog to a woman in a jeweled emerald-green sari, a delicate tail of vibrant silk behind her, her cat eyes unbothered by the crush of humans.

She was staggeringly beautiful, perhaps made more so against a backdrop of unapologetic havoc. I kept my eyes on her until the throng swallowed her up.

"Overwhelming?" I offered.

Each traffic-clogged street was lined with buildings teetering skyward in clustered tangles, their walls held together by a mess of electrical wires and layers of ancient gunk. Not a single square inch was boring. It was absolutely thrilling. I just didn't know if *hiking* through it was the smartest idea.

"Torre, I don't . . . I mean . . . this place is . . . I can't . . . " She paused to find her words. "People always tell you India is confronting. I've read so much about this place and knew it would be difficult to walk through, but . . . "

We both squealed as we leapt out of the way of a car pushing straight into the crowd, fist to horn and bumper to flesh, trying to cleave space for itself to pass through.

" . . . but apparently cars drive straight into people here, and I didn't know about that part. And I really like it when my body isn't bleeding and broken, you know?"

The air we breathed was not so much oxygen as it was a muddy brown syrup of mixed pollutants that tasted like a pack of grit-filled cigarettes. Piles of toxic plastics smoked on the roadside. Passing trucks coughed up great burps of smoke that had nowhere to dissolve in the pea-soup air. Even the yell of car horns seemed to get trapped in the soup, resonating a constant discordant *wahhhhhh* like a bad case of tinnitus. The smells could not blow away either, and they floated like invisible stench bombs that would explode over my face with unimaginable awfulness. As we walked down the street, I smelled the worst thing I've ever smelled in my life. A few steps later, I smelled something even worse than that.

This hike was going to be the opposite of John Muir's idea of adventure.

"So, we're really going hiking here?" A part of me hoped she would say, "Let's call it off. This was all a bad idea."

No answer.

"I have an idea," I said. "How about we skip this whole walking-on-foot-through-India idea and just take up chain smoking and hard drugs for three weeks? It will probably be healthier. And safer."

She mumbled something inaudible from under the wad of scarf she'd stuffed over her mouth. Her eyebrows were fixed in panic—an expression I'd only seen on her before when there was a snake around, or a rope or a stick, and seeing her afraid here made my body rush with adrenaline. I realized how much I'd been following Masha for emotional cues, latching on to her for guidance, barnacled onto her confidence.

But I couldn't look at her for long, because as we walked I was trying to work out whether to keep my focus ahead on the careening human and vehicle traffic, to each side at the stores spilling out glittering saris and jewelry, or down to avoid tumbling over potholes, poo, and beggars draped across the footpath in various poses of human suffering. Despite their circumstances, the people smiled and bobbled their heads as we passed. A man tried to hand me his baby. Instinctually, I opened up my arms to accept it, but Masha stopped me. "Torre! Do not take the baby!"

I left the baby.

We carried on, looking for a place to retreat so we could hear each other talk, passing cows and dogs who had gathered on giant mounds of waste, looking for something to munch on among the already well-foraged pickings. I tried to remain neutral about the situation, to observe rather than judge, to keep an open mind. The animals looked pretty happy—they didn't know any better, and since I've never tried masticating on plastic wrappers or empty soda cans, who was I to judge it? Maybe it was more chewy and delicious than it looked. Just because it was different to what I was used to eating at home didn't make it automatically bad.

Okay, it was bad.

But is it ethnocentric to describe the quotidian details of another city as "bad"?

Yes.

No.

Shit. I don't know.

But if I was going to get all politically entangled over the trash-eating livestock, what emotional energy would I have left to use on the skinny old man lying in the street with only one atrophied leg to scoot around with? He looked perfectly happy, though, and when he saw us walk by, he shot up a hand, smiled a giant toothless smile, and yelled, "Good night!".

It was morning.

I wanted to hug him.

I wanted to hug everything until it was all better and every living being on earth was properly nurtured and healthy and clean and nobody died of poverty and injustice and incomprehensible suffering and everyone lived happily ever after forever and ever, the end.

Is that too much to ask?

My mind began to rework *The Worrier's Guide to the End of the World* with these new impressions of human and animal suffering. The cogs of my brain spun, trying to work out how to keep myself safe, how to keep everyone safe, how to save the world from all its wrongs and evils. It whirred, clanked, and then began to billow smoke.

Anxiety!

Breakup!

Death!

Climate change!

WILD FIRES!

MELTING PERMAFROST!

Killer robots!

INDIAAHHHHHHHHHHHHHHHHHHHHHHHHHHHHHHH-
HHHHHHHHHHHHHHHHHHHHHHHHHHHHHHHHHHHHH-
HHHHHHhhhhhhhhhhhhhhhhhh

There was so much of it. So much need. So much suffering. Too much to try to troubleshoot within the confines of one busy brain. As I looked around, the concept of manifesting strawberries and kittens on demand became the silly play of our childish former selves as my attention dashed from one broken human to the next, one limping animal to another.

All I could conclude was: *Life's a bitch and then you die.*

I looked to Masha for a dose of her optimism, searching her eyes for their normal infectious sparkle. She looked back at me with unseeing blankness and said, "I need a pack of cigarettes."

"Wait, you smoke?"

"I used to. Years ago. I'm starting again."

We found ourselves faced with two options:

1. Be like Gandhi: March on as two fearless warriors, two shining lights of empathy and love, interacting with wide-open hearts, without judgment or ego.
2. Be like Torre and Masha: Run and hide in hotel; order overpriced room service. Cry.

We chose option two. Or should I say option two chose us.

✦

When life gets you down, all you have to do to come back to center is to find a restaurant with delicious food and wine, and a credit card—yours or someone else's—and then simply take a deep breath in, hold it, and begin shaking out your fingers as you feel your paralyzing middle-class self-hatred begin to loosen up. That's right, just keep shaking—it may take a while. When the waiter next approaches, saying, "Can I get anything else for you, ma'am?" You say, "Wine. By the bottle." Because how many humans and animals in the world are suffering once that bottle of wine arrives?

None.

None, just so long as you stay mildly anesthetized at all times.

Masha sipped her glass of chilled white. "Torre, I think this plan to walk through Gujarat may have been a bad one, and I'm sorry."

We'd been sitting in the restaurant for four hours, trying to avoid going back outside to walk three hundred meters to our accommodation. Though we hadn't yet started our pilgrimage along unknown roads for six to eight hours a day, I'd already been involved in a small traffic accident when a car had pulled out of a parking space, lurched into the thicket of humans, and hit me in the thigh. I was, thankfully, uninjured—if severely spooked.

Every day in Delhi felt like a month, and in the course of a single day, we were ripped off, leered at, pushed and shoved by crowds, and kissed and pinched by women. We saw monkeys making love on a rooftop, an elephant on a highway moving cargo, a donkey painted with polka dots, a guy getting beaten on the side of the freeway, and several instances of non-ironic bell-bottom business slacks paired with spectacular connoisseur mustaches. While I was walking up a set of crowded stairs, a skinny preteen boy, not even twelve, took hold of my butt with two firmly committed hands and invited himself to a squeeze. It's a uniquely confusing experience to be molested by a child.

We could only manage to be outside in bursts, and then, burnt out, we'd go back to our accommodation to recollect inside the four blank walls of our refuge. Inevitably, hunger would drive us back out into the jostling masses. The prospect of being fully exposed to the outdoors for five to ten hours per day was unimaginable.

When we looked at the terrain on Google Maps, it seemed that we'd be walking through flat, dry farmland, highways, and industrial zones for 240 miles. Would we even find a place to sleep each night? Was this the stupidest idea ever? Nobody had the answer to that. I'd asked two Indian friends of mine what they thought of the idea, and they'd said: "Whatareyouthinking?!"

People don't commonly walk this route: not tourists, not Indians, not pilgrims, and especially not women. There was no guidebook for this. Many of the villages we'd be passing through didn't even come up on a Google search. It isn't a friendly, meandering trail through enchanted woods like a European pilgrimage. All that remains of Gandhi's legacy is a historically documented route dotted with a series of ashrams built in each town that he slept in along the way, many of them dilapidated and uninhabitable—all of them abandoned midway through construction. Like so many other projects in the country, the funding for the ashrams was squandered by corruption, and development was stunted.

I looked Masha in the eyes. "Do you still think we should do this?"

I hoped she would have some sage traveler wisdom to offer. In our months apart between Italy and India, she'd finished walking to Rome on her own, hiked to the top of Kilimanjaro with her husband, and completed a two-week pilgrimage through Turkey with her dad. He'd carried an ax in his backpack for safety, much to Masha's amusement—she did not share her father's neurotic fears. And yet here she was in Delhi, terror-struck by the hardship. What had happened to her trust in the universe? Her faith in the divine?

Instead of any sage wisdom, my optimist, my alchemist, my candle of hope in the darkness had only a string of nonsense to offer: "I . . . can't even . . . don't . . . what is . . . Torre, I . . . *donkeys?*" Her cheeks were flushed from wine and stress. Delhi was unsettling her core. I could tell by the way her eyes dashed around, hyper-aware, the way the corners of her lips were fixed downward, tugged by invisible strings. And she was smoking. Relentlessly. India Masha was an entirely different person to Italy Masha.

We sipped our wines and gazed at the planet outside the window. Cars pushed their way through crowds of people, honking and nudging bodies to make room for themselves. You don't wait for space in the world's most congested cities; you take what you need where you can get it, because aggressive opportunism overrides diplomacy when you're competing for survival with one and a quarter billion people. It's hard not to slip into cynicism when surrounded by such ruthlessness. Every piece of Western self-help advice becomes null and void, and coping mechanisms need to be formed afresh.

Masha stubbed out her cigarette, lit another one, and disappeared into the furrow of her brow. "Something happened when I was in Istanbul," she said.

"Oh no, what?"

"I really liked it there."

"Well, isn't that good?"

"No, it's bad, Torre. I felt really at home there." Her eyes were conflicted, both overjoyed and saddened. "It's the only place I've ever been that feels like home. You should see it, it's so amazing. There is so much to do, so much going on. It's like New York, but not like New York at all, and I could just see myself living there."

"That's wonderful. Why is that a bad thing?"

"Because my husband is in New York."

She lit another cigarette and gazed at the street. "So many people don't have basic rights here. Women can't wander the streets alone. Kids can't get medical care. So many people don't even have a toilet to shit in, and here I am complaining about not wanting to live in one of the world's richest cities. People are dying outside, and here we are drinking our third glass of eight-dollar wine and I'm complaining."

"I think you're preaching to the white choir over here."

She sank into her sadness. "You know, before I came to India I thought I had everything worked out. But god, Torre, this place . . . Being so close to all of this suffering is just not something you can prepare yourself for. Now I realize that Italy was all unicorns shitting rainbows and us rolling around in fields of dildos and daisies."

"Dildos?"

"Yeah, well, people seem to like dildos. I was just trying to think of something that people really like."

"Oh, right."

She ashed her cigarette.

"Do you think it's possible," I said, trying out a hypothesis I'd been dwelling on for a while, "that the earth is a giant cancer growing inside a much larger being, and we humans are the antibodies whose purpose is to destroy it?"

She stubbed out her cigarette. "Holy shit, dude, I think that's the darkest thing I've ever heard you say."

"It would explain a lot," I continued, "about how humans behave. Why we go to war, why we kill each other, why we exploit other cultures, why we're killing the planet with toxic waste from greedy consumption."

Her eyes became distant and watery. "Oh, that's great. Thank you very much for that, DeRoche. I'm going to kill myself now."

Her cheeks were pink with irritation. I tried to soften my statement. "I almost find the thought of it to be peaceful, because, like, maybe things don't matter as much as we think they do. George Carlin said, 'The sanctity of life doesn't seem to apply to cancer cells, does it? You rarely see a bumper sticker that says: Save the tumors.' He had a point. I mean, we make enemies out of anything that's parasitical to humans, but aren't we proving to be parasitical to the earth?"

Masha looked shattered.

"I'm just . . . saying," I stammered, nervous at the effect my words were having on her. In Italy, she'd seemed almost unshakable; there was no conversation too crass, no topic that was taboo, but now . . . "When you look at climate change and politics and everything that's going wrong with the planet, it's hard not to think that—" I stopped my rambling when I noticed her chin had began to pucker and wobble. Tears sprang into her eyes and began to roll down her cheeks.

My casual nihilism had accidently upended her.

I tried to backtrack. "I mean, that's just a theory, but we're probably not—"

It was too late. She erupted into tears and whimpered, "If that is the truth, then I have no reason to live anymore."

"Oh, Masha," I said, reaching for her arm, "it's just a stupid idea. Don't listen to me. Being in Delhi is difficult and I'm scared about our walk, and this stress has brought out the worst in me. I'm sorry. It doesn't mean anything. It's philosophy, a hypothesis; it's not real. I'm talking nonsense. I'm not going to make a Disney film out of it or anything."

She used a wad of thick napkins to collect the tears streaming down her cheeks, her pink face twisted by anguish. I'd never seen her this way before. She wasn't just crying. She was weeping a river of loud, wet pain, as though I'd accidently unbalanced the core of her entire sense of being. Words are powerful. Nihilism is contagious. Finally it had happened: I'd pooped on Masha's rainbow.

16

Wʜᴇɴ ɪᴛ ᴄᴏᴍᴇs to adventure, it's not always easy to know if what you're doing is inspiringly bold or recklessly stupid, and, really, the single distinguishing event between those polar opposite classifications is whether or not you die. Therefore, depending on the end result, an adventure like this was either a trailblazing expedition in the footsteps of a great thinker, or a harebrained voyage that two idiots agreed upon while living off Chianti, endorphins, and the delusion that they were wizards.

I pictured the headlines: "Two American Women Raped and Murdered in India During Soul-Searching 'Pilgrimage.'" The opinions would crawl the mediascape like bedbugs for days, weeks, maybe longer if the story made it to meme level. *Eat, Pray, Die.* We'd become celebrities for all the wrong reasons. "Today we don't burn witches, we just shame them," said writer Rhian Sasseen in her article "She Wants to Be Alone." Our stupidity might even get Songified as our choices became public property, free for the picking, beginning with our epic foolishness at deciding to walk across a country known for violence against women, right through to the way we walked and talked and styled ourselves. "They wore pink! They were asking for it!" Perhaps Guy would come forth to speak on a special news report: "Yes, that's right, they weren't even carrying a guidebook, and the blond one led us straight into a river."

The world might *tsk tsk* at our airheaded American carelessness, and *tsk tsk* again at India fulfilling its cliché. I didn't want to feed the media with those stereotypes. In her TEDGlobal 2009 talk, Chimamanda Ngozi Adichie coins this phenomenon as "The single story" as she dissects the problem of relating to a country and its people based on one cliché, saying, "Show a people as one thing, as only one thing—over and over again—and that is what they become."

It was December 2012 when India's singular story gathered strength. A woman in Delhi was gang-raped on a bus at night, and, when questioned, her attackers held her responsible for their crime, saying that a woman shouldn't have been riding the bus at night. She later died of her injuries, and it was brutal and bleak enough to make global news, angering the whole world. India was furious too: The incident set off protests in Delhi against the systemic disregard for the rights of women, and words like "sexism," "patriarchy," and "misogyny" became a part of the mainstream vocabulary, fueling an important conversation about human rights for half the country's population. Women took a stand for their rights: their ability to go to work without worrying about how to get to and from the office without being violated and their freedom to marry whom they wanted, to wear what they wanted, to report crimes against them without fear of shaming. Progress. India—like the rest of the world—is a country in a state of constant development. It is not a single story.

The unfortunate reality is that no matter where in the world a woman is born, from the moment a girl can speak, she's warned—from parent to politician—to be careful: *You're fragile, you're weaker, you're less capable, you're rape-able.* That is the single story of women. It's the single story of the world being a hostile one. And because women hear that story over and over again, it can so easily flourish into a spectrum of generalized fears. Fear of the outdoors, of adventure, of being alone, of men; fear of wearing the wrong clothes, taking the wrong street, inviting the wrong person in . . . Fear that an act as harmless as a long walk might lead to rape, death, and public shaming.

This single story is perhaps the biggest oppressor of women. It can keep us in self-doubt. It can keep us inside comfort zones. It can narrow our vision and blind us to opportunity. It can limit our ability to find our own potential and impair our willingness to put ourselves out in the world with all our power and all our courage and be a force for positive change. In even the most beautiful and benign places in the world, like the backcountry, fear lurks always in the shadows, dark and ominous, imbedded into our cells from as early as fairy tales. But actual monsters and the fear of monsters are two very distinct phenomena. While we can't control the fact that barbarians exist, we get to choose whether or not we want to be oppressed by the single story. *We* get to choose.

There was no doubt about it: What we were planning was dangerous, but there was no way to know how dangerous it would be until we were on the road. Given the number of hours we were planning to spend exposed in the streets in completely unknown and untouristed areas, we decided to hire some protection in the form of a male chaperone, a token dude and a nationally respected mascot that announces: *Don't mess with us. We have a man!*

Well before arriving in India, we'd begun emailing tourism companies, but nobody had replied. Just before giving up, we heard back from Naveen, the owner of an adventure company who said he could put his explorer Ajit on the ground with us for the three-week walk. Naveen seemed to think it was a great idea, which he would happily help us out with for the low, low price of a great chunk of money. We had found him via the

Internet, which may sound dodgy, but the company had a sleek logo with great website functionality and . . . Okay, it was dodgy, but after two months of emails, he was the only person who had replied. Our struggle to find a guide had thrown out our plans to get home in time for Christmas. We couldn't keep waiting around for better options.

Masha and I weighed our risks, did as much research as we could, talked it over from various angles, panicked, argued, napped, decided it was all a very bad idea, closed our eyes, held our breath, and then clicked "Transfer" on the direct deposit to the adventure company. We'd come too far to give up.

This was happening.

"It's been fun, DeRoche," said Masha.

I gave her a firm salute, and we booked flights to the city of Ahmadabad, the starting point of Gandhi's walk.

✦

The day was golden and warm as we sat cross-legged on the green lawn of Gandhi's ashram. Locals in saris glided around the property, pausing mid-stride to stop and gape at us. I gaped back; the fascination was mutual.

We were a small group of four—Naveen, Ajit, Masha, and myself—and then five when a young Indian man wandered over and said, "Do you mind if I join you?" Nobody objected. He sat down, cross-legged and straight-backed—an enthusiastic pupil at our gathering. He told us he was a student, studying to become a doctor. "Thank you very much for letting me sit in on your meeting," he said in singsong Indian English.

"Let us now go through the rules," said Naveen, handing Masha and me a printed list of terms and conditions. "First of all, Ajit is not your bodyguard. He is an explorer. He will translate for you and help you to negotiate and find places to sleep along the way, but it is not his job to protect you, and we can take no responsibility in matters of your personal safety."

I looked at Masha, wide-eyed, one eyebrow arched. She met my expression and raised me one more eyebrow. I looked over at Ajit. He looked asleep. Were his eyes even open? Yes, but he was so calm that his eyes appeared to be resting. His trimmed black beard hid full lips, and he had the paler skin of an Indian who lives indoors, along with the body of a man who lives indoors: doughy and rounded.

"Excuse me, but where are you going?" said the young pupil.

"We are walking the Salt March, in the footsteps of Gandhi," I told him.

"Gandhiji," said Naveen, correcting me. "In India, you put a 'ji' on the end of a name if you wish to show your respect to that person. Here, we always say either 'Gandhiji' or else 'Mahatma Gandhi.'"

"Oh, okay. We are walking in the footsteps of Gandhi*ji*."

The boy's eyes were orbs of amazement as he sucked back his own breath. "You mean to say you're walking all the way to the seaside in Dandi? In Bapu's footsteps?"

"'Bapu' means 'father,'" Naveen explained. "Gandhiji is regarded as the father of our nation."

"Yes," I said. "That's our plan."

"Oh!" he said, his head bobbling furiously, his excitement so pronounced he was almost bursting out of his skin. "That is very impressive! What inspired you to take this journey?"

I wanted to offer him an impressive cause for undertaking a very long stroll in the footsteps of one of the world's greatest human rights advocates, like world peace or women's rights or even an act of protest against the $1 price hike on coffee at my local hipster café, but the truth was far more self-indulgent than that: *I, like, broke up with someone and my dad died and I'm scared of everything all the time, and so I thought that maybe if I started wandering aimlessly, I'd be somehow less scared, and also . . . well . . . I want to lose weight while eating large quantities of Indian food.* My brain grappled for the least dishonest lie. "To learn about India."

"Oh!" he said. "Oh, ma'am, I'm so very, very proud of you. Even the people in India do not do these kinds of activities to learn about their own country."

"Thank you," I said, while thinking: *Dammit, now I have to learn the complete history of India to make good on a promise.* Three seconds into this adventure, and I was already a fraud.

I'm not going to lie: Before landing in India, my knowledge of Gandhi . . . *ji* . . . was limited to a brief scroll through Wikipedia, a film about him I'd once fallen asleep in, and a bunch of Internet memes I'd seen floating around with quotes Photoshopped over his face, which may or may not have been things he once said, which may or may not have been Gandhi's face. It could've been Tina Fey doing a skit on *Saturday Night Live* in a latex bald mask with a rubber nose and round spectacles—what would I know? I'm going to level with you here: I don't know that many things about stuff. Let's just say that nobody ever puts me on his or her trivia team *twice.*

"Excuse me," said the boy. "But can I ask what it is that you do for jobs?"

"We're all freelancers," said Ajit, pointing to himself, Masha, and me. "I'm a photographer, and these two are writers."

"Oh, I'm sorry, sir, but freelancing is not the answer to this country's problems. We have a social responsibility to work hard as a hive, not as separate individuals. I have traveled here today to Gandhiji's ashram from my hometown, because I am a great believer in the principles of the great Mahatma Gandhi, and I believe we need to reinstate them to improve the circumstances of this country and ensure a prosperous future. Don't you agree?" he asked, looking to me for a response.

I shrugged, realizing I was way out of my political depth on this topic.

Naveen continued the meeting. "We will provide you with some pepper spray and a whistle. While we feel that you will be safe and that you will have no problems at all, these are some small items you can carry to help you if something bad should happen."

I imagined Masha and me standing in a circle of heavy-breathing men as the *squeeeeee* of our two plastic whistles was absorbed into the cacophonous mass of sound coming from horns and generalized havoc.

"Oh, great," I said. "That's really helpful." My fingers reached around inside my pockets for better solutions. There was my small multi-tool, which comforted me, even though I'd never tried to fend off an attacker with a pair of retractable scissors, a nail file, and a plastic toothpick. I felt around in my other pocket: a phone. Excellent. But who would I call? And how would they reach us? What happens when you hashtag #emergency on Twitter?

Naveen turned back to his list of meeting items. "To be honest, we have no idea where you're going to eat or sleep every day, and won't for the entire duration of your trip, because this is the first time we've led this expedition. I will be calling ahead to try to find you accommodation, but I can't guarantee that we will find anything."

"Oh," said Masha.

"Oh," I said.

"But," said Naveen, "Ajit has walked this route before, so he knows the way and will surely keep you safe. And I will be here at home base while you two and Ajit are in the field, and I'll be doing my absolute best to phone ahead and arrange accommodation for you. I don't imagine it will be a problem to secure your accommodation each night."

Masha and I let out our tense breaths in unison.

Naveen shook out the list of terms and conditions and continued reading. "The state of Gujarat is a dry one, so there will be no alcohol."

Both Masha and I sighed.

"And," he continued, "it's also a vegetarian state, so there will be no meat throughout your journey."

No meat, no alcohol . . . what was next? No fun?

"No sex," Naveen said. Of course. "We ask that you refrain from engaging in any sexual relations with Ajit."

The grass became very interesting to all of us: how green it was, how thick and how grassy, how unlike the burning crimson of our faces. Though the three of us would be spending the next three weeks together—walking together, eating, sleeping in the same hotels—hookups of any kind were the last thing on my mind, falling well behind other priorities such as not getting hit by a truck, avoiding rabid dogs, learning how to effectively target rapists' eyeballs with pepper spray instead of my own, getting Masha to forgive me for suggesting the planet is a giant ball of cancer, becoming fearless like Gandhi, and, last but not least, learning the complete political history of India to make good on my word to some arbitrary Indian boy who was preemptively proud of me.

Who has time for fun with that kind of schedule?

We agreed to all the terms and signed the dotted line.

✦

The next morning, we gathered once again at Gandhi's ashram on the banks of the River Sabarmati, the official starting point for the pilgrimage. Dressed in our moisture-wicking pants and hiking shoes and carrying colorful hiking poles, we were an eyesore among the saris, rickshaws, and old-world beauty around us.

Our faces were puffy from a lack of sleep, our bodies fidgety with fear. I felt foolish.

"I have a gift for you both," said Naveen. He handed each of us a gift bag. Inside was a pocket-sized can of pepper spray that seemed to contain only a single squirt of defense, a cheap whistle made from orange plastic containing a ball of dried cow poo as the whistler, and a polyester T-shirt with my name on the back shouted out in all caps, TORRE!, alongside the adventure company's sleek logo.

Stranger Danger Rule 1: Don't wear your own name emblazoned across your clothing, or else creeps might approach you on familiar terms—"Oh, hey, Torre, how have you been?"—and ask you to take the candy and get in the van. I put the pepper spray in one pocket, the whistle in the other, and stuffed the shirt into my backpack to dispose of later. "Thank you so much for the gift."

His head bobbled. "Don't worry. Ajit has walked this path before. He will guide you well. I will be at home base here if you need anything."

We stood silently in the calm before the storm. The light of the morning turned the river to liquid gold, and on its banks devotees sat in lotus position reciting prayers or tossing handfuls of seeds to pigeons. Compared with the ceaseless hustle and bustle of Ahmadabad outside the gates, the grounds were a relieved sigh of tranquility. I'd never been so conscious of the sound of silence before.

Inside that momentary calm, looking around the gardens of what was once Gandhi's home, I tried to develop a sense of gravitas about our journey ahead. On the green grass by the river sat a larger-than-life bronze statue of the man himself, poised cross-legged. Around his neck was a loop of white *khadi*, his iconic homespun cotton, made on a loom.

We were to begin following the ghost of an activist so important to India that his is the face on their currency. I'd begun to soak up his philosophies at the exhibit of his life on the property. Gandhi believed "a small body of determined spirits fired by an unquenchable faith in their mission can alter the course of history," and so, on March 12, 1930, he left the ashram to walk to the coastal town of Dandi, along with seventy-eight followers, where he broke the law by picking up a lump of sea salt from the shoreline. The British Raj had not only monopolized the salt trade but had imposed a tax on this popular condiment, savior of bland meals everywhere, and because Gandhi believed in the basic human right to deliciousness, he was like: *Hey, you guys, watch me stroll 240 miles to the beach so I can bend down and pick up a handful of salt as though it's a free mineral that washes up on beaches, because it is a free mineral that washes up on beaches, you assholes.*

He didn't say it exactly like that, but he did it, and they arrested him—along with thousands of others who had joined the movement. He generated worldwide publicity, making it a brilliant act of performance art that demonstrated the power of nonviolent civil disobedience, which not only paved the way for India's independence but inspired many of the world's greatest misfits throughout the decades since: Nelson Mandela, John Lennon, Martin Luther King Jr., Aung San Suu Kyi . . .

That is what you can achieve if you're fearless.

I looked back at Mahatma Gandhi's statue and thought about all he fought for. An end to mass production. Independence and self-sufficiency. Freedom for all. Had we listened to his message, the world would be a very different place.

By walking in his steps, I hoped that some of his superpowers would flow into me through osmosis, so that I'd leave Gujarat ready to save the world with stronger compassion, bravery, and wisdom, along with the svelte body of Raquel Welch in *One Million Years B.C.*

On the head of Mahatma Gandhi's statue sat a pigeon, its feathers the same slate-grey tone as the weathered bronze, as still and immortalized as the great Mahatma himself. I felt more of an affinity with that bird than the great Gandhiji, given that, instead of leading a country toward its liberation, a more likely result of my efforts would be roosting on the head of a noble-man while shitting all over the face of India.

"Are you ready to begin?" said Ajit.

"Not really," I said.

"Not at all," said Masha.

"Okay, *chalo*," said Ajit. "Let's go."

17

You're never more sober than when you think you're going to die.

Car horns, piles of trash, a wide berth given to a buffalo's rear end, truck horns, A NEAR CAR ACCIDENT!, bumping into Masha—"Oops, sorry." Rickshaw horns, staring men, grit in my eyeball, temporary blindness!, more staring men, beautiful saris, horns, OH MY GOD, WHAT IS WRONG WITH THAT DOG?, stepping over poop, stepping *in* poop, bumping into Ajit—"Oops, sorry"—Ajit's warm brown gaze set into the broad face of a lion.

"No-prob-ah-lem, Tanya."

"It's Torre. My name is Torre."

The energy of our walk was crazed, horrifying, exhilarating. Our feet danced to find space; our eyes darted to make sense. It was like a blockbuster film that has no plot, just a nonstop barrage of loud action scenes and money shots.

We didn't belong in this place. Everyone knew it. Our appearance wouldn't have been any more shocking if we were an ambush of hot-pink Bengal tigers.

Even the buffalo knew we were strangers. They went goggle-eyed when they saw us and tried to flee their tethers in a heavy scramble. Dogs barked and snarled. Babies cried. Toddlers hid behind parents' legs or ran screaming, arms flailing. Teens dared each other to get close enough to say "Hello," dashing away in a fit of exhilarated giggles. A new mother clutched her baby, and another dragged her toddler by the arm to cross the road, well away from the stranger danger. As we passed through Indian villages, we were causing a wave of trauma. It wasn't just that we were one fair-skinned Indian man and two white women in a sea of dark-skinned, non-touristic India—Masha and I were tall, ghoulish freaks dressed like men, wielding long metal walking sticks. Aliens with vaginas, basically. No wonder the kids were screaming.

Lucky for us, cars and trucks gave us the wide berth of a holy cow. Rickshaw drivers would slow their vehicles beside us, and we'd shake our heads, *No, we don't need transport*, but they'd hover beside us revving their engines, backing up traffic behind them into a choke of horns. "Where are you going?"

"We're going to Dandi."

"But where are you walking to?"

"Dandi, Dandi."

"No, I said where are you *walking* to?"

"We are *walking* to Dandi!"

It didn't make sense because it was too far for a sane person to walk on foot. What fool would push their body through heat, dust, horns, crowds, livestock, cow patties, trucks, clusters of men, and toxic burps of diesel fumes when you can catch a train for the cost of a coffee? More specifically, what kind of white—and therefore presumably *wealthy*—fool would choose to travel in such unpleasant conditions?

After ignoring a driver for a hundred more feet, he would leave, and a new rickshaw driver would immediately take his place—"Where are you going?"—clogging the traffic behind him, so that wherever we went, a crazed tangle of vehicles would follow.

I was getting dizzy from whipping my head back and forth at every spectacle. On the sidewalk a man was lathering the face of another man for a shave; next to them was a vendor selling figs coiled like serpents; next to that a shabby lemon-yellow wall painted with blue Sanskrit letters, in front of which was a mange-ridden dog with her litter of itty-bitty scabby pups, all writhing for a nipple. Every inch was either disastrous or beautiful, and I didn't want to blink in case I missed any of it.

A produce vendor, sitting cross-legged on the dirt and surrounded by a spread of vegetables, asked Ajit why we were carrying canes used by crippled elderly people. Failing to understand his answer, she offered us free carrots, saying that if we needed crutches to walk, we must be in need of more nourishment. She pulled her chin back into her sari and cackled, her belly laugh as loud and vibrant as her neon-blue and hot-pink outfit.

Our undertaking made no sense to anyone. It was starting not to make sense to me either. I packed my walking poles away into my bag, hoping to lower our profile and stop scaring the children and animals. As if that would make any difference.

"Would you like some bananas?" Ajit said, stopping in front of a cart piled high with fruit. We nodded, and he bought three. After I'd eaten mine, I searched for a trash can.

"Just throw it on the ground," said Ajit.

That didn't fit well with my standards. Sure, there was trash all over the ground, but contributing to it was not the way to improve the situation. I held the peel until it grew warm, slippery, and brown, and then, twenty minutes later, realizing I wasn't committed to carrying organic waste for three weeks, flung it into a bush with a quick snap of my wrist. What would it matter? The bush was already drooping under snagged trash and thick dust.

"Now you're getting it," Ajit laughed.

With long black hair and pale skin, Ajit fit no stereotype. He didn't look like any other Indian man I'd seen: he had glossy hair pulled into a ponytail that flowed down as far as the small of his back. His wide face reminded me of a lion's, with a narrowed gaze and irises like tiger's eye, taking in everything before him with studious reflection. One year out of a photography degree in India's best art school in Ahmadabad and, always ready to capture his vision, he carried a Nikon DSLR in his hand.

Because of his long hair and pale skin, every Indian we encountered assumed Ajit was Western, and they would communicate with him in English. When he'd reply in Hindi, they would bobble their heads with impressed delight and say, "Your Hindi is very good, sir."

"Thank you."

"Where are you from, sir?"

"Delhi."

"But *where* you from?"

"Delhi, Delhi. I'm from the city of Delhi."

"Yes, but which *country* were you *born in?*"

"India."

They would return a prolonged blank glare, shake it off, and then change the subject: "So where are you walking to, sir?"

"Dandi."

"But where are you . . . "

We passed a small outdoor factory, where men hurriedly ran handfuls of magenta clay along taut rows of white string. It was a shock of color against the surrounding buildings and trees, which were muted to monotone from layers of pollution.

"They're dyeing kite string," Ajit explained.

"Oh, how pretty," I said, snapping a photo.

The factory workers' hands were dyed pink, and the pigment had fallen into the dirt below their feet, staining the ground the color of lipstick. Their hands were wrapped with swaths of fabric to protect their palms as they ran them up and down strings at frantic high speed.

"This pigment is mixed with glass," said Ajit. "That is why their hands are covered."

"What is the glass for?" I asked.

"Every year in India, we have a popular kite festival. The objective of the game is to fly your kite and cut the string of another person's kite. This glass makes the kite strings very sharp. Of course, the strings fall from the sky and get snagged in roofs and so on, and drape across the road. And because they are very sharp, motorcyclists collide with them at high speed. A lot of people get decapitated every year."

"Oh . . . my god." As I looked down at the pink dirt, I imagined a Monty Python–like rolling of heads and was overwhelmed with the urge to laugh, followed up by the urge to cry. These contrary emotions neutralized me to indifference, and we carried on walking.

As I looked down at the wrinkled skin on the backs of my hands, I noticed they had aged since we set out. They were layered with dust and lined with wrinkles from the dryness of the air. The white scarf at my neck had turned brown from dust, and my sinuses were sore from inhaling pollution. I felt like the flu was coming on from the throb of toxins lining my nasal cavities. We weren't in Tuscany anymore. It seemed we'd been walking for fifty years, and if I were to look in the mirror, I'd see a weary, grey-haired woman staring back at me, saying "Why are you doing this to yourself?"

But when I checked the time, it said we'd been walking for only two hours.

✦

Ajit rhymes with unfit, which is what he was. He kept falling far behind, half a mile or so at times, and Masha and I would find ourselves walking alone. For hours we walked down the median strip of a featureless freeway that looked like any other freeway, only busier, dustier, and cow-ier.

Under a slither of shade from a road sign, we stopped to wait for Ajit to catch up, and ten minutes later he limped up, sweating and suckling the teat of his water bottle like a desperate lamb. "I ran out of water," he gasped, and I offered him mine.

He hung the water bottle above his head, dropped his neck back, and poured it straight down his throat in a long stream, sweat pouring from his hairline in rivulets as if his body were dumping hydration as quickly as it was being consumed.

He had the stricken, bloodless appearance of someone who is in the deep throes of cardiac arrest, but when I asked him if he was okay, he said, "Yes, I'm fine, Taroo."

"It's Torre. My name is Torre."

"Okay, Taryl." Maybe I should've kept that name T-shirt after all.

"How old are you, Ajit?"

"I'm twenty-eight. How old are you?"

"I'm thirty-four."

"Don't worry, Tara. It's just a number."

"I wasn't worried, but thanks?"

The sun was hot. The air was dry. Masha and I were feeling it, but coping. Ajit, it appeared, was not. His idea of navigation was to stop every five minutes and ask a rickshaw driver for directions, which would not only back up traffic but would lead into five or ten minutes of the standard circular Delhi/Dandi/Delhi conversation. Hovering behind Ajit, Masha and I would wait for these conversations to end so that we could get moving again, hoping to arrive to more welcoming places than the median strip of a freeway. But Ajit seemed to be stalling, buying himself some recovery time, using the scarf at his neck to mop his brow once again, puffing his lungs back to life.

We were responsible for having gotten him into this. He didn't seem cut out for this kind of physical activity.

All the while the sun arched up over its apex to begin its fall toward the horizon, and we were not making the distance we needed to in order to reach our destination before sunset.

"Ajit," said Masha, "I have GPS on my phone. You don't need to ask people for directions. Just ask me." She waved her phone in the air.

"No, it's okay, I know where to go, and I have GPS too," he replied, but five minutes later, he'd stop another person in the street for directions. Oftentimes the locals' directions would conflict with our digital maps, and Ajit and Masha would end up in a debate at the crux of an intersection.

We took stock at a roadside chai stand, sitting in the center of a swarm of men who gathered to gape at us up close, in silent disbelief, encasing us in a claustrophobic ring. They were so close that I could've reached out and poked their bellies. My fingers found the can of pepper spray in my pocket. I hoped that, if the time came, I'd remember to turn the nozzle outward, away from my own face.

The tea—milky, sweet, and spiced—was calming. The cups and saucers were dirty, but those kinds of details were starting to become irrelevant, given the amount of dirt we'd inhaled. A more pressing concern was getting to an accommodation of some kind before sunset.

Masha looked at Ajit. "You've walked this pilgrimage before, right?"

"Only a portion of it," he confessed.

"Why won't you use the GPS on your phone?"

He looked coy. "Actually, I don't yet know how to use this phone, but do not be worrying. I will get us there. We just need to turn left at the end of this road here."

"But the satellite says we need to go right."

"Well, I asked a rickshaw driver, and he said left, so we go left."

"But . . . "

"*Chalo*. Let's go."

Ajit was not a guide. He was a liability.

18

As the sun lowered after sixteen miles of walking, or perhaps sixteen years in hiking-through-India-time, we found ourselves sitting on plastic chairs inside a dark, ramshackle community hall—the first of Gandhi's overnight stops on the Salt March in a village called Aslali. Mice scampered in the corners of the room while a cluster of men stood in a semicircle watching us, silent apart from their mouth breathing.

I tried to make eye contact with Masha, but she wouldn't look my way. She seemed annoyed at me. All day, she had kept to herself, and when I tried to joke with her, she'd look at me blankly and then return her troubled gaze to the road.

I looked up at the ceiling, waiting for somebody to say something. Anything. A fluorescent light flickered, and a fan knocked and buzzed with poor installation and electrics.

I had no idea what was happening—with Masha, with our accommodation arrangements, with India as a whole . . . I hoped the strange puzzle of it would all slot together soon.

"Ajit, *where* exactly are we sleeping tonight?" Masha asked.

He replied with a head bobble.

"Was that a yes, no, or maybe?"

His head bobbled again.

The men began speaking in Hindi. Ajit could speak perfect English but did not enjoy the chore of translating. When he did, it was most often cryptic.

"This is where Gandhi slept on his first night on the Salt March," he said.

"So . . . does that mean we're sleeping here?" asked Masha.

Ajit's head bobbled, loose-necked, as though his spine was made of rubber. The fan knocked and buzzed; the light flickered.

"Is that a yes?" Masha asked.

More bobbling.

She turned to me. "Is he saying we're sleeping here?"

I shrugged and said, "Maybe?"

When the men began unfolding dusty mattresses, we deducted the answer was yes, we were sleeping our first night in this dilapidated community hall, which was disappointing news for anyone who enjoys fine luxuries such as bathing, privacy, and the absence of rodents in one's sleeping space. The good news was, the men were caring and generous, willing to feed us and do everything they could to make us comfortable. It was touching to be welcomed and cared for by people who had not expected our arrival.

One of the men came over to us carrying a tray with stainless steel cups of tap water. "Drink," he said, and when we shook our heads to say, "No," he pushed the tray at us and insisted.

Ajit explained in Hindi that, to a Western belly, drinking tap water in India is a sure way to get sick. Since there are no public bathrooms available on the streets of India, there's no place to relieve oneself in an emergency—unless, of course, you're cow, dog, or man, and in that case the toilet is everywhere, anytime. Walking all day, every day meant we had no bathroom handy, no hotel to dash back to, doing the Delhi belly toilet tango. Getting sick was not an option. Still, the man didn't understand, and he kept pushing the tray at us, urging us to drink, because we'd walked such a long way and must be thirsty. To save us, Ajit downed all three cups of water in quick succession.

"Thank you," we said.

One of the men asked us a question in Hindi, and Ajit translated. "They want to know which of Gandhi's philosophies you most align with."

"Ahhhhh . . . " said Masha.

"Errrrrr . . . " said I, feeling like a fraud. Here we were in a sacred space, the rest stop for Gandhi on the first night of his pilgrimage, and I was wordless, my knowledge of Gandhian philosophy still somewhat thin.

"Simplicity?" said Masha.

"Truth?" said I.

Ajit translated, and heads bobbled, seemingly content with our answers.

Ajit turned to me looking miserable. "Taroo, I don't think my feet are doing so well." With a loud sigh, he removed his shoes to reveal a ripe blister the circumference of a tennis ball on the soft padding of his sole. It was in the worst possible place.

"I have shoe bites," he said. He looked at me, terrified. "What do I do, Tanya?"

I pulled out my first aid kit and wrapped his feet in thick bandages to try to prevent further damage. "That will fix it," I told him, hoping my confidence would set off a placebo effect.

He calmed at this. "Thank you, Tahrye. I'm sure it will heal quickly and will be no prob-a-lehm."

I was not so sure. His feet were filthy. We were *all* filthy— head to toe—and trying to fend off infection in these conditions would be difficult-to-impossible.

The men made beds for us in the foyer, beneath a ceiling fan that knocked so violently it sounded like it might fall and drill through the concrete by way of our bodies. The townspeople caught wind of our presence, and people began to arrive to have their photos taken with us, whispering a coy "Hello" in English as they peered around the doorframe.

The head of the office, a wiry man with serious eyes, brought us an aluminum pail full of home-cooked food, hot and delicious. We ate with our hands, using pieces of *chapati* to scoop up the sweet and salty lentil curry, washing it down with sour *kahdi*—hot yogurt soup flavored by a blend of *masalas* (spices).

Afterward, I wandered outside to find a place to wash and found a dark concrete space with a lockable door, perhaps a laundry, where I filled a bucket, got naked, and dumped cold water over my body. The day's dust loosened from my skin and clothes and a muddy river of dirt went down the drain. I brushed my teeth and combed out my hair and, in clean, dry clothes, stood outside and enjoyed the silky sensation of clean skin.

The air had cooled, and the sky was golden, silhouetting temples and smoke, buffalo grazing trash, and the easing tumult of the day. I could smell rotting produce and stagnant water, but also, on the breeze was the scent of fresh flowers, like freesias. It was divine. I'd smelled it now and then, but Ajit and Masha swore they couldn't smell it. I breathed it in and held on, feeling the euphoria of it swelling in my chest.

When you're unspoiled by luxury, happiness is measured by a different baseline. It's a phenomenon I first discovered when I lived on a boat on the Pacific Ocean, where life is so often wrought with physical and emotional trauma. Whenever we'd pull into a dry port—alive!—I'd find myself rolling in ecstasy over tiny luxuries like clean, dry clothing, the smell of clean hair, or a tin of unheated baked beans, eaten with a fork. Joy is relative. When you're accustomed to a life of milk and honey, it's much harder to be impressed by little pleasures, because small luxuries so quickly become entitlements. *Why isn't there enough foam on my fucking cappuccino?* But when you're roughing it, something as simple as not smelling shit for ten seconds can be heaven. The world's wealthiest countries might be cash rich, but one could argue that we're terribly poor at appreciating tiny pleasures.

With the doors locked, Masha and I laid side by side. "Torre?" she said. "Do you know what I want to get out of this pilgrimage?"

It was the first time she'd opened up to me all day, and I was relieved to have her back. "What?"

"I want to learn to do a headstand."

I waited for her to elaborate, thinking it was some kind of quirky metaphor, but she put her head down on her mattress and began flipping her legs up toward the ceiling in jarring spasms.

"What are you doing?"

"Headstands!"

"Why?"

"Why not!" She kicked her legs up high and then tumbled over herself, laughing.

I had no idea what was happening. So far, my experience of India had resembled a peculiar fever dream. Up to this point I'd believed Masha was a wise and well-traveled pilgrim, a magical wayfarer with flowers in her hair, but it was starting to look like she was just plain unhinged. I'd been following her compass— but where on earth was she taking us?

If you want to erode the entire foundation of what you think you already know about humanity, life, death, and the space-time continuum, go for a stroll with Masha. Do you feel certain that you know things about stuff? Oh really? You know nothing. Everything you once believed with firm conviction—your logic and values, your sense of right and wrong and good and bad and funny and sad—turns into M. C. Escher staircases, twisting around into infinity loops, folding back into themselves, leading, ultimately, to absurdity.

"Do headstands with me, Torre," she urged, and I began to walk the Escher staircases with her.

I tucked my head under my neck and pumped my legs up toward the ceiling. We fell down with a thud on our beds, sending a puff of dust up in the air, laughing and breathless.

Lights out. The doors were bolted to keep us safe. I stretched my sore limbs out over the hard platform of my dusty bed, pulling the thin sheet up over me and nestling into a pillow made of my own piled clothing. Mice busied themselves in the corners of the room and the fan knocked and squeaked.

From toes to head, euphoria began to flood my cells like a warm bath, as gratitude for having survived the day's harshness rolled through me. We had eaten. We were safe, warm, sheltered. Such simple pleasures. Masha was still in a weird mood, Ajit's foot was a bloody mess, the day's walk had been brutal, and in the morning we'd have to wake up early to do it all over again. But those were all problems for other moments.

If you were to string together all the moments in an average life, it would amount to about 2.5 billion seconds if you eat kale and forgo fun. If you divide that by three—the feeling of nowness—you get 833 million beats. Now, imagine if everyone was given $833 million in cash to spend over a lifetime, only with one key condition: you can only spend a dollar at a time. Those are the rules of our moments. We can't save them up or steal them from anyone else; we are equally rich with what we have to spend, give or take an early death or the invention of immortality by Google. How we choose to spend each beat is a personal choice: happiness, acceptance, resistance, misery . . . In his book *Man's Search for Meaning*, Auschwitz survivor Viktor Frankl said: "Everything can be taken from a man but one thing: the last of the human freedoms—to choose one's attitude in any given set of circumstances, to choose one's own way."

In this peculiar makeshift bedroom—fan knocking, mice scampering—I was the happiest person in the world. You can find bliss in the strangest places if you let go of *what should be* and fall, instead, into *what is so.*

I melted away into the deepest of sleeps.

19

SILENCE IS UNNERVING in India. Noise is so constant it becomes a comfort, and once it's gone it can feel like you're missing an irritating, but loved, companion—maybe an obnoxious and dominating in-law has dropped dead at a family function, and finally there is peace and quiet but, dammit, Dorothy is dead.

Wide-open space is equally unnerving. The road we followed in the morning was empty, straight, and hushed, and as miles passed, busy cities eased into small villages and villages into open farmlands, where buffalo grazed on thirsty grass. Our only company was the occasional passing shepherd moving members of his herd with a bamboo staff, ushering them to feeding spots. Their breakfast could be anything from roadside scrub to the piles of colorful trash that dotted the parched, yellow landscape. This would be an effective scrap recycling system if not for the toxins and plastics covered in famous logos.

Inside the space of that silence, I could hear our percussion: the *crunch* of our shoes on the roadside, the arrhythmic drag of Ajit's limp, the *clank* of trinkets on Masha's backpack, the *clack* of hooves from passing buffalo. Together, we made a beat, a song, a band of pilgrims.

I watched the shells on Masha's pack bounce to her quick skip and missed the times when she traveled at the same pace as me, chatting and laughing. She'd gone so far inside that she couldn't be coaxed out unless there was a kitten, donkey, or large cauldron of chai tea in her immediate vicinity. She wouldn't laugh at my jesting; I was lucky to get a vague smile. She was absorbed in her own troubled mind and refused to come out. No matter what beguiling spectacle was going on around us, she kept her eyes fixed on whatever it was that was going on in her mind.

I skipped to catch up to her. "Hey, Masha. Are you okay?" The dry, hot air made my throat hurt when words came out.

"Fine."

"Are you mad at me?"

Head down, brow stitched, she said, "No." The trinkets on her backpack jingled as she walked a little faster to break off on her own once again, and I let her be, hoping her mood would pass in time. She'd been so inspired and resolute in Italy, and her dramatic change of mood threw off my own. We carried on in mute silence, sweating and weaving and dodging, looking for negative space to occupy, looking for ways not to be negative.

As we walked, I would often write journal entries or thoughts into my phone. Thumbs wriggling over the screen, I would type a thousand words or more onto my tiny computer, watching the road out of my peripheral vision as I tried to capture all that we'd seen and done so that the strange little details wouldn't be forgotten.

Day two. Navgam. 15km walked. Stayed the night in a Hindu temple. Walked past a head-shaving ceremony of a small child, called a Mundan ceremony—for a calm and peaceful life, and was invited to join in. Asked, "How old is the child?" Was told, "Actually, we don't know. We celebrate happiness, not numbers." Was fed lunch. Taken into temple where men have been feeding people in need for thirty years. They played a weird electric gong drum for us while we all stood around being accosted by this head-splitting cacophony. Much staring, people looking bewildered and shocked, even scared. Much hospitality. Many free chaos. (Chai got auto-corrected to chaos—also true.)

"Whazhappening, Torreji?" Ajit said from behind me, singing in his musical intonation, finally getting my name right.

"Nothing's happening. Whazhappening with you?"

"Nothingzhappening with me. Are you writing to someone on your phone?"

"No, I'm writing notes."

"While walking?"

"I'm good at multitasking."

"Be careful, I do not want to have to peel you off the front of a truck."

"I'm fine. At home, I read entire books while walking around the park, and I've never run into anything."

Our strange percussion filled the silence and then, "Torreji, for what reason are you doing this pilgrimage?"

I thought for a beat, wondering whether or not to give him a polite and respectable lie or the raw and awkward truth. I looked up at his puffy, relaxed eyes and decided on the truth. "Well, first of all I'm here to keep Masha company. Second, because doing this walk through India seemed like a really scary thing to do, and I suppose I thought that if I could conquer this, I could conquer other things in my life that scare me."

"What are you most scared of, Torreji?"

"Going home. I lost two of the most important people in my life this year, and now I have to start again from scratch." My words hung in the dusty air like a bad smell. We'd walked past slums with plastic tarps for ceilings, cardboard for walls, roadsides for toilets, and phrases like "Start life from scratch" felt almost grotesque coming from my mouth in this environment.

"I understand," he said. "I know that feeling. And what about Masha? Why is she doing all this walking?"

"I'm not really sure. I used to know, but now I don't."

He bobbled his head.

"What about you, Ajit? I know you've been hired to do this job, but do you have something else you'd like to get out of it?"

"Well, I'm not doing it for the money, that's for sure." He laughed.

"You're not getting paid well by the company to do this?"

"No, but I'm not doing this trip for the money. I left a good-paying job to come on this pilgrimage. I finished my photography degree last year and then I started working at a corporate job in Delhi—an excellent job that a lot of people would want. The money is very good. But I don't know if that's what I want to be doing with my life. I want to make art. I want to be a freelance photojournalist and tell stories that are important. But this is a risk. I don't know if I can make money being a freelancer and maybe it is a stupid idea to leave a steady job that many people would want to become an artist. And so right now I feel a bit lost about which direction I should move in."

"So you're doing this walk to try to figure out if you should pursue security or passion?"

"That's right. I'm walking for the same reason as you two are. Because, through seeing this country and being in a new environment in a new way, I might learn about myself and what I want."

That made us a trio of navel-gazers, three rebels without a cause, wandering aimlessly after the ghost of Gandhi, hoping we might stumble across answers to personal questions. Introspection gets a bad rap from some, but if we can understand ourselves from the inside out, perhaps that gives us a stronger ability to empathize with others and what it means to be human. It's like putting your eye up to the small tunnel of a telescope in order to peer out into the universe.

He stopped to snap a photo with his Nikon, adjusting the focus on his lens with expert flicks.

"And what have you learned so far, Ajit?"

"I don't know. This whole experience has been very weird so far." He laughed and bobbled his head.

"I agree," I said, catching on to the head bobble and wobbling my own in reply.

A man with a decorated buffalo passed us, both animal and man looking one part terrified, one part intrigued as we crossed paths.

"You know," said Ajit, "we should all make artworks while we are doing this pilgrimage and then have an exhibition at the end, in Dandi. We can make art about what this pilgrimage means to us, what Gandhi means to us. What do you think?"

"I love the idea. I don't know what I would make, though."

"Think about it. We have time and many, many miles to go." He laughed and then winced, carrying his blistered foot outward at a sickly angle to lift the pressure off the wound.

"How are your shoe bites?"

"Not good, Torreji." His expression was anguished.

"Do you need more bandages?"

"No. But I think I need to rest. A little rest and then it will be no prob-a-lehm."

We found a spot of shade under a tree and sat cross-legged next to arid farmland. Ajit offered us a packet of mixed nuts, and before I put my hand into it, I inspected my hands. They were filthy. My nails were packed full of grit. Dust was impregnated in my pores, and brown had settled into every crevice of my skin, accentuating the lines in my palms. My long lifeline was now perhaps not so long, because the dirt and pollution were all over us, around us, inside us. We were not just walking the country; we were becoming it.

I shrugged and ate the nuts from my hands anyway. At this point, what would it matter?

In the distance, I spotted a pack of men coming straight toward us with bamboo staffs in their hands.

"Oh shit," said Masha, spotting the same threat on the horizon.

My body turned rigid. "Men."

We were far from the safety of crowds. No cars had passed us in some time. We were alone in a field, exposed and vulnerable. My fingers found the can of pepper spray in my pocket and I flicked the lid off with my thumb. *Nozzle out.* I counted the men. There were six. How could I possibly take down six men with a single squirt of pepper spray? It would be like trying to bowl a strike with a shuttlecock.

"It's okay," Ajit said. "Do not worry; we are safe."

I tried to trust Ajit's words as the men closed in on us. They stood feet apart from us in a semicircle, clutching their sticks, staring without inhibition. Cross-legged on the grass, we returned the stare, necks craned and shoulders tight with apprehension.

One of the men spoke in Hindi, and we looked to Ajit for a translation.

"The shepherd says you are the first Westerners they've ever seen," said Ajit. Among them was a boy, maybe only three years old, who held in his clutch a short bamboo staff, cut to his tiny proportions. He regarded us with the same intense curiosity as the adults. Their luminous brown eyes were wide open with awe.

"They are curious about you," said Ajit. "Do you mind if I ask them to sit with us?"

We both nodded our approval, and I relaxed my shoulders.

They dropped their bamboo staffs and sat straight-backed and cross-legged beside us. More men gathered, on bikes and motorbikes and on foot, and truck drivers pulled over to stare out their windows.

"Ask the men a question if you like," said Ajit. "Ask them anything you want to know. I hope they will answer honestly.

This is a very informal setting. I think you can ask anything, whatever you want to."

Masha took up Ajit's open invitation and delved into India's patriarchal value system. "What do you think the role of women is in Indian society?"

I braced myself for their answer.

The men spoke between themselves for several minutes while Ajit listened and replied with, "Accha, accha, accha," a multipurpose interjection that means something along the lines of, "Hmm, okay, good, yes, I see." He addressed us with the translation: "They're saying they all want to give freedom to females in their houses, but they say there are traditions, and they can't break that culture. It's very difficult. And then they're saying they would like the females to be like you guys— to travel and wear whatever they want to—but it's society that won't allow it."

Ajit turned back to the men and asked, "But who makes the rules of society? The culture: who makes it?"

The shepherds reflected on this and said, "Accha, accha, we make it." They reflected on this concept for a few beats, adding nothing more.

Masha said, "And what value do you get from your wives?"

A long dialogue exchange and then this: "What we value is the partnership we share with our wives. We speak to them at the end of each day about problems and successes. A successful marriage is a balanced union of both sexes. The Hindu Gods Radha and Krishna are an equal union of both sexes, devoted to one another, working harmoniously together. That is what we aspire to."

My heart softened to hear their answers. Because of warnings before we'd set out, I'm ashamed to say I'd anticipated misogyny and aggression from these rural shepherds, but they were gentle with their answers. The single story sells us on a big, bad world crawling with monsters and terrorists, when, in fact, the world is crawling with kindness and curiosity. And yes, there are bad people, and sure, it's important to stay alert, but being habitually closed-off and suspicious ends up blocking opportunities for meaningful connections. How can you be moved by random encounters if you're guarded? How can the world show all of its stunning dimensions to you if you're unable to let go of fear?

"Your skin is so white," said one man to Masha, his expression one of enchantment. "How do you keep your skin so white?"

She showed him her tube of sunscreen.

Ajit translated, "He wants to know if he can put some on his face."

Masha handed it to him with a clear instruction, translated by Ajit, "Whatever you do, do not rub it into your eyes."

"Accha, accha," he said as he rubbed the cream on his skin and straight into his eyes.

His faced twisted up in burning agony. To make the pain go away, he rubbed his eyes some more.

"Don't put it in your eyes! Don't put it in your eyes!" we chimed.

He was crying now. Crying and laughing at the same time. All the other men laughed and we laughed and the other men laughed harder, and the sunscreen guy was all rapture and agony—raptagony—and then Masha offered him her pink flowery scarf so he could wipe out his burning eyeballs.

We sat in the sigh of a delightful silence, a slight warm breeze rolling in off the paddocks to dry the tears from our laughing. It smelled of livestock, smoke, and dust—a mix that was starting to grow on me.

One of the men spoke, and Ajit said, "He is asking if you'd like to go into the paddocks to watch them milk a cow for some chai."

We nodded and then followed the men way out into the paddock alone, while Ajit rested in the shade. Out in the paddock, among a thousand cows and buffalo, the men picked a suitable cow for our chai and squeezed her milk into an aluminum pot. If the herd got too close, the shepherds would use their bamboo staffs to bump their horns and startle them away. The men were smaller than us in stature. We towered over them, Western Amazonians that we are.

Back under the shade of the tree, they set up a triangle of bricks and began stuffing sticks underneath it. A fire was lit and from somebody's pocket came a sachet of sugar, from another a sachet of masala—cardamom, cinnamon, cloves, ginger, and peppercorn. They worked as a team, collecting sticks, stoking the fire, stirring the milk, adding sugar, adding more sugar, lining up the mugs, pouring, offering us cups of steaming chai.

We sat cross-legged on the dirt in silence together, sipping tea and smiling at the shared specialness of the moment. When you travel in an unconventional way, even if it's only taking a different route to work, your chances of having serendipitous encounters go way up. Alchemy is the magic that emerges when we give up needing to have certainty and instead open up to the world, so that the world can open itself up to us.

In the end, when we're old and grey, we are made up of the sum of what our eyes have noticed, how our ears have listened, and the ways in which our hearts have responded to this stimuli. Eyes closed, ears closed, heart closed, you let nothing new in. You become a house with doors and windows closed, stagnant and cobwebbed, never seeing the light. What is the point of that kind of life? The cost of fear is a life half lived. The only way around it is to offer trust before skepticism, calm before vigilance, and grace before suspicion.

The older of the men asked Ajit to translate to us. "He said they are very impressed that you are walking in the steps of the great Mahatma Gandhi. And he wants to know which of Gandhiji's philosophies you most align with."

"Ahhhhh . . . " said Masha.
"Errrrrr . . . " said I.
"Truth," said Masha.
"Fearlessness," said I.
Ajit translated and heads bobbled with approval.

20

Aⱼɪᴛ's ʟɪᴍᴘ ɢᴏᴛ worse and he began to fall farther and farther behind. More often than not, Masha and I walked alone, single file along the highway, dipping off the road whenever a screaming truck barreled toward our bodies, bouncing on unstable suspension.

Masha walked in a daze, often headlong into traffic while looking at the screen of her phone, and I worried that she was so caught up in her inner world that she was no longer aware of the dangers all around us. She'd been so shrewd in Italy; in India she seemed to have checked out. Despite my growing frustration with her moodiness, I knew I wasn't going to give up on her. I'd stick this out until the end, even if it meant we hated each other in Dandi.

I kept one eye on her and the other on the road, looking for potholes, poo, and dead animals. Whenever I'd find a particularly good roadkill, I'd stop to inspect it up close, and then take a photo like a crime scene detective.

Ajit caught up, breathless and clutching his phone. "A journalist from a local Gujarati newspaper wants to speak to you."

"Why?"

"He wants to interview you about the pilgrimage you're doing."

"I don't really want to speak to a journalist," I said.

Masha frowned. "Why not?"

"What is the point of generating publicity? It's not like we're performing a protest. We don't need exposure. If we are written up in the paper, a lot of people are going to know there are two women walking alone. They will know our route. Doesn't that concern you?"

"Not really, no."

"What would we even tell a reporter, Masha?" The truth was, I was embarrassed and didn't want to draw any extra attention to our senseless journey. All three of us had fallen so far down the rabbit hole of our self-involved inner worlds that any meaning outside our own navels—world peace, for example—had been forgotten. "How can we capture any of this? I mean, what are we going to talk about with a journalist? The headstands? The monkeys?"

The monkeys: This was how we referred to all the worried, obsessive thoughts that were dancing madly around in our minds as we walked, otherwise known as What Ifs. Between the three of us, we talked often of our monkeys and would check into each other's emotional states by asking, "What are your monkeys doing right now?"

"They're possessed zombies," Masha would reply, "who are swimming around inside a cesspool of filth. Yours?"

"My monkeys are currently jumping off cliffs, like lemmings."

"What are your monkeys doing, Ajit?"

"My monkeys have many shoe bites, and they are in pain."

"Aw, poor monkeys."

The sum of our journey had become a series of obscure in-jokes, meaningful only to us. Attempting to recount any of this to a journalist would be the equivalent of trying to explain the meaning behind a delirious fever dream in succinct, print-ready sound bites.

Ajit told the journalist no, hung up the phone, and, once again, fell far behind as we walked on.

Masha fell behind me too, and that is how we all walked: alone.

✦

It's amazing what you start to notice when you move slowly through a landscape rather than inside the bubble of a vehicle. By train, car, or plane, a landscape tends to appear as a big sweep of large features: sky, trees, roads, signs, passing towns. But on foot, the scenery becomes a collage of tiny, obscure details.

I was just ahead of Masha when I saw the snake, a dead one, severed at the neck, presumably by a shovel. Its body was a fat S-curve with distinctive markings: a Russell's viper, responsible for more incidents and deaths than any snake throughout Asia, killing around 46,000 Indians per year and maiming countless others. Farmers who work all day long in the fields face the greatest risk. The snake is fast, with long fangs and rapid injection, striking victims from five feet away within seconds, and unlike most other venomous snakes, it almost never delivers a dry bite, preferring instead to inject its maximum dose. But that's not even the worst part: If you survive a bite from this moody beast, the venom destroys the kidneys or shuts down the function of the pituitary gland, which causes a kind of reverse puberty. Pubic hair drops out. Men lose facial hair and muscles, women lose curves, and both genders lose sex drive and fertility.

Russell the snake is one deranged motherfucker.

We were walking daily alongside grass and farmlands, our ankles tickled by dry underbrush as we edged into scrub to avoid oncoming traffic. Some fears are reasonable, and this was one of them.

I snapped a photo of Russell to add to a growing collection of dead animal photos. It was the most beautiful dead animal yet: a beguiling and deadly S-curve in the photo frame. It looked like my contribution to the art exhibition in Dandi was going to be a colorful collection of dead things.

I backtracked to Masha. "There's a snake on the road," I warned.

She looked disgusted but was still too far inside her own head to react as she passed around it and walked on in silence.

The dirt on the roadside was flecked with bits, bobs, and oddments: some gross, some strange, but all captivating for the fact they could break up the monotony of pot-holed roads lined by dusty trees and dirt.

"Oh, look, I found a peacock feather," I said to Masha, offering it like an olive branch.

"Oh, wow, it's only half damaged."

I found another treasure. "Look, I found a black tassel. I have an idea. Let's make a bouquet of found objects together."

She gave me a vague smile and nodded, and we filled half a morning with scavenging.

Each discovery was a small thrill. We searched the dust for treasures as we walked, filling our hands and pockets with random junk. As we combed for flotsam, we were in good spirits, and I began to weave the junk into a hodgepodge bouquet.

"I just found a jar of hot-pink nail polish," I said.

"Is it still good?"

"No, it's sticky."

"Why have people thrown all this great stuff away?"

"Holy shit, I just found the Hindu God of money on a sticker!"

"That's amazing!"

Outside the busy city of Nadiad, we broke free from the thrust, sweat, and shriek of a busy epicenter to the straight path of a calm road. The roadside was an Aladdin's cave of incredible finds. Okay, it was all junk, but everything is exciting when you're looking at dirt and road for eight hours a day. Deprived of other stimulation, you can find pleasure in the smallest things. For the first time in days, we were working together, assembling the treasures into a nasty, but lovingly created, bouquet of utterly useless bric-a-brac. We were creating an offering of some kind, perhaps an entreaty for our friendship to go back to the way it was before.

"Where should we put it?"

"Let's wait for a place that feels right."

We searched trees and bushes, looking for a home for our offering. An hour after searching, we came to a line of huge, shady banyan trees hung with hundreds of colorful scarves swaying in the warm breeze. The space was hushed, sacred. I turned to Masha. "Let's put our offering here."

She said, "I was just thinking *exactly* the same thing. That must be a sign."

I was relieved to have the old Masha back, the one who believed in magic and trusted in everything.

We approached the temple with our assembled bouquet of roadside treasures, wrapped together into a bundle with a piece of dry grass.

"Wait!" said Ajit, stopping us just in time. "I wouldn't leave any kind of offering here. This is a temple for the God of bad spirits."

"Oh, gross."

"People come here if they need a quick favor to get themselves out of a bad situation, and they make an offering, but they do so in exchange for becoming indebted to evil. They only come when they are desperate. Or they come here when they're possessed by evil."

"That's truly disturbing."

I looked up at the trees hanging with colorful scarves, and now they looked demented, like a cluster of restless spirits caught up in the branches of the trees, unable to escape up to the sky. My skin crawled.

"And," Ajit went on, adding insult to injury, "if you put that bouquet here, it would be offensive to the Hindu religion."

We abandoned our cluster of trash in the crux of a nondescript tree up the road. Ajit fell behind, Masha broke off ahead, and we walked again in single file, alone and lonely. We stopped meddling with magic and instead began our fall toward madness.

21

WE WALKED HIGHWAYS wobbling with heat from the parched farmlands that lined them, through villages writhing with trade and the racket of pumping embroidery machines, past monotone industrial zones, eerily empty, before easing out along the sigh of a calm road lined with green trees full of monkeys. Though there were always curiosities to observe at walking pace, the landscapes were mostly a continuum of nondescript features, blurring into a montage of passing days that lacked the sense of arrival you otherwise get when distance transforms landscapes into new destinations.

Under the heat of the sun, we walked all day to reach the same place we'd started out from, it seemed. It's not difficult to understand why Gujarat isn't a popular tourist destination for either foreigners or Indians. Best known for its farming, industry, and commerce, it's a place of productivity and big business, of textile manufacture and the production of petrochemicals, fertilizers, engineering, and electronics. It wasn't the most thrilling part of the country, but it was home to Gandhi's legacy, and so onward we pushed, never knowing where the path might take us, whether we'd find a safe place to sleep before dusk, whom we might meet, what we might eat.

Hungry, we sat down in a featureless village at the only snack shop we'd seen after miles of barren road. Whatever they were selling at the shop would be lunch. Ajit ordered a plate of *namkeen*, and we sat outside on plastic chairs sharing the nuts. As I sat there spooning the spicy mix into my mouth, my peripheral vision caught a cheeky brown mouse in the store's window display, ducking in and out of the various hessian sacks of nuts.

That meant our food was contaminated with rodents.

I looked down at my nuts and waited for my gag reflex to kick in.

It didn't.

"There are mice in the nuts," I announced to my companions.

Masha and Ajit looked down at the plate of namkeen. Perhaps a former version of us would've gagged, screamed, or at least stopped eating the nuts. But fussy eating is a privilege of choice, and in the more remote areas we passed through, sometimes it would be 4 p.m. by the time we found a restaurant or food stall. By then we were ravenous, and if the only item on the menu was old, dry, deep-fried snacks buzzing with flies, an oily curry from the world's grimiest restaurant, or mice-infested nuts, then so it was. Despite our eclectic eating, nobody had suffered even the slightest stomach upset.

We'd spent so much time resting in the dirt on the side of the road and sleeping on ashram floors shared with critters that the lines that normally separate rodent from human and dirt from food had become blurry.

I ate one more bite of namkeen before Ajit and Masha finished it off. If you are what you eat, then we were nuts.

While Masha played on her phone and Ajit thumbed through photos on his camera, I pulled out the book I was reading. Often when we'd stop to rest, I'd read from Gandhi's memoir, *The Story of My Experiments with Truth*, to find out whom, exactly, we were following. I was captivated by his confession of suffering from various irrational fears in his youth: "I used to be haunted by the fear of thieves, ghosts, and serpents," he wrote. "I did not dare to stir out of the doors at night. Darkness was a terror to me. It was almost impossible for me to sleep in the dark, as I would imagine ghosts coming from one direction, thieves from another and serpents from a third."

Yep. I hear ya, Gandhiji.

I wondered who—or what—had traumatized the great Mahatma Gandhi. I thought about a time in my teens when Dad's talent for terrifying the shit out of people grew stronger, after he discovered the omnipotence of Photoshop. On the wall outside my bedroom were three framed oil paintings of women, all prints of classic portraits that had hung there for as long as I could remember. One day, while walking into my room, I noticed something in my peripheral vision. One of the portraits seemed different. When I turned to look, I noticed *one of the women had fangs!* This wasn't a movie; this was real life, and I must've cleared at least two feet of air before running teary-eyed and breathless to my dad, crying, "Something's wrong with the painting!" He chuckled with satisfaction as he explained how he'd taken the picture down; removed it from the frame; scanned it; Photoshopped in fangs, curled lips, and evil eyes; reframed and rehung it; and then—perhaps most masterly of all—stayed silent for *months* until somebody noticed his prank. It was all meant in good fun; Dad just didn't quite grasp where entertainment ended and trauma began.

But there was hope for me yet. Out of a determination to be strong and daring, Gandhi had worked at becoming fearless. He was valiant not by nature but by strength of character, and it reassured me to know that even a great force like Gandhi had to learn how to be strong in the face of imaginary ghouls and serpents. Turns out, everyone has their own monkeys to battle, but, as he said, "There would be no one to frighten you if you refused to be afraid."

Gandhiji was my new hero. As Masha drifted further away, I latched myself onto his teachings.

I delved deeper into his memoir, and with that, and the help of Ajit's commentary, my experience of India began to change. "That is where the wealthy live," said Ajit, pointing to a huge Hollywood-style estate. "And that is where their slaves live." He pointed across the street to the slum. "Those are the people who built it and who tend to the estate."

The contrast was overwhelming. Due to a lack of toilets and running water, the people of the slums were living on top of their own waste. Outside the estates, they would fill pots from the taps used for watering the gardens, and carry it on their heads back home for cooking and drinking. Meanwhile, these estates looked like a faux-Hollywood dream.

A place of spiritual happiness, said the slogan to an estate constructed from clean lines and Western modernity, with a view out over the people that built it, living ankle-deep in waste. I wondered if anyone could feel spiritually happy with that kind of sweeping panorama over the cost of their privilege.

"Torreji, I have never seen a rainforest, only on my computer wallpaper. Have you seen a rainforest?"

"Yes. In Thailand. In Costa Rica. In Australia."

"Oh, you've done lots of travel. I hope to travel too some day, when I can afford it. Was it beautiful?"

"Yes, it's beautiful."

"These estates we are seeing: they are selling a dream to live close to nature, but nature is only a souvenir." The properties had fake grass, fake trees, and even stuffed monkeys hanging from wires.

All over the world, we're paving paradise, turning communities of forests into bigger and taller houses that smell of cut pine and fresh paint, that sigh at night with unsatisfied emptiness. In

the morning, we get in the car and drive our commute, discon-
nected from our surroundings as we move at high speed toward
bigger and better and newer and lonelier. Trees come down and
wildlife scatters, and we don't even notice because the car windows are tinted and the radio is loud and if a tree falls in the
woods, nobody hears it.

We have insomnia, anxiety, depression, or the malaise of
general discontent, but instead of focusing on our quality of
life, we focus instead on digits. Money is our God, and that,
unfortunately, is where our cultural values have rested since the
industrial revolution. We chase more of the same, focusing our
time and efforts on better and newer, and trees fall and wildlife
scatters, but maybe all we get from it is lonelier.

"The world has enough for everyone's needs, but not
everyone's greed," said Gandhi. He pushed for self-realization,
believing that only through a higher sense of purpose, above
and beyond the pursuit of wealth and pleasure, could we hope
to improve the human condition. This is not an Indian issue;
this is a global issue.

"Do you think Gandhi was successful?" I asked Ajit.

"I think he has had great influence on the world. He was
a powerful protester, and his great skill was in generating publicity for his causes. So in that regard, yes. But I don't think
Gandhi's mission was successful. His ideology of self-sufficiency
did not take hold. Weaving one's own clothing on a loom, living
minimally, nonviolence, truth . . . Great human injustice is still
happening, here and around the world."

As we passed slums and estates at walking pace, I started to
see what could not be unseen. "Desire World" was the name of
one estate. "Heaven 444," was another. Money changes hands
around the world over this lure of heaven and desire, a place
superior to the here and now; a place you can get to if only you're
one part lucky, one part hardworking. We celebrate the wealthy

and ignore the poor, chase the money and waste the moment. Though this is a global issue, in India the puppet strings are more obvious, the production more awkwardly executed. The truth hangs out like a fly undone.

We passed a slum where we were invited in for chai that tasted like sugary drain water—and possibly was. We drank it quickly and returned the cups, but when three more cups of lukewarm tea arrived from our generous hosts, we said "Thank you!" and sipped the tea more slowly, so as not to invite a third.

Kids with ratty hair and torn clothing sat on our laps and looked at our faces with bright and curious eyes. They lined up to take selfies with us, writhing in an excited tangle and punching each other with balled fists to compete for front and center. They bent down to touch our toes, but Ajit stopped them. "No, no, no, no!" *Pranama* is an Indian greeting that shows respect for grandparents, parents, teachers, gurus, gods, and others of great wisdom or virtue by bending down to touch their feet in an act of "reverential bowing." Because the feet are close to the dirt and the elements, they're the least honored part of a body, and so bowing down to touch them is a show of submission and respect. By virtue of being white and therefore wealthy and therefore power-wielding demigods, oftentimes when we would meet new people, they would bend down to touch our feet. Ajit would stop them in their tracks. "No, no, no, no!" He would offer his hand, and they would smile broadly and shake it, and we would all greet one another on equal terms.

Through Ajit's open heart and mind, along with inspiration from Gandhi, we were brought into contact with everyone's stories—not just those of the upper caste, but the stories from every tier of the hierarchy. Ajit had the inquiring mind of an artist, and so he helped us to *see* what we were seeing.

When we would stop to rest, he would engage anyone at all in lengthy chats in Hindi, learning their personal stories and then reporting back to us. "He immigrated here two years ago from Nepal. He doesn't like his job at the restaurant because he says it's all older people serving here and he's young and this isn't the right job for him."

With expert flicks of his lens, Ajit snapped photos everywhere we went. It was often hard to see what his vision was, as he would point his lens at the strangest places: an old wall, a half-built construction site, the corner of a room with Masha's sad and distant face reflected on a wardrobe mirror . . .

"Why did you study photography?" I asked him once.

"Photography is a catalyst for me. A catalyst to ask questions. Even when there are no answers."

✦

No answers.

That is what I had after I began to query deeper into the details of Gandhi's life, only to stumble upon *Gandhi: Naked Ambition* by Jad Adams, a biography that delves into Gandhi's disturbing "celibacy experiments." According to Adams, as well as a range of other journalists brave enough to write about this lesser-known side of the man, Gandhi was kind of, sort of, a tiny little bit of a . . . maybe . . . I don't know how to tell you this, but . . . *a sexual predator?*

As part of his experiments, Gandhi took a vow of *brahmacharya*, committing himself to a spiritual life of chastity, which, I can only imagine, was terrible news for his wife when he made the unilateral decision. Could you imagine? *Honey, I'm home, and guess what? We're never having sex again.* As Adams describes, Gandhi had an "almost magical belief in the power of semen," quoting Gandhi's own words on the topic to prove his point: "One who conserves his vital fluid acquires unfailing power."

Like vegetarianism, sobriety, and nonviolence, it was a puritanical ideal that he encouraged others to follow, preaching his message to readers of his newspaper *Indian Opinion*: "It is the duty of every thoughtful Indian not to marry. In case he is helpless in regard to marriage, he should abstain from sexual intercourse with his wife."

Okay, so he was a little eccentric. Who isn't a little eccentric? But then I read that, at his ashram, he encouraged young boys and girls to bathe and sleep together to test their temptation, and then reprimanded them for any sexual talk or activity. Meanwhile, as he was instructing the women of the ashram not to sleep with their husbands, he had them sleep naked alongside him in bed to test his celibacy, though it seems he didn't always pass. "Vina's sleeping with me might be called an accident. All that can be said is that she slept close to me." Okay, so he was extremely eccentric.

One time, after discovering that a young man had harassed two of his female followers, Gandhi cut the girls' hair off. In his writing, he used this incident to demonstrate his belief that women are responsible for sexual attacks on them, because, ladies, you're really provoking the boys with those long, silky locks. He believed that a raped woman had lost her value as a human being and that contraceptives were for whores. You won't often see this angle of Gandhi's wisdom quoted on a meme. The single story of Gandhi is one of do-no-wrong sainthood.

Like many "saints" who suppress sexual urges, Gandhi's experiments began to truly warp right about the time he decided to sleep with naked young women, including his own great-niece, Manuben, as a way to test his temptations. "Despite my best efforts," he's reported to have said, as captured in Joseph Lelyveld's book *Great Soul: Mahatma Gandhi and His Struggle with India* (a book that was banned in Gujarat), "the organ remained aroused. It was an altogether strange and shameful experience." I can't be certain, but I'm pretty sure he wasn't talking about a piano. Ew.

Bapu was a creepy uncle?

I didn't know what to make of this incongruous information about the man whose legacy we were tracing—a common problem, I suppose, given that, in an effort to protect his image, letters and other evidence of Gandhi's sexual forays have been suppressed or destroyed. Only in 2010 did Manuben's diaries find their way to the National Archives in Delhi. In them, Manuben says "Kaka (Gandhi's youngest son Devdas) warned me not to disclose the contents of my diary to anyone and at the same time forbade me to divulge the contents of the important letters. He said, 'You are very young but you possess a lot of valuable literature. And you are also unsophisticated.'"

Some are tempted, I'm sure, to give Gandhi immunity for his wrongdoings because "the times were different" or "he was imperfect like anyone else," in order to avoid the cognitive dissonance of this visionary being flawed to the point of disturbed. But failing to acknowledge and condemn the severity of this misdeed blurs the lines between right and wrong. It was a violation of power. To whitewash this invalidates the experiences of anyone who has been personally violated and makes space for it to happen again—particularly when the role model happens to be a national hero.

What was I supposed to do with all the inspiration he had given me? I'd been following not only his footsteps but his moral compass, and it had ended up leading me to the intersection of Deep Confusion and What the Actual Fuck, Gandhi.

22

DEAD ANIMALS MARKED out the growing distance between Masha and me. They were everywhere, all day, every day, flatted on the side of the road like overcooked pancakes, dogs' faces fixed into expressions of permanent two-dimensional shock. It was so confronting that it was almost funny, but when I tried to laugh, only a dry wheeze came out of my pinched lips.

Puppies with their ears chewed off, dogs foaming at the mouth from rabies, an unidentifiable animal knocked clean out of its skin from a road accident, a dog in a tree thrust into the foliage by the walloping heft of a vehicle some time beforehand. The corpse had, over time, turned into a skeleton wedged in branches, like some kind of grim Tim Burton Christmas decoration, but with less curlicued whimsy and more bleak reality.

Ajit's phone rang.

"The journalist from the *Times of India* wants to speak to you," he said, holding his phone out. Masha did an interview, and then it was my turn. I gave in and took the phone, ducking off the side of the road into a bush for privacy, covering my ear to block out the noise of trucks barreling past only inches from

my body. Masha and Ajit walked onward and disappeared from
my eyesight.

"How are you enjoying India?" The phone line dropped in
and out.

"The people are lovely. We are encountering a lot of generosity. We have felt very supported by every person we've crossed
paths with."

"That's great. And what have you been eating?"

"Everything."

"Is there any particular Indian dish that you enjoy?"

"All of it."

"Can you give me the name of one dish that you enjoy?"

"Those deep-fried ball thingies with the dipping sauce that
you get from the street stalls. I can't remember what you call
them: um . . . something-something . . . they have cilantro in
them." I wasn't being facetious; I just hadn't learned the names
of all the food. They were often our only meal for the day, and
I'd been too focused on shoving them into my face to remember the local name of the something-somethings. They were
edible and they had carbs; that had been my main concern. We
often marveled at how sixty-one-year-old Gandhi had not only
walked the same distance as we were each day, but he also had
the energy left over in the evening to deliver an impassioned
sermon in each of the villages where he slept.

"Err . . . okay . . . so . . . um, what are your impressions of
the country?"

Kids in blue school uniforms. Dry grass hiding snakes.
Tobacco and cotton farms. The smell of burning sugar cane.
Small bodies bent over crops. An ultramarine kingfisher flying
over a lake thick with scum. Limps on dogs. Bright smiles on
children. A filthy woman with a half-clothed baby selling Santa
costumes on the side of a highway. A hundred other stalls selling
the exact same red-and-white costume. The country of uncom-
fortable truths. The complete deconstruction of any rational

narrative that I once believed in, tallying up to absolute mental blankness.

"Um . . . " I looked down at my clothing, searching for something to give her. "It's very dusty here, and we are covered in dirt." I laughed.

She did not. "Are you not bathing every day?"

"Yes, we are bathing every day."

"Then why are you dirty?"

A truck drove past, sending up another giant plume of dirt, which swirled in the air before settling as a fine coating on the trees, on my shoes, in my lungs. Everything here was snowed on by dust particles, and having spent so many days walking, I was observant enough to understand that the dust was made up of not only pollution and earth but the fine powder of dried shit and decomposed animals. Dirt. Shit. Death. We couldn't escape it.

The phone dropped out for a second and then she asked, "Are you there?"

"I'm here."

How could I have told her over a bad phone line that my nails were so full of black gunk that I couldn't scrape it out anymore, and that stuff was coming out of my nose that really shouldn't have gotten up there in the first place? How could I tell her that every day I tied my small bath towel to the outside of my backpack to dry, and when we'd stop to rest and I put my bag down, it often sat in dust and poo? And how could I explain that, in the evenings, after my shower, I'd have to dry my body with that poo towel, and then put on the same outfit I'd been wearing every evening for twelve days—my one change of clothes that I also slept in—clothes that smelled of all the places we'd stayed in like an olfactory map of our travels: strangers' homes and run-down hotels, ashram floors and incense from temples, mothballs and curries and soaps and drywall.

Should I have told her that, one day, when we stopped to rest, we put our bags down on the ground and sat cross-legged in the dirt, and only after I'd been resting for minutes, snacking on a bag of nuts, did I notice the toe of my shoe was lodged in a dead mouse? I could see its tiny ribcage where its skin was flayed at the edges, little paws curled up and frozen solid near his buckteeth. Not only was I indifferent to the fact that my shoe was wedged in a corpse, I didn't even bother to shift my foot. I saved my energy for the walk ahead. My eyes made their way back to the horizon, hooded and indifferent. I kept eating nuts.

At some point, perhaps even as early as the first day, we all stopped caring about the specifics of what touched our skin and mouths. How could I tell her that without sounding crazy? How could I tell her that walking brings you so intimately close to the earth that the separation between you and dirt or you and rodent becomes inconsequential? Where once you saw yourself as a superior being, a clean and shiny thing, you start to know yourself as a mass of decomposable flesh, moving through a landscape of decomposing things, atoms through atoms, particles coming and going. We go to such great lengths to avoid dirt; avoid shaking hands with anyone who seems unclean, thinking that, if only we can keep ourselves clean, we can avoid diseases and dying. We won't catch the miseries of another human. It creates separateness. But to become so intimate with dirt is an exercise in humility and humanity. By not being afraid of dirt, I stopped being afraid of death, and by not being afraid of death, I was starting to get closer to fearlessness.

"I'm dirty because there's a lot of dust on the side of the road, and we are walking along the side of the road for five to ten hours per day."

A long beat of confusion, and then—"So anyway, which of . . . " A truck barreled past and I couldn't hear the question.

"Pardon?"

"I said, I'm wondering which of . . . "

Another rickety truck zoomed past, all banging metal and slapping chain, carrying goods to places along a highway built to honor Gandhi's protest against corporate greed, pumping out the sticky mud of exhaust. A fresh storm of dust snowed down over the bushes, over my head.

"I'm sorry, what?"

"I said, which of Gandhi's philosophies do you most align with?"

No answers.

23

It was official: Ajit was crippled. His blisters had turned into huge open wounds, too tender to tread on. Man down.

"Mashaji, Torreji, you need to keep walking, or we won't make it to Dandi on schedule." Knowing we weren't going to make it back home in time for Christmas, Masha and I had booked flights to Varanasi to spend our Christmas in this famous holy city. Any delays on the pilgrimage and we'd miss our flights. I thought about what the yogi had said in Bangkok—"You will get very lucky on Christmas"—and a hopeful part of me wondered what might unfold in Varanasi.

"I'm going to catch a rickshaw to the next village," Ajit declared. "Trust me, it will be no prob-a-lehm," he insisted, eyes calm. I'm pretty sure that if a team of thugs was coming at Ajit, smacking their palms with the worn handles of sharp objects, he'd still be bobbling his head from side to side and insisting, with an untroubled expression, that there was "No prob-a-lehm." Such was the nature of his unshakable inner tranquility; if he had a superpower, it would be ejecting lightning bolts of peace from his eyes.

I dug around in my pockets to make sure the pepper spray was still in there. "Are you sure this is a good idea, Ajit?"

"I can't walk anymore," he replied. "The pain is too much."

I felt terrible for having gotten him into this, for having gotten ourselves into this.

"So exactly where will we meet you?" said Masha.

"The next village. Call me if you need anything."

He hailed a rickshaw, and it putted off into the distance with our translator and token male. We were alone. It was the first time we'd had the luxury of privacy since we'd first set out walking, and so we used the opportunity to do what we'd been waiting to do for the longest time: explode at each other.

"Masha, have I done something to upset you?"

"I'm not doing anything."

"Exactly. You're not speaking to me!"

"I am speaking to you!" She walked on, silent once again.

I rushed to catch up. "Why are you not talking to me?" The anger in my voice was sobering as I said, "It's like I'm walking through India alone."

We ducked off the road and sat in the dirt. The sun beat down on our heads, accosting us with the kind of heat that gropes like a pair of clammy hands, but that was the least of our problems. We were two loitering women on the shoulder of a busy road, collapsed in the dirt, in the shit, in the dust of dead animals, attracting the attention of every single passing being— man, child, or holy cow. Eyes watched us from every angle, but we were too caught up in our own personal drama to pay them any notice.

"Oh, *I'm* the only one to blame here, Torre? *I'm* the only jerk?"

"You're angry all the time," I said, my own anger grazing my throat to raspy shreds.

"You're angry too."

She wasn't wrong. I was angry because I didn't know what I was doing on a route like this with a person who didn't want to talk to me. The scenery for most of the journey had been industrial towns, clogged freeways, flat farmlands, and busy highways. What was wrong with the two of us? Masha's clothes were filthy. Her blond hair was gathered up into a scraggly, unwashed plait. Her hiking shoes were pulling apart at the seams, and the tread was so compacted with cow shit that her feet might've been locally regarded as holy if not for the fact that her toes had become so frighteningly deformed from walking halfway around the world that they'd make a podiatrist dry-retch. She had circles of sweat under her boobs and nails black with muck, and she smelled of something rancid, sweaty, and unwashed.

Like, for example: me.

But none of this mattered anymore. We both had seemed to stop caring, seemed to stop noticing any trivial details outside our own navels, such as the danger we were putting ourselves in by sitting on the side of the road, screaming at each other.

"What's wrong with you?" I yelled. "Why won't you talk?"

"I AM TALKING!" she screamed back.

"YOU'RE YELLING!"

"I'M NOT YELLING, *YOU'RE* YELLING!"

The irony was not lost on either one of us that we were arguing on a road built to pay homage to a famous peacekeeper, in a country weighed down beneath appalling poverty, pollution, and corruption. It was embarrassing, and yet—

"Fuck you!" My throat was raw, and I coughed on the rough edges of the pointiest words I had to throw at her.

"Fuck yourself!" she said, a tone louder, coughing harder.

Had we been violent types, this would've been a moment to uppercut this bitch in the chin and have her punch me right back in the nose. We'd wrestle backward to the ground, shove each other's faces in the dirt, and battle with brawn and animal instinct. Instead, we had only word weapons, and no amount of swearing seemed to land satisfying punches. Little did we realize that the biggest threat from being left alone would be each other. No pepper spray or rape whistle was going to help this situation.

Sweat dripped from my hairline and rolled down my shoulders, crawling down my back. My water bottle was almost empty. The dirt under our knees was cracked and crusted over from thirst, and the sun overhead was a brutal inferno. We couldn't just sit here all day fighting. We needed to keep moving, but there was no resolution to this in sight.

Our faces, sticky with sweat, were dusted with grit and exhaust funk. As she began to cry, she wiped at the tears with her fingers, making brown grime whiskers across her cheeks. What a mess.

"I don't know how to talk to you anymore," I said, my voice quiet now.

She exhaled. "I don't know how to talk to you either."

Somehow her calm voice was more frightening than her shouting voice, as if all the blossoming enthusiasm for our friendship had decayed into apathy—the opposite emotion of love.

An ashy-colored cow walked by wearing an amused grin, her giant curved horns bouncing along with her heavy swagger. Tiny bells on her horns set her rhythm. She ogled us with curiosity and a touch of apprehension, and for a moment I wanted to laugh at the absurdity of all of this.

I missed Ajit. Calm, openhearted, open-minded Ajit. If he had been listening, he would've told us, in his melodic Hindi accent, "Mashaji, Torreji. Whazhappening? Let us move into the shade and drink some water. Rest. Do not worry. Everything will be okay. Now, *chalo*—let's get walking."

That would be calm, rational advice, but Ajit wasn't there, and neither Masha nor I was good with rational. We were good at daring and impromptu. We were good at inappropriate jokes and hysterical fits of laughter. We were good at "I love you" and

"I love you too," and "I'm so glad you came into my life," and "I don't know how I would've coped this year if I hadn't met you."

But that was before.

Times had changed.

"Masha, please." My tone was pinched and desperate. "I can't handle losing you too."

"Torre, I'm sorry, but . . . " A flicker of regret crossed her eyes. "But that's really not my problem."

I looked at the dirt. "So I guess that's it between us then?" I asked, bracing myself for her answer, hoping she'd say "No, of course not," that she'd hug me, that we'd laugh and move on, that this would be nothing but a funny story, that everything would go back to how it was before we made a mess of it.

"I guess it is," she said, looking away.

I had hoped to leave India ready to save the world with stronger compassion, bravery, and wisdom, along with the svelte body of Raquel Welch in *One Million Years B.C.* What a joke. We couldn't even save ourselves.

My bag had been a light seven kilos, but as we walked on, I began to load it up with a heavy sense of loss and failure, too. Unhappiness can feel like a welcoming refuge to a homeless psyche because it knows the space so well: the stony walls; the dark, chilly air; the hard floor made of dust and the bones of the dead. I curled up in that place.

Nine years of relationship lost.

Father gone.

A friendship destroyed.

Time passing.

Heroes fading.

Hope slipping.

Though I was walking forward, my mind began to track backward into memories. I could hear the sound of a motorbike rumbling in my ears, feel its vibrations on my legs, smell the wet soil of another time and place—an adventure had, now lost. I tried to stop the memories, to tell them *No, please not now,* but in they flooded . . .

Damp earth, motorbike roaring, months and miles and spooning each other at thirty-five miles an hour, stopping only to pitch a tent before nightfall.

On that motorbike, we were happy once again, but it was a temporary kind of happiness: a happiness stolen from our future selves, payable with interest later on. If you live your life inside a motion blur of backdrops—if you move quickly enough, stay busy enough—none of yesterday's problems can keep up. The past takes time to orient itself within a new environment, and so, if you move fast enough, for long enough—toward exotic places, distant horizons, toward anywhere but here—you might be able to escape that which you most fear. The only catch is, you can't stop moving.

We were escaping. It was working. It was exhausting.

"Where to?" he asked.

"North?" I suggested.

The *where* never really matters that much to an adventurer, just as long as it's anywhere but here.

The motorbike's engine clapped and growled, and we merged onto the open roads that ran along Thailand and Myanmar's lush border, swerving around potholes and scooters teetering with entire families. The bike's reverberations sent tingles through my hips, up into my limbs, and through to my fingertips. Our bodies tilted in sync around the bends. In the stillness of that moment, inside that motion blur, life was beautiful.

Day after day, in the early morning, before we could orient ourselves, we'd pack our small bag, strap it to the saddle of the motorbike, and kick-start the engine back to life. We'd put on our helmets, straddle the bike, and push up against each other on the narrow motorcycle seat—him at the handlebars, me squished in at the back. I clung to him with all my strength.

On the motorbike, the wind swept forming arguments straight off our lips. It was a refuge, as long as we were speeding forward. We climbed switchbacks up mountaintops, where the road curled around jungles, green and alive. Roosters crowed at the pink dawn sky as we cruised past thatched-roof homes, where shirtless men with bare feet and fisherman's pants stopped their chores to wave at us. Women in sarongs swept dust from porches with straw brushes, while puppies chased naked children around an orbit of the household. Every square inch was photogenic, but only because it was exotic to my eye. To the Thais, this was their domestic everyday. Kids, pets, family, home . . .

I need to go home to see my dad before he dies.

We can't spend our lives sitting around waiting for people to die.

YOLO: You Only Live Once. It's the acronym of our generation, second in popularity only to FOMO: Fear of Missing Out. Forget sitting in hospice rooms waiting for others to move along; we've all got the ticking clock of our own mortality to contend with. You've got to get busy living or else get busy dying because the world is a book and those who don't travel read only one page, and twenty years from now you will be more disappointed by the things that you didn't do than by what you did do, and so we must travel not to escape life, but for life not to escape us.

Or so they say.

Of course, it should've ended there, clean and simple, because you can't reconcile core value differences like those, and nobody will ever win a battle of Family versus YOLO, but losing two people at once was a crisis too monumental to fathom. I had made my home inside a series of daring pursuits, but that wasn't the home I belonged in. This wasn't the man I belonged with.

Denial is a wonderful—if temporary—refuge, and so I tried to pretend it wasn't happening, but at night my heart would flutter in my chest like a trapped moth and then stop for one beat, two beats, three . . . The mind can lie, the body cannot, but the body can be ignored so I ignored it.

I went into action. All I needed to do to rescue the situation, I believed, was state the obvious enough times in enough ways with the correct italic emphasis—*My dad is dying!*—and it would fix the misunderstanding. I penned long letters of heartfelt prose, drew Venn diagrams of overlapping conflicts and poster-sized charts of possible solutions, created Excel spreadsheets of finances versus time versus dreams, yelled until the veins in my neck swelled, flung my limbs around in an angry lover's jitter-bug . . . Fool that I am, I even wrote him a song, hopeful that poetry and rhythm might fill the gaps between us left vacant by ordinary logic. But it didn't work, of course. The only thing that worked was travel.

At elevation in the mountains, the air was crisp and not the same sweaty heat of the lower altitudes, so I buried my hands inside his jacket and wrapped them around the flesh of his torso, sharing the heat from his skin. After almost a decade of companionship, I knew how to read him by the rhythm of his heartbeat, the pace of his breath.

From the top of the hill, the valley below was a carpet of rice fields, hatched in different shades of green and glittering wet. On the side of the road, a Buddhist temple shone gold in the light of the rising sun, and monks in orange garb walked with mindful devotion.

Dressed in our protective gear and silver helmets, we couldn't hear each other talk. The only way to communicate was to yell out in the kind of thunderous voice that strips your throat of delicate skin tissue.

"THIS LANDSCAPE IS SO BEAUTIFUL!"
"WHAT?!"
"I SAID THIS LANDSCAPE IS SO BEAUTIFUL!"
"WHAT?!"

"DON'T WORRY!"

"WHAT?!"

"FORGET IT!"

"WHAT DID WE FORGET?"

But on that early morning along the switchbacks, I wasn't bothering to speak. There was nothing to say. The moment was perfect, and we were both feeling it. I could tell by the short, shallow breaths under the palms of my hands, combined with the long, deep breaths he'd take to catch up.

We were escaping. It was working. It was heartbreaking. The pressure was building day by day. I was spooning the person I loved at thirty-five miles an hour, 5,000 miles from where I needed to be, heading north when home was south. The agony was a knuckled fist up under my ribs, pushing deep. It was tightening. It was hurting. I could hardly breathe. It was time to go home—not now, but yesterday. I had questions to ask my dad, the kinds of everyday trivia about a person's life that plague you after they're gone. "What were you like as a boy?" or "What did you think when you first met Mum?" You believe you have forever to ask a person those kinds of questions, but you don't, and then the answers are gone. Unknowable forever.

My helmet fogged up when the tears came, but it didn't matter. I wasn't the one driving, so I didn't need to see the road ahead. The tears made my chin itch, but I couldn't reach it through the bubble of my full-face helmet to scratch, and so I held on and endured the tickle. I was good at endurance. Too good at it. I squeezed my wet eyes shut until I could see nothing ahead and clung to him, trusting his direction despite myself.

From the outside looking in, it was just us and the road and the sea fog and each other's warmth, but inside the bubble of my helmet—my silent room for one—I acted on the most primal urge inside of me. I screamed. I screamed, but nobody could hear.

Tears came like rain after a tropical thunderstorm, and with my eyes squeezed shut, I felt the road move below our hips and the mountain air swirling around our bodies. His heart sped up on the switchbacks, and I hoped that maybe, if I could only cry enough of them, the tears might fill my helmet up to the brim.

Far ahead up the road, India came back into view, and I watched Masha walking solo with her head down. One more person lost.

Can a love story still be a love story if it doesn't have a happy ending?

24

"Ajit, are you sure you're okay?" He was back on his feet, limping along on a sandal strapped around his bandaged foot.

"I'm fine, Torreji. I just need to go slowly."

I left him to hobble at his pace behind us.

Masha charged well ahead of us on the opposite side of the road, and we all walked alone, confronted by our own monkeys. Nobody was happy. It was becoming more and more difficult to rationalize why we were enduring, but giving up was not an option for any of us, it seemed. We'd all traveled too far through tough conditions to give up without the catharsis of reaching the end point where, we hoped, some sense would come out of the grueling effort. Though carrying on was excruciating, pulling out at the halfway point felt akin to walking out of a surgery when your chest is still splayed open on the gurney. Somehow, I hoped we'd all be stitched back together again by the time we reached Dandi and, at the very least, restored to the same imperfect condition we were in when we set out.

I kept my head down. In the dirt I spotted a pink rock. Rose quartz. I picked it up and dusted it off, putting it into my pocket. The love stone.

"Torreji," said Ajit, his voice surprising me from behind, "whatzhappening?"

"Nothingzhappening, Ajitji."

"You're walking very slowly. And Masha is walking very fast. You both seem upset."

"We had an argument."

"Why are you fighting?"

"I don't really know why, but it started when I suggested to her that the earth was a giant ball of cancer and that the purpose of humanity is to destroy it, and that's why we've made such a mess of the world. It made her sad. But it was just a silly idea. I don't really believe it, I don't think."

He chuckled under his beard. "But isn't that true?"

"I don't know. I don't really know anything anymore."

"And why are *you* sad, Torreji?"

I thought for a beat, wondering whether or not to give him a polite and respectable lie or the raw and awkward truth. I looked up at his puffy, relaxed eyes and decided on the truth. "Ajit, do you think a love story can still be a love story if it doesn't have a happy ending?"

He gave me space to elaborate. I listened to the drum of our feet, the crunch of the gravel, and said, "I went through a breakup this year. I was launching a book and it was a story about us, but then everything started to fall apart. My dad got really sick. End-stage cancer. I was watching him die while the relationship broke down, too, and it was just . . . really . . . I swallowed hard. "Awful."

"I have had bad breakups too, Torreji. Maybe not quite that bad. I wasn't launching a book about it." He chuckled again. "But I know how much it hurts when love ends. I am still hurting myself."

"You are?"

His head bobbled. Our feet strummed the straight single-lane road, which cut through a field of tall sugarcane, hazed with smoke. The warm air smelled like burnt sugar. "I was with a Muslim woman, but my parents couldn't know, because my parents wanted me to marry a Hindu woman. We had to hide it the whole time. It was very difficult. It has been two years since we broke up, but it still hurts. I still think about it often. I have thought about it very much while we've been walking. We met in high school."

"Oh, she was your high school sweetheart."

"Yes, my sweetheart."

"It seems like such a waste, don't you think? To spend all of that time with someone and then have it fall apart?"

"But is it a waste, Torreji? Endings are part of the package. They come with love, and so we must accept it going in."

"I suppose," I said. "Even if a relationship lasts until old age, someone ends up dying first."

"Right. It's a guarantee of love. It always ends. Always."

Though it seemed obvious when he said it, I'd never considered it that way before. My parents had been married for forty-six years, but it had ended when my dad passed away. My mother and I had formed a unique bond when we both found ourselves freshly single—by breakup and by death. The only way to escape heartbreak is to die simultaneously in a perfect Nicholas Sparks–designed ending, or to close your heart off and refuse to let love in to begin with. Endings are guaranteed, but what miseries we endure to strive for longevity, what guilt and regret we feel if it fails, what anger. But to have it end doesn't mean it wasn't worth the effort given.

I thought of the flow state I'd found in the Tuscan woods, that tiny window of perception through which each of us perceives our realities: the three-second timing of the human spirit. How busy we all are trying to plot out futures and happy endings when the only time frame within our absolute control happens inside that tiny window of nowness. And inside the space of that rightnowness, I was walking along a quiet road lined with euca-lyptus trees in an incredible country, healthy and intact, with two working legs and one kind and intelligent friend by my side.

I touched the boney dip in my chest that held the squeezing fist of my heart and told it everything would be okay. Pain is not forever. In the dirt I spotted another powder-pink crystal, and another, and I began to fill my pockets with love stones. My pants were getting heavy.

Ajit began singing lyrics from Hindi songs, bending notes in the distinctive Indian style.

"What do those lyrics mean, Ajit?"

"They mean: 'If you read so many books, why can't you read the expression on my face?'"

A car pulled up alongside us, interrupting our conversation. The window came down and a man poked his head out. "Where are you going?" he shouted.

"Dandi," said Ajit.

So accustomed were we to these questions that we didn't bother to slow our pace. The man continued to follow us in his car. "I've heard you're walking the Salt March," he said. "Is that true?"

Ajit bobbled his head at the man. Apparently word had trav-eled. Perhaps he had read about it in the newspaper. We picked up our pace, hoping to shake him off, but still the man followed.

"I would like to invite you to my house," he said. These kinds of invitations from strangers were so common that they were almost a nuisance. On the days we said yes to every invite for chai or lunch from friendly strangers, we would make poor progress and end up rushing to find accommodation danger-ously close to dusk. For this reason, we had to say no more often than not. It was a good problem to have.

"No, thank you," Ajit said. "We are on a schedule, and we must keep walking."

"But I would like you to meet my father," said the man in the car. "He has met Gandhiji."

✦

The old man was dying in the middle of the family's hot-pink living room. The color of the walls clashed with the blueness of his ancient skin, where angular bones protruded. He was sitting upright on a small bed, hunched into himself and mostly oblivious.

"This is my father," said our host. "Please. Take a seat." We pulled up chairs alongside the old man. "This is my wife," he said, gesturing to the woman who was placing a tray of namkeen and chai in front of us. She smiled and nodded at us.

The old man couldn't raise his head. He was blind. His white clothing was soaked in bodily fluids, and he wore a sweater and a beanie despite the heat. His large, veined hands looked like my dad's just before he passed away.

He moaned and began to ramble in Gujarati. The son translated it into Hindi, and Ajit translated the Hindi into English. By the time the old man's words reached us, they were but a single sentence, translated to us piecemeal.

"He says he met Gandhiji," Ajit explained. "Gandhiji visited his school when the man was eight."

"How old is your father?" I asked, and Ajit translated.

Our host hesitated. "I think he's ninety-four. Or maybe ninety-eight." He didn't know the exact age of his father. I did the math. Gandhi walked the Salt March in 1930. The old man said he was eight when he met Gandhi. That meant he was ninety-two. Those with firsthand memories of Gandhiji are a dying generation.

The old man's wife, equally ancient but in much better condition, came over to sit on the bed. Although we couldn't understand each other's languages, she watched our faces as we spoke, her eyes glittering with curiosity. Despite the awkwardness of it,

I held her gaze and fought the impulse to look away. We peered at each other from only a foot apart, sharing a moment of wordless connection. Her eyes were wells of kindness, so deep with compassion that my hair stood on ends.

"Ajit," Masha said, "can you ask how he felt when Gandhiji came to town?"

"He said that Gandhiji wore only pants."

"Yes, but how did he feel?"

"He said Gandhiji brought watermelon for all the children."

"He didn't tell you how it felt to meet Gandhi?"

"His memories are very fragmented," said Ajit. "His sentences often repeat themselves."

The old man began to ramble.

"He said that Gandhiji stayed at the cotton mill and washed there. He said Gandhiji wore only pants, no shirt."

Sometimes during the pilgrimage it felt as if we were following a ghost, piecing together the fragments of Gandhi's past by the stories people shared with us, told through the distortion of Telephone down the family line, through the warp of several language translations until it settled into legend. What we ended up with was a collage of peculiar details: that Gandhi walked with a goat, that Gandhi had one arm longer than the other, that Gandhi's arms came down past his knees, that Gandhi fed the children watermelon. Everyone we'd encountered spoke fondly of him. He had pushed for equality between rich and poor, across caste and religion lines, and devoted himself to making a better India, and I could see his legend radiating brightly through people's facial expressions as they offered any memory or story passed down the line. Because of the fact we were walking in his footsteps, we were welcomed liked protégés of Gandhi, fawned over and admired by association.

The old man grew restless, moving his head back and forth, rambling under his breath. Nobody was translating. We looked to Ajit for an explanation.

"I think a lot of what he says makes no sense," said Ajit, his head tilted with sympathy. "He is just repeating himself over and over. Gandhiji bought watermelon. Gandhiji stayed at the cotton mill. Gandhiji wore only pants. He keeps saying the same things."

We listened and waited, watching the old man ramble. Now looking emotional, he lay down on the bed. He began to cry. Tears soaked his ancient cheeks. He closed his eyes, and still his index finger and thumb fidgeted. His digits were blackened with bruises from so much anxious rubbing.

Ajit spoke. "He said that his father couldn't afford to keep him in school."

The old man wept openly now, his rambling wet with tears and saliva.

"He said that Gandhiji gave them hope when he came, that they might be able to afford to go to school, but his ideology was not successful. He said he had to quit school. He had to leave school to help his father on the farm. He is wondering what his life might've been like if he had continued his schooling and if Gandhi's teachings had stuck."

This old man had, from such a young age, latched his hopes onto Gandhi's ideals, and would die with the sorrow of that deep disappointment. I fought an overwhelming urge to cry. I swallowed a mouthful of chai to ease the throbbing lump in my throat.

"I think my father is tired and needs to rest now," said the son, and we nodded, thanked them for their hospitality, and went outside to put our shoes back on.

I waited until we were back out on the road to let out the tears. Apart from the sadness of watching the old man suffering, I was conflicted by the contradictions of Gandhi, a character of incredible courage and charity entangled with morally warped experiments. Western society doesn't like confusing blends. We want absolutes. We love answers, pedagogy, and neat little peer-reviewed conclusions. We want Hollywood endings. The hero saves the day! (He isn't a sexual predator.) The girl gets the guy! (They don't break up when her dad is dying.) Two traveling women become BFFs! (They don't scream at each other and never talk again.)

Absolutes are nimble yet deceitful. They get away from you. They morph and change and evolve over time, shaped by infinite variables, which means there can be no peace in expecting absolutes. It's like building your home on a fault line: Eventually it's going to cave in and you'll end up wandering aimlessly on rubble, looking for something to salvage.

I picked through the rubble of my broken nine-year relationship and found the beautiful adventures we'd shared together. In the rubble of my anxiety, I found the problem-solving skills I'd developed. In the ruins of my friendship with Masha, there was the magic of the unknown she'd shown me in Tuscany. In the disaster of our Indian pilgrimage, I found the alchemy of meeting Ajit, the shepherds, and all the others who had shown me the world is a kind place worth trusting in and fighting for. In the wreckage of Mahatma Gandhi, I found, once again, all he achieved with courage.

Perhaps there is no one person to turn to in this world— politicians, CEOs, the Kardashians, medical doctors; gurus, saints, philosophers, artists, scientists; parents, lovers, sisters, friends . . . They're all human. They're all flawed. They're all capable of being wildly disappointing fuck-ups. But as my grandma once told me in a dream: "Honey, there is nothing in this world that exists outside you that you don't already have within you."

With my heart full of salvaged treasures, I decided it was time to start following my own compass.

25

"Goddammit, that dog is alive," Masha muttered.

We were walking on the outskirts of a small city when we passed a dead dog on a pile of trash that looked like all the other dead dogs we'd seen—bloody, gnarled, tragic—only this one turned its head and looked at us as we passed . . . with only half a head.

It looked at us with its single remaining eye and then rested its half head back into the trash pile. My brain ran through solutions. I thought about using my tiny pocketknife to end its misery but knew it would be a messy job with such a small knife, and, besides, I knew I didn't have it in me to save a wretched creature with savage violence.

Since being absurd is how we all coped with trauma, we named him Half Head McHalfy and laughed feebly to fend off gutting agony.

Ajit, too, was noticeably shaken by McHalfy, pained by his own powerlessness. As a trio, we came crashing down to rock bottom, defeated in both body and spirit. Our stomachs churned; our monkeys screamed. Any sense of equilibrium we once had was now a million light-years away. The devastation of it was a sucker punch to the solar plexus, and all three of us fell into defeat.

Burnt out, we decided to take two days of rest in a run-down hotel. The walls were streaked with ancient, dried gunk, and old furniture sat stacked in the hallways, covered in stained sheets. As we passed the dark kitchen, I looked in to see that every surface, from wall to table, was coated in the drips of presumably every meal prepared within it since the 1970s. It would've made a perfect set for a horror film about an Indian chef who murders guests and serves them up in oily curries. When life gives you horrors, make horror movies.

But it was the only hotel in town, and it had beds, a shower, and a door that locked out the rest of India, and so, to us, it was a palace.

Ajit retreated to his own room while Masha and I lay side by side in our respective beds, doing what we'd become best at: not talking to each other. She had disappeared into the world inside her laptop and was typing to someone who wasn't me. I felt jealous of whoever it was. Even yelling is better than the silent treatment. There is nothing worse than being left to guess why someone is angry with you. Actually, that is not true. Lying on a pile of trash with only half a head is definitely worse.

Hours passed.

The fan spun.

A tap dripped.

A sign on the wall read: "Liquor is strictly prohibited."

I decided to dig deep into my box of charms to coax Masha into engaging with me: "I'd kill a dog for a glass of wine right now," I said, using Masha's most favorite shade of humor: black.

She laughed.

Success.

"I feel like everything would be okay right now if we could've been drinking wine this whole time," she said with a smile.

"This would've been so much easier to handle with Aperol Spritzes."

"And cappuccinos."

"Ugh, I miss Italy. That feels like it was a lifetime ago."

The tension softened, and we were back to our friendship, however briefly.

Silent tears rolled down her cheeks, wetting her trembling lips. Her face was raw, her eyes glazed and tired. She looked haggard. We both did. "I'm so sorry I'm being such an asshole, Torre. This year has been unimaginably hard for you. Not only did you lose your dad, but you lost a man you'd spent almost a decade with. You were each other's universe. I can't even begin to imagine what you must be dealing with. I'm so sorry. I'm not being a good friend to you."

I smiled at her. "It's nice to have you back to me, Masha. I want to talk about all the crazy stuff with you."

"How insane was Half Head McHalfy?"

"I've never seen anything so gruesome in my life. I just hope that the dogs are more skilled than we are at being present, so that they're not suffering."

"Maybe. I don't know. Torre, I don't know anything about anything anymore. In Italy I felt like I finally had things worked out, you know? Do you ever look back at a low point in your life and think, 'I am so glad I will never be that insecure, scared, angry, etc., ever again. Who was that crazy person who lived in her pajamas for a month and made all the children sad?' I thought that part of my life had been bulldozed and turned into a kitten sanctuary years ago, but yet here I am, wandering around in old, familiar neighborhoods."

"I might still be in the making-children-sad phase. I'm sorry for saying that the earth is a giant cancer growing inside a much larger being, and we humans are the antibodies whose purpose is to destroy it. That is very nihilistic and I shouldn't have said it."

"Huh?"

"In Delhi. Before we started walking, remember? I made that remark and you said it was bleak and then it made you cry into your wine."

She laughed. "Oh, don't worry about that. I don't care. It's probably true anyway." A silent beat. "Torre, can I ask you something?"

"Yes, of course."

"How do you know if you're living the life you're meant to be living?"

We sat in silence while I thought about the question. Louis C.K. calls it "the Always Empty." Aldous Huxley calls it "the urge to escape from selfhood." Despite the newness of being fed a never-ending stream of Instagram images of all the beautiful places we are not, the urge to dive deep into the warm waters of YOLO is not new to humanity, because nothing is more alluring than the experiences we've not yet grown bored with, the people we've not yet been disappointed by, the happiness that surely exists in a destination called Anywhere But Here, that other, better life we're *meant* to be living. Oh, how the heart lusts for such a place; just keep running, keep longing, keep sailing over horizons and you'll catch it sooner or later—won't you?

The world is a book, and those who do not travel read only a page has to be one of the most shared, liked, and shared again quotes on the Internet, so often published on social media over images of hikers on mountaintops or sailboats in tropical waters, telling us that a life well lived—a life we should all envy—is one of daring adventures against color-saturated backdrops. YOLO. What tension that provokes. FOMO. What crushing urgency there is to always be living interesting, Instagramable lives when, in fact, we're all quietly hiding the parts that don't make for good photos. Sometimes life is mundane. Sometimes you have to break the heart of someone you love in order to live your own truth. Sometimes life is hospital rooms that smell of antiseptic and defeat as you watch the body that held you as a newborn wither into the folds of his hospital gown, the blue eyes you inherited darting with fear. Sometimes this one wild and adventurous life is excruciating. How easy it is to imagine there's a better one we're meant to be living.

I looked into Masha's glassy eyes. "Remember what you told me in Italy? That the pilgrimage always brings you what you need to learn if you just look for the signs?"

"I'm confused about the lesson, though. How can you extract lessons from this place? Everything is so random, so absurd. There are dead dogs everywhere, Torre; what does *that* mean? What is that a sign of? I'm trying to work it all out, I really am, but everything that made sense to me before doesn't make sense anymore. Is that the lesson I'm supposed to be learning? That nothing makes any sense, so stop trying to work it out all the time?"

Life's a bitch and then you die. "I've kind of come to the same conclusion, to be honest."

She took a deep breath in and held it. "I love my husband."

"Okay?"

"I really do, Torre."

"That's great, but what does that have to do with—"

"He's kind. He makes me laugh. He supports me. We've had a lot of fun together."

She breathed out and sank back into the bed, fixing her eyes on the ceiling fan. I waited while she formed her words. "In Istanbul I made all these great friends, Torre. Two Syrian refugees, a twenty-seven-year-old doctor who is incredibly brave, four Italian women, an American photographer . . . people with the warmest hearts you could imagine. We'd have these incredible conversations about politics and why the world is suffering and how maybe we could make it a little bit better somehow. People don't really talk like that much in New York. They don't really talk the way you and I talk, Torre. Everyone is so focused on their own image, their success, their comforts. That used to be me too. I'd wander around thinking about what I could do to get that little bit more ahead of everyone else, because if you're not ahead in New York, then you're nobody. You're invisible. So you play the game, just so you can be a somebody, but that game becomes your whole life."

"So Istanbul is more authentic to you?"

"That's right." She sighed. "Torre, my husband is such a nice person. He's supported me. He let me go walking around the world for a year. What kind of husband supports his wife to go wandering around the world for a year without giving her a hard time about it? He's been so understanding."

"That's a nice quality. He must be a kind person."

"He is. And I love him so much. But we don't talk politics or philosophy or what's wrong with the world: the big issues, the hard stuff, the important stuff. We don't talk hopes and dreams. He runs a bar and we used to drink together and that was fun, but now . . . Torre . . . " Her chin began to shake. "He moved to New York for me, from Ireland. He won't move again. I know him. He won't want to move to Istanbul; he won't want to leave New York. All of his friends live in New York now. He doesn't like to travel." Tears rolled down her cheeks. "I just want to be happy. But I don't know how to get there." She sobbed hard as she said, "I'm a bad person, Torre."

"Don't feel bad. There's probably not one single human on the planet who hasn't wondered what life might be like down a different road than the one she's on. Most people don't have the courage to even think about change, let alone declare it out loud, let alone put on a backpack full of rocks and other crap, and walk around the world alone for a whole year to try to work out an answer, risking death, forming blisters, losing toenails, battling snakes and USB cords."

Tears were streaming down her cheeks as she laughed.

"Your courage astounds me, Masha. Every single day I get energy from watching you do what you're doing. I mean, how many people are clinging to dull office jobs or shitty relationships or their shitty single life or a religion they don't truly believe in because they're too scared to face the unknown void of living between answers? They're afraid of the dark, and so they put their heads down and endure. But you: Your kind of bravery is contagious. It's a gift to the world. You're out there doing something really hard while many people are hiding away in the safety of the herd, but that doesn't mean they don't wonder about the exact same questions, that they don't feel the same guilt. You're facing the void, Masha, and that's scary as hell, but it also means you get to . . . well . . . you get to be in India with your friend, covered head to toe in shit, and crying in the world's most disgusting hotel."

She laughed.

"I think walking is a catalyst for you. A catalyst to asking questions. Even when there are no answers."

She nodded.

"I totally stole that line from Ajit, by the way."

She smiled and wiped her wet cheeks with the backs of her hands. "This adventure has gotten kind of intense, hasn't it?" She laughed through her sobs. "Thank you. For being here with me in this insanity."

"I wouldn't want to be anywhere else."

"Okay, now I know you're lying."

"It's true. I'm lying. But if I'm going to be crotch-deep in dead dog for three straight weeks, I can't think of anyone else I'd rather be with, Mashaji."

26

"Come in, come in," said the caretaker, welcoming us into the ashram. "You've walked such a long way. Here, let me get you some water."

"Oh, thank you, but we can't drink the . . . "

He dashed off before we could object and came back carrying a tray with three cups of tap water in stainless steel mugs. "You must be thirsty," he said, pushing the cups at us. Offering us hydration was always the first gesture that every kind host welcomed us with, and, though I felt bad declining his hospitality, I didn't want to get sick.

I held up my bottle. "We actually have our own water."

"But this water is from our village tanks," he said proudly.

Ajit cleared his throat. "They are from the West and cannot drink the water here."

"What?"

"It makes them sick."

"But this water is very clean."

"Yes, but their bellies are not accustomed to it."

"But the first thing that Gandhi did on the Salt March in every village he visited was drink the water from the well. I can assure you that our tanks are very clean, sir. I drink it every day."

Cornered, Masha and I smiled and each took water from the tray, and when the man wasn't looking, Ajit slammed all three cups like a row of tequila shots. He sputtered for air and wiped off his chin before the man looked back at us. We had lost count of the number of times he'd done this for us.

"Thank you so much," we said, returning the cups to the tray, and then quietly to Ajit: "*Thank you.*"

"Let me show you to your rooms," he said. He led us through the ashram's courtyard, a peaceful and empty space that, enclosed within the parameter of high walls, was tucked away from the street noise. A lone set of child's eyes peered over the top of a boundary wall, no doubt standing on someone else's shoulders, and when I spotted him and waved, he giggled and ducked from view.

The caretaker keyed the door to one of the many rooms. It creaked open to a dusty space with a single chair, an old desk, and a pile of miscellaneous items swept into one corner with a thick blanket of dirt. Spiders hung in corners, ants crawled in single-file along the concrete floor, and a black cockroach the size of a peach pit scattered under the door to the bathroom.

"This looks perfect," I said, in all earnestness. Finding a private room was a luxury we never took for granted, no matter the condition of the place.

"Please allow me clean it for you first," said the caretaker, and he began sweeping. Bugs scampered from all corners as dust flew up into the sunbeams to pirouette.

I went outside for air. As with all of Gandhi's ashrams, the centerpiece of the courtyard was a large block of plain grey concrete that, we'd been told, was supposed to be sculpted into a statue of Gandhi, but the ashrams had run out of money to complete their construction. Funding had been squandered by authorities, as often is the case. Many of his ashrams are in a state of disrepair, some have become schools, and others have been appropriated for paid functions, like weddings. One night we had locked ourselves in a room while the world's loudest wedding exploded in the courtyard, with fireworks and gongs ringing all night.

"Why do people get married in the middle of the night here?" I asked Ajit.

"People get married at different times depending on what is most auspicious for the bride and groom. But between 4 a.m. and 6 a.m. is *Brahmamuhurta*, the 'Creator's Hour,' which is considered to be auspicious for Hindu religious practice. It is a very spiritual hour. It's said that prayers reach directly to the God in this time."

When we asked Ajit if we could go outside to witness the wedding, he said, "This wedding is too big, and you will be in danger. The whole town is here. It is unsafe." It was the only time Ajit had ever spoken a warning, and so we locked ourselves in an ashram room and tried to sleep through bells and explosions. Though it was like trying to curl up and nap inside a jet engine, we eventually passed out from exhaustion.

"There," said the caretaker. "Your room is clean now." I went back in just as a large lizard, displaced by the cleaning, shimmied across the floor to seek safety. The caretaker swung his boot out and kicked it with a loud, meaty *pop*, and the lizard sailed out the door in a long arc, before landing on concrete with a *splat* and limping off toward the compound walls.

"Oh, I think that's clean enough," I said. "Thank you so much."

"It's no problem." He rolled out two thin mattresses onto the less-dusty floor and promised to bring us chai first thing in the morning.

I joined Masha for headstand practice on our mattresses. Walking such a long distance activates the body, making it strong and energetic, and when it comes time to rest, it doesn't always want to stop moving. Even after long days, one of the first activities we'd do after taking our bags off and having showers was a bunch of haphazard yoga poses, or even an outburst of random jumping and pumping and throwing our limbs about like a pair of children on a sugar high. In twenty days of nightly practice, I could use my core strength to lift my legs up into a perfect headstand. I would say that it made me feel like I was eighteen again, but I never had that much energy or strength at eighteen. I felt strong and capable inside this new body.

While Masha disappeared into the private thoughts of her journal writing, I went outside to see Ajit. He was setting up a mattress for himself beneath the large concrete block from which nobody had yet carved a statue of Gandhi. In a way, the uncarved cube was a better likeness to his legacy: a solid plan for a fully realized ideal, but incomplete. Despite the work still left to do for human rights and equality—in India and across the world—Gandhi's innovative use of nonviolence as a powerful force for change will remain a guiding light for future generations. These tools in good hands might carve a better future.

"I want to sleep under the stars tonight, Torreji," said Ajit. The sky was a vignette of dusky indigo blending to orange. I sat down next to him.

"That sounds like a nice idea."

"I think it might be cleaner out here. There are definitely less bugs outside."

I laughed. "Did you see that man kick the lizard?"

"Yes. It went *pop*."

We both chuckled and then sagged, heavy-hearted.

"You can sleep outside too if you want, Torreji."

My cheeks flushed, and I shuffled awkwardly.

He tipped his head back to gather his long, silky hair into a ponytail. "Look!" he said, pointing. I followed his finger up to the muddy sky. Colorful kites were flying high up in the air.

Near the horizon, the sun was a giant pink ball, as pink and tender as love. As pink and tender as a skin infection, maybe. Soon it would disappear, stars would spin in an arc, and then it would climb back up toward the opposite horizon, and it would be time to get going again.

Every morning, the alarm would go off at six a.m. to signal the start of another one hundred years of solitude, and then, once again, I ask the same old questions: *What am I doing here? Why am I putting myself through this pain? Why am I suffering this self-inflicted agony when I've already been through a cataclysm of grief? Is this some kind of masochism?*

Back on the road, we'd swim through a dense syrup of dust and exhaust fumes, which would dry our throats and sting our eyes and color our clothing brown. We would dodge traffic beneath the blistering sun while listening to a soundtrack of insistent horns coming from all directions at once, risking ourselves by stepping out onto the road in order to give a wide berth to an angry dog or an irritated buffalo or a cow's rear end as its tail flexed and shifted to one side. *What am I doing here? Why am I putting myself through this pain?*

And then we'd turn a corner onto a road that would cut through leafy, shady trees, alive with monkeys. The traffic would thin out and the crowds would dissolve and the silence and cleanliness would seem like a gift I'd never expected to receive. Fragrance would fill my nose, and I'd search everywhere for the flower or perfume, before realizing that it wasn't anything in particular, only the temporary absence of stench. A rest in the abuse to the senses. A space in between so many somethings.

But what is perhaps the strangest thing about walking through India is that you can come, over time, to love every minute of it, from the funk to the beauty and all the bits in between. You come to love it because, in order to cope, you have to give up on trying to mentally categorize a thousand simultaneous encounters into "good" and "bad" and instead let things be what they are. You stop judging and become an observer, which allows you to begin to see the moment just as it is: horrible and flawed and exquisite all at once. In India, despite your privilege, you are not the center around which everything else orbits. All of your whims and desires aren't met in the same way as they can be in the West. You get what you're given. You don't get to shape or form your surroundings, to push them in the direction you want them to move in, to swap money for granted wishes. You have very little say. You're merely one of the many irrelevant masses of fleshy guts occupying space among many others, and there are bigger, more important masses than you, like herds of horned buffalo breathing heavily in your direction, like the single shitting cow clogging a highway. So you give in, because there is no choice, which sounds like a bad thing but it's not, because it's humbling. And only when you're humbled can you fall into a state of surrender. Now in flow, your brain is no longer buzzing with the useless narration of "I like this" and "I can't stand that" or "This should be another way" or "I wish I hadn't done that." Instead, you are giving everything around you the permission to be as it is, in all its flaws, because with or without your permission, that is the way it is for now. And it's only there for you to behold for that single three-second window, before it will move on into the swirling dust storm of atoms and become a new version of itself.

So long as you keep your senses and soul peeled open, there is stunning magic inherent in every small detail, like the feel of a breeze on sticky skin or the call of a bird in an empty wood, and why not, therefore, the texture and temperature of your father's hand as life leaves it, the taut fullness of love in your heart just as it breaks. What beauty. What privilege there is, even in pain. The richness of experience can be found in every moment—anywhere, always—as long as you remain humbled. You can feel awed by the divine rush of celestial wind in your throat even as you exhale your final breath.

Ajit walked over to the edge of the ashram and asked a small boy if he could borrow his kite. It was a cheap homemade job, made from recycled plastic covered in logos. The kid handed him the string and reel, and Ajit took over the piloting. His sleepy eyes widened with boyish excitement.

Masha came outside to watch. We stood in the courtyard together, necks craned, chins angled skyward, watching the kite fly as if it was the most beautiful sight we'd ever seen. It reminded me of being a kid, watching my dad fly his model planes in the park.

With his head tilted up to the sky, Ajit made the plastic bird dance, his eyes full of euphoria at the simple joy of a cheap plastic kite dipping and swirling on the currents of a breeze, tail tassels flapping behind it.

Life is beautiful and then you die.

27

"You guys really can't smell that?" I asked Ajit and Masha. I searched the bushes for flowers but found none. "It smells so good. I don't think I've ever smelled anything so sweet and fresh before."

"Torreji, I think you must enjoy the smell of shit," Ajit teased.

They both erupted into belly laugher. We were standing by a chicken abattoir at the time, and smells of sweet rotting meat and poultry feces oozed out into the street in a thick and eye-watering spew.

"You don't know what you're missing," I told them. "Just you wait. I will find the source and prove you wrong, and then you'll know I'm not insane."

After almost three weeks of walking, nearing the end, I was able to fall into meditative flow on command just by giving in to the smells and noise, the pain and discomfort. It was as simple as relaxing a squeezed fist. Now armed with this ability, I felt like I'd mastered a skill that I could call on anytime.

As we walked along dusty roads and ugly industrial centers, I began to build a home with my imagination, brick by brick, made with wet earth. Inspired by the simple mud-brick houses of rural India, my home had stained-glass windows and little Persian-style archways embossed into the walls for holding candles. Indians make great use of cow dung in their constructions, coating the floor and walls with this sacred material that, once smoothed and dried, smells earthy and agreeable, and feels silky to bare feet. I decided to skip the cow poo in my imagined home, but in my warm nest, there would be walls of books and objects from my travels on display, and I'd build it close to my sister and best friend, Summer. There, in my little mud-brick nest, my sanctuary, I'd finally feel at home. We walked miles and miles as I created this visualization over and over, brick by brick.

A commotion on the road ahead stirred me from my dream. A shepherd with a herd of goats was standing by one of his flock, who was lying in the middle of the road on her side, panting and bloody.

We rushed over just in time to see a slimy kid being pulled by the legs from the mother's slippery rear. She was the second of twin babies.

As the doe licked the film off her kid, we danced around in giddy joy, snapping photos of messy new beginnings being born in unlikely places. The shepherd insisted we shoot from the doe's best angle—her non-business end—and he posed for us with his arms crossed, his lips pursed like a proud father.

If only the tube of pepper spray in my pocket was a cigar.

✦

When rural India merged into bigger and bigger cities, we knew we were getting close to the end.

For breakfast we had chai, tamarind from the pod, and sweet, exquisite sugarcane chewed fresh off the stick—all gifts from passing strangers. It took forty minutes of chewing at hard, green bark to break into the juicy nectar of the sugarcane.

An old man working a field took off on his motorbike and came back with fried snacks and chai, and we sat with him in the dirt and shared a moment of language-less connection together. Both Masha and I now spoke fluent head bobbling, which you can use to say anything you want. That meant we were never out of our depth, even when an entire conversation was taking place in Hindi. The bobble is all-purpose like that. It says everything and nothing and anything else in between, too.

"We are almost at the end," said Ajit, as we walked along an old train line.

"I know," I said. "Are you excited?"

"Not really. I'm going to miss you and Masha very much."

"I'm going to miss you too, Ajit."

Along the final stretch to Dandi we passed under a shady archway of banyan trees, three hundred years old and all growing together in tight-knuckled twists. On the wide and quiet road, we walked side by side, our feet forming a strong and steady rhythm. We were a united team of three: strong limbed and strong willed.

Our clacking percussion made our familiar pilgrim song. I was strangely nostalgic about the journey's end, knowing I would miss the ritual of getting up every day to meet a cool morning, the smell of smoke from the fires that huddles of locals made to warm themselves. How weird it is to breathe dust and exhaust all day, to battle heat and truck horns and piles of shit on the road and yet want to be nowhere other than where you are. Since my plan was to head home and settle, I knew this would likely be my last big drifting, impulsive travel adventure.

"So do you have enough photos to make an exhibition in Dandi?" Ajit asked.

I flicked through the photos on my phone. Dead dog. Dead dog. Dead bird. Dead boar. Ball of black fabric that looked like a dead dog. "I have only photos of dead animals, Ajit."

"And what is the meaning of your art, Torreji?"

"I'm fascinated by the darker aspects of life that nobody else wants to talk about or put on their Instagram accounts because I think that, while it's confronting and ugly, facing up to it instead of pretending it's not there makes life more beautiful. Knowing it will all end one day makes the little moments sparkle with magic, you know? And that's a gift."

"Yes, I know."

"But I think I kind of overdid it with the whole dead-animal theme. I don't think I should inflict this on anyone else."

He gave me an all-purpose head bobble, saying everything and nothing and anything else in between, too.

"What about you, Ajit? Do you have photos for an exhibition?"

"Not really, no. I have taken a lot of photos, but I don't really know what any of it means."

"This was a confusing experience, wasn't it?"

"It was very confusing, Torreji."

I looked down at the ground and spotted a chunk of pink rose quartz, and I brushed it off and stuck it into my pocket.

The smell of freesia flowers was once again radiating in the air and, determined to locate it, I followed my nose to its source, knowing this might be my last chance to find it. I wandered down a driveway until I found a line of trees with tiny, nondescript clusters of flowers. On my tippy-toes, I smelled the common-looking flower. My nose filled with the scent of clean soap and green things, sweet fruit and the nectar of honeysuckle. I'd found it: the most divine smell in the world.

Using my pocketknife, I clipped a small bouquet from the tree and held it in my palm, breathing in its sweetness, dizzy with bliss.

I ran up to Ajit and Masha. "Smell it!" I demanded.

They did.

"Oh my god, that's amazing!" said Masha, burying her nose in the flowers, and Ajit agreed.

It was real. I wasn't imagining it. As we carried on, we all smelled it everywhere, this trailing perfume of floral loveliness that had kept me hopeful for weeks, a tiny, exquisite refuge from the stench of waste and decay.

Ajit spotted a family on the side of the road who'd made a small business from weaving names from lettered beads onto bracelets and key rings. They were a poverty-stricken family of four—a mother, a baby, a small boy, and a grandmother.

"Let's all pick a word or phrase to have made up," Ajit proposed. "Something that has been relevant to you on this journey."

On a piece of paper, we each wrote what we wanted. Masha wrote "Chai baby" to express her great devotion to sweet Indian tea. Ajit wrote "Monkeys" to pay his respects to the unbridled chaos that lives inside us all. Since I'd been dreaming nonstop about having a home near my sister, I penned her name, "Summer," deciding I would give my key ring to her after I survived this pilgrimage and found my way back home. For the first time since I'd left home at age twenty-four, I felt not just ready to return for good, but inspired by it.

Squatting with her baby on her knee, the mother picked out the letters, and her small boy plaited them onto string. The grandmother burned the edges with matches, sealing the knots. We paid them, and I tied my key ring to the zipper of my backpack. The mother and grandmother pressed their hands together in Namaste to give thanks.

Along a quiet highway, I was writing a thought onto my phone as I walked, as I so often did:

> Everything is very messy in life, but we strive for clean edges. Neat hair, straight teeth, smooth skin. White skin. We think there's something wrong if our own lives are jagged and gnarled, and so we use all our energy to strive. But nothing is clean—not really.

My toe struck something large, hard, and chalky, and it went *thunk*. My body lurched forward from the impact, and I clutched my phone, catching it just before it flew out of my hands. My big toe throbbed from the impact.

When I looked up, I spotted a giant brown ball flying out into the road as if it had been scissor-kicked by Lionel Messi.

"You kicked a dry poo!" Ajit squealed. He started to laugh, smacking his thigh and cackling. "Torreji, you kicked a poo!"

We started howling, doubling over and gasping until we couldn't breathe anymore, and then, after minutes, we straightened up and calmed down, breathing hard to recover.

Moments of silence passed, and then Ajit sputtered and exploded once more. "Torreji, you kicked a poo!" And then we doubled over again, wheezing and roaring.

Maybe it was the endorphins from all the walking, or maybe madness had finally become us. Perhaps watching that meaningless piece of shit go flying through air was analogous to the last three weeks of our lives. But either way, punting the top off a semi-wet ball of cow dung was the funniest thing I'd ever seen in my life, and somehow, from that point on, I knew everything was going to be okay.

28

"ON THIS SUNNY day, in this beautiful space, I welcome you to the end of the journey," said the caretaker of a museum built to honor the Salt March. Using two hands, the man looped hand-spun raw cotton wreaths around each of our necks in ceremonial fashion. "We don't give these to everyone, only those who follow the ideologies of Mahatma Gandhi."

"Thank you," we chorused, though I wasn't sure we were among his most devout followers.

On the beach, Ajit wrote the words "Dandi Walk" in the sand with a stick, and we stared at them for a while in a cardio fog, trying to compute what we had just done. There was no salt at the seaside to collect in handfuls, just a collection of Indian vacationers pottering about on the sand, fully clothed.

"So it is finished," said Ajit. "Now what?"

"Rest?" said Masha.

Next to a larger-than-life bronze statue of Gandhi collecting his handful of white salt, we took off our shoes and sprawled out together in silence, soaking up the sun. This was it. The end of our journey. I tried to reflect on what it was all for, but my mind was blank. The monkeys were quiet—passed out from cardio exhaustion in a pool of their own saliva, maybe. There was no moment of great insight, no *ah-has* or *yee-haws!* or high kicks. Actually, there were high kicks. Masha tucked herself into a ball, kicked up her legs, and held her first awkward headstand.

We each had 833 million single moments of life to spend any way we pleased, and this was how we spent a portion of ours. The earth kept spinning, the sun rose somewhere, babies were born, and the sun fell over a horizon the way it always does. The climate kept warming and countries were still warring and refugees were still washing up on shores, and there we were: a trio of odd friends in Dandi, India, sweat-soaked and lazing in the shade of an immortalized man holding a handful of salt, pondering the endless sky in silence.

"I love you so much, Ajit," said Masha.

"I love you too. Very much."

The clock ticked on. Time passed, I have no idea how much of it. Without the beat of walking, there was no way to measure time. For thirty minutes, or maybe two hours, we floated together inside the hush of one moment giving way to the next.

Ajit clapped his hands together, startling us from our stupor. "Shall we get something to eat?"

We found a small food stall that sold deep-fried something-somethings. Exhausted, we fell asleep sitting upright in plastic chairs, mouths open and gargling on deep-fried crumbs and peculiar dreams. Who knows how long we were passed out before the storeowner woke us. "You're putting off other customers," she said. "Please leave."

We wiped the dribble from our cheeks, stretched, and left the restaurant wearing our spun-cotton Ghandi garlands.

"Okay," said Ajit. "How would you like to celebrate?"

My stomach moaned. It craved meat, alcohol, and general debauchery for no other reason than to rebel against three weeks of hard effort.

"Wine," said Masha.

"Chicken," said I.

"Cocktails," said Masha.

"Champagne," said I.

"What else are we forgetting that's bad?" said Masha.

"Ummm . . . "

Ajit tilted his head. "Unfortunately, we can't drink alcohol or eat meat within the state of Gujarat. We could catch a taxi across the border and out of the state, but it will take many hours and it is quite far, and the taxi will be expensive, and—"

"Let's go!" we cried in unison, and Ajit dialed the taxi.

✦

In a hotel that looked like kitsch Florida circa 1983, we set down our filthy backpacks and took long, hot showers, washing the accumulated dirt down the drain. It took forty minutes just to shave my legs and, after I emerged from the shower sparkling clean and restored, I dressed for our big celebration in my fanciest outfit: my not quite, but almost, pajamas. They hadn't been washed in three weeks. Masha wore a new scarlet-red skirt to her ankles that made her want to twirl fast and often. Cheeks glowing, dimples showing, she looked vibrant and happy.

In the most luxurious restaurant we could find, which wasn't luxurious at all, we ordered beers and cocktails and meat and fish, which we consumed while overlooking an alien seascape. The small strip of sand tapered into pockmarked rock that stretched out all the way to the horizon. There was no sea to this seaside. It looked like a shore you might find if someone pulled the plug on the ocean and it drained down to black volcanic rock.

"Do you want to go back to the hotel, drink beer, play *bhangra* music, and have a dance-off?" said Masha, eager to twirl her skirt.

We all nodded.

But back at our hotel, dancing gave way to pure exhaustion, and we collapsed into sleep with tight bellies, like three little piglets.

✦

It wasn't easy to say goodbye to Ajit. I knew I might never see him again. We all hugged on the platform until the final call for our train blasted over the loudspeaker. Masha and I both carried bulky bags of swag, sent to us by the tourism company to congratulate us for the accomplishment: books of Gandhian philosophies, a miniature wooden model of Gandhi's loom with a tiny spool of cotton ready for weaving, and a framed photo of Gandhi working his loom.

"Please stay in touch," we told Ajit, exchanging emails and addresses. "Thank you for everything you did for us."

We waved out the window of our train to Mumbai until he disappeared out of sight.

Within an hour of the four-hour journey, I'd developed a burning fever. It was the meat we'd eaten, I think. It wasn't surprising that I'd fallen sick in India; it was only surprising that it hadn't happened much sooner, in harsher conditions. After weeks of eating home-cooked meals and street-stall food buzzing with flies, it was a fancy restaurant in a blue-collar resort town that took me down. I was so desperately thirsty, but we were out of water. I tried to sleep it off, but my dreams were restless, disturbed, parched.

I walked the train, asking strangers where I might find water, but was told, "There is no water on this train." I wanted off. I was trapped inside a fast-moving steel prison when I longed to be back outside on my own two feet. It was the freedom of being outdoors that now felt safer to me.

Masha pulled my legs up onto her lap as I lay across the train seat. Two Italian women sitting across from us offered help. They told us they were from a town in Italy off the Via Francigena pilgrimage we'd walked. A touch of magic.

Once in Mumbai, they helped us into a taxi, because I'd fallen into a stupor and had little idea of what was going on. I crawled into bed in our hotel and fell asleep to feverish dreams, waking to find myself sweat-soaked and tangled in twisted sheets. I'd roll back to sleep and come lucid to find Masha talking on her phone, or smoking a cigarette out our window, or eating toast, and then I'd roll over again and lose hours, nights, days? . . .

Masha roused me one evening to say that we should abandon our flights to Varanasi for Christmas because I was too unwell. She made sure I was breathing and hydrated, but then fell ill herself. Her fever wasn't as bad, but whatever bug we had ripped through her like a gastrointestinal freight train. We didn't leave the hotel. We lay in our beds, doing nothing for days.

This meant we were set to spend Christmas in Mumbai, stuck in a hotel. I thought about the yogi I'd encountered in Bangkok who'd told me I'd get lucky on Christmas Day, and a very small part of me was still hopeful that something magical would happen to prove him right. *You have the snake between your eyes. There is no need to worry anymore. You will get lucky fifty days from now.*

I dashed out of bed to vomit once again. This was not the kind of luck I was hoping for.

The Snake

29

"MY GOD, LIFE is so hard, isn't it?" I said to Masha.

"I know, right?"

"I can't work out if I want the Toffee Nut Latte or the Gingerbread Frappuccino."

She gave me an empathetic nod and then turned back to the menu board. "Ooh, look! They have white chocolate and red velvet cake. But they also have chocolate cake. All these choices! Oh Torre, this is so difficult!"

After weeks of dust and slums, curries and dals and deep-fried something-somethings, concrete ashram floors and deep immersion within the glaring divide between wealth and poverty, we were back where we most belonged: in the cosmopolitan city of Mumbai, in a Starbucks that looked like every other Starbucks, debilitated by choice.

Christmas jingles played in the background. It was as though we'd stepped into a teleportation machine to home. It smelled like the best time of year—cinnamon and pine, gingerbread and burnt sugar. "Have Yourself a Merry Little Christmas" began to play, and the warm, chocolatey voice of Frank Sinatra filled the café along with stringed instruments and choir accompaniment, plucking at heartstrings. I looked up at the tree decorated with baubles and tinsel, all the pomp and circumstance of Christmas, and a lump formed in my throat.

"Oh, Masha," I said, patting my bulging neck, "this place is just so breathtakingly beautiful. I can't handle it."

"Isn't this just the best thing ever?" Her eyes were watery too.

"I feel at home. In Starbucks. How dire is that?"

"*Shhh,* DeRoche, just focus on the menu board for now."

"Do you think we've had too much truth serum by walking through India?"

"Absolutely."

"Is it too late to unsee all the bad things?"

"Absolutely."

"I think we might've just traveled a very long way to end up more confused than ever."

"Absolutely. But don't you think that's what always happens when you travel? The more you know, the more you know you don't know. What is it you want?"

"I suppose I want more equality. It doesn't seem right that so many people are thriving in certain parts of the world while other people are suffering in order to facilitate that. I don't want animals to be injured and dying on the side of the road and—"

"No, DeRoche, I mean what kind of *coffee* do you want?" She tapped her credit card against her palm.

"Oh. A Toffee Nut Latte and . . . oh wait, no . . . the Gingerbread Frappuccino . . . oh wait, no . . . the Toffee Nut Latte and . . . oh wait, no, no, okay, yes, yes, the Toffee Nut and a slice of white chocolate and red velvet cake. With whipped cream. Actually, no cream."

Have yourself a merry little Christmas . . .

The lump in my throat got bigger.

"Actually, I will have the whipped cream."

Masha placed the order.

I said, "I thought we would be different after walking three weeks in the footsteps of Gandhi, you know? More clear on everything?"

"I think we *are* different. Like, probably worse off. But, DeRoche, we're only human."

I inspected my hands. "I've certainly aged."

"Torre, I have no idea what that whole pilgrimage was. I mean, what the fuck was that? It was like some kind of bad dream, mostly. And why was I such an asshole the whole time? I am so sorry. I don't know what came over me. I know nothing. The only thing I know for certain is that all I want for Christmas is to not have gastrointestinal disturbance anymore. And a latte."

"All I want for Christmas is to be at home. You know, this is the first Christmas since I lost my dad and I won't be home to—" *Let your heart be light* . . . As Frank Sinatra sang his chocolatey song, my heart grew heavy and words snagged on the lump in my throat. My three-second window became a gut punch as memories flooded in, images of Dad waiting for me by the door after I'd been away to give me a hug and say, "So, how was your trip?"

I wrapped my arms around my stomach and erupted into tears.

"Aw, dead dad hug." Masha pulled me into her warmth and held me there, her eyes wet with empathy. "I know, I know," she said. "I can only imagine how much this must hurt."

"We walked such a long distance. All of those miles. I thought I'd feel better by now."

"You lost two of the most important people in your life this year. And these songs bring up memories of times from the past we can never get back to, and that is understandably painful. It will probably always be a bit painful. That's okay; just let that feeling exist, because it will. You don't need to try to change it."

She handed me a wad of napkins and collected our coffees. With trembling lips, I sipped my latte. "My sinuses are swollen, and I can't taste my Toffee Nut Latte." I howled and laughed at the same time, gasping for air.

"That is a true tragedy, DeRoche, but don't worry, I am here with you."

"My nose is so blocked right now that it's squeaking." I laughed and squeaked. "I'm crying in Starbucks. In India. I'm such a moron."

"But Torre, you're a wonderful moron. I love you so very much, and you wouldn't be this Torre without all that you've seen and experienced, including the really shitty things. Including the nose squeak."

"I love you too."

Frank Sinatra gave way to Bing Crosby's "Mele Kalikimaka," changing the mood to upbeat ukulele, and, just like that, the three-second window had passed over into a sunnier one. With tears still streaming down our cheeks, we began to dance in our chairs, doing an interpretive dance of pooping and vomiting and opening presents together and celebrating and crying and vomiting again.

My belly ached from laughing so hard. Tears fell as we choked for air in between heaving guffaws. We were a disaster, but it didn't matter. We'd walked 240 miles looking for neat and tidy answers but found mostly poo, dead animals, and a truck-load of new questions. Yet we were laughing together in this suspended moment, and that was everything.

"Torre, if we can make it out of the hotel tomorrow, can we spend all of Christmas Day here doing exactly this?"

I thought about the yogi's words—"You'll get very lucky"— and reasoned that drinking Toffee Nut Lattes with a person who knew how to love so abundantly, with her heart peeled wide open to the rawness and rapture of life, is about as lucky as one could ever hope to be. "I wouldn't want to be anywhere else."

She beamed and pantomimed retching into a toilet bowl while she sang, "A very Merry Christmas . . . a very, very, Merry, Merry Christmas . . . "

I clutched my belly in mimed illness and sang, " . . . to you."

✦

The worst possible film combination was playing on television: *Melancholia,* followed by *Snakes on a Plane.* It was a nihilist's night before Christmas and, of course, I loved it.

Despite our better judgment, we stayed up late, watching both films with dry, hooded eyes.

"Maybe we shouldn't be watching this, given that you're flying back to Australia in a few days and I'm flying back to Turkey to work out what to do with the rest of my life." Masha smoked a cigarette out the open window of our small hotel room as snakes writhed around Samuel L. Jackson.

Wide-eyed, I said, "Maybe." But sprawled out on the bed, I was too gripped to change the channel.

It was early on Christmas morning by the time the films ended and we turned out the lights. I checked the time. It was 4 a.m. Brahmamuhurta: the Creator's Hour, as Ajit said, the time when prayers reach directly to the God.

"Merry Christmas," I said to Masha.

No reply. Her sleeping breaths formed a gentle rhythm while I sat under my covers, too wired to sleep. I rolled over, hoping to find a better position, and scissored my legs out into the white sheets of my single bed.

Within a second, I felt a tugging, stinging pain on my leg. Odd.

I reached down to find something adhered to my leg, like a piece of soft plastic, pierced into my skin somehow. Thinking nothing of it, I used two fingers to pry it off, rolled over, and tried again for sleep, but my leg began to radiate with burning pain. Really odd.

Not wanting to wake Masha, I used the flashlight on my phone to peer under the covers. The skin on my lower leg was beading up with two distinctive drops of blood, an inch apart.

Fang marks?

What the hell?

I scrambled up to the top of my bed and hit the room lights. Searching the sheets for a moving object, I saw nothing. Under the bright lights, I inspected my leg again and saw that the side of my calf had two unmistakable punctures.

A snake?

Really?

Did Russell just bite me?

In bed?

It seemed absurd, the stuff of peculiar dreams, only I was quite sure that I wasn't sleeping. I checked the bed for clues. Maybe a piece of plastic with a staple in it had punctured my skin, but I couldn't see anything in the bed, and, besides, I had merely stretched my leg out into the sheets. There wasn't enough pressure in that motion to push a staple into skin.

I did a quick tally of the circumstances: Masha had left the window open for much of the day while she smoked. Our hotel was under construction—maybe the jackhammering would displace snakes. Maybe one came in the window. Maybe I was going to die now. Maybe *Melancholia* followed by *Snakes on a Plane* is a bad late-night double bill for a person with a history of horror movie PTSD.

Was this unreasonable panic? I checked in with my body. It felt calm. My pulse was steady. My mind was placid. These weren't the typical symptoms of anxiety. And yet it seemed unreasonable, so I didn't wake Masha. I knew how terrified of snakes she was, and waking someone with ophidiophobia on Christmas morning to say, "Surprise! There's a snake in our room!" is a very cruel gift indeed, one with enough power to trigger posttraumatic stress at holiday time—forever.

I chewed my lip over what to do, inspecting the wound again, going over the circumstances, deconstructing my logic, reassembling my logic, measuring my sanity, doing complex mathematical calculations in my mind of my possible death over the likelihood of inflicting psychological trauma on Masha, divided by the chances of getting bitten by a poisonous snake in a four-star hotel, multiplied by the square root of India.

I decided that I needed to wake her for an opinion.

"Masha," I whispered, trying to rouse her gently.

Nothing.

"Mas*shhhhhhhhh*aa."

Her eyes cracked open and, annoyed, she said, "What?"

I said, "Look at my leg."

"Huh?"

"My leg. It's bleeding."

Her bloodshot eyes made their way to my calf, dazed and indifferent. And then she vaulted into a standing position on her bed, crying, "HOLYSHITISTHATASNAKEBITE?!"

Still whispering, I said, "I don't know. Is that even possible?"

"ISTHEREASNAKEINOURROOM?"

"Perhaps?"

Her limbs were jelly as she danced on her bed, eyes dashing around the floor for signs of a tail.

As calm as can be, I said, "What do you think I should do?"

Her expression sobered. "Get some clothes on, DeRoche." She surprised me by jumping off the bed and onto the snakey floor to pull a sweater and skirt on over her pajamas. "We are going to a hospital *now.*"

30

"SIR? HELLO? EXCUSE me?" Masha said.

There were two men in the hotel reception, both dead asleep on the reception couches in their hotel uniforms, unresponsive and mouths ajar.

We stood over one of them as Masha tried to stir him from sleep. "Sir? Hello? Sir?"

His eyes shot open.

"I'm sorry to wake you, but I think something has bitten my friend," she said, urging me to hold my wound up to his field of vision. I pulled up my pants.

He gazed at my leg with bloodshot, unseeing eyes, looking like he was still inside the thrilling arc of an action-adventure dream. Maybe we were *all* inside the thrilling arc of an action-adventure dream.

"I think something has bitten me," I said, raising my voice and hoping to rouse him from dreamland. "It looks a little bit like fang marks."

He rubbed his eyes and stared at my leg, swaying slightly. He let out a big yawn and smacked his lips. "Fangs?"

"It looks like a snakebite," I said. "See?" I pointed to the two dots of blood.

"No, no, no, not a snake," he said, bobbling his head with slight amusement.

When the other man came over to have a look, he agreed: "No, no, not a snake."

"Well, then, do you know what might have bitten her?" Masha pointed at the two pin dots of blood. "It looks like fangs, don't you think? Could it be an insect, maybe?"

"No, no, no, not a snake. Impossible. A snake cannot get into your hotel room."

"But we've had the window in our room open all day." I pointed to Masha. "She's been smoking out the window."

He sprang off the couch and said, "We go to hospital *now*."

✦

The night was chilly, the dark streets cloaked in fog.

"It's not a long walk to the hospital," said the hotel clerk. "Please follow me."

Masha led the way, tugging me behind her to rush me toward help. Shapes stirred from doorways and footpaths, and homeless men scowled from under their shawls, roused by our presence in their domain. Dogs unfurled from rest. Creatures stretched. As more and more sets of eyes began to blink from the shadows, we hurried our pace. This was no time to be out on the Mumbai streets.

I thought of the yogi's words. What on earth was "lucky" about this situation?

The hospital was an old converted government building—a large, unlit warehouse that echoed with the sounds of the sick coughing into the void. Equipment sat abandoned in corners—wheelchairs, steel trolleys, science beakers, empty glass tinctures. Bird poo was streaked down the walls from all the nests in the ceiling. People rested in corners, under blankets that shook with coughing and moaning; their nondescript bodies forming small lumps in the darkness. I wasn't sure if they were sick or homeless, but if I had to take a guess I would say both.

We were ushered into the doctor's office. It was lit by a shock of fluorescent lighting that punched me in the retinas.

"How can I help you?" said the doctor. He had a gaggle of young interns surrounding him, all thick spectacles and pens scribbling in notebooks. Their white coats and stethoscopes looked too large. That there were so many people crushed into a small room in the middle of the night made me feel as if I'd awoken into some kind of art house Indian dark comedy. There was a pharmacist in the corner of the room, face on desk and sound asleep.

"I think something bit me," I told the doctor. I pulled up the leg of my pants to show him the bite. "I was lying in bed when I felt a little sting on my leg, and I reached down and tugged off something that felt like plastic, and when I looked down I saw these marks. It's burning a little bit around the bite. Do you know what it might be? It looks a lot like fang marks, and so I thought I should come here to get it looked at."

He glanced at the wound and then back into my eyes. "No, that's not a snakebite." Interns' pencils scribbled notes.

"Okay, good. Well, do you think maybe something else bit me? Because I couldn't find anything on the bed and—"

"It's not a snakebite," he chuckled. He looked amused, as if I were a terrified traveler who had just landed in Mumbai, who mistook every piece of rope or string for a deadly snake. Five sets of baffled eyes blinked at us.

"We've just walked the entire length of Gandhi's Salt March," I explained to the doctor. "We slept on ashram floors, in temples, and in people's homes."

"Okay? . . ."

"We've been walking for almost a month. On foot. Through farms and long grass and into traffic and . . . and, well, I just want you to know that so you don't think I'm being alarmist." As soon as you start to think that people believe you're crazy, you start sounding crazy.

"Okay? . . ."

Time was ticking on. Precious venom-spreading time. Time that might result in the onset of heart palpitations, breathlessness, bleeding gums, or the reversal of puberty. I abandoned that approach. "So anyway, I came here because the bite marks seem odd, our window was open, and the hotel clerk also thought it would be a good idea to see a doctor just in case."

"Calm down, ma'am."

"I'm very calm, thank you." Strangely, I was as calm as a sloth on Xanax. I turned to Masha. "Am I being calm?"

"You're super-calm! Weirdly calm!" Masha took over. "Can you tell us what has bitten my friend?"

"We have antivenin right here." He pointed to his drug guy, who was nose to the desk and snoring.

"Antivenin?" Masha said, looking at me.

"But don't you need to know what type of snake it was to give the right antivenin?"

"Please tell your friend to calm down, ma'am."

"She is calm. We're just trying to understand what is happening."

"We have antivenin."

Masha looked at me and then back at the doctor, trying to make sense of the situation. "So just to be clear, you think maybe it *was* a snake?"

"No."

"Okay," I said, "so what could've bitten me, then? Maybe a rat or a bat or some kind of insect?"

"Calm down, ma'am."

I turned back to Masha. "Am I not being calm? Because I feel like I'm being calm; I really do."

"You're totally calm!"

"This whole situation is very weird, right?"

"I have no idea what is happening!"

"Maybe we shouldn't have watched *Snakes on a Plane*. And *Melancholia* was probably a bad choice too, because—"

"Shhh, DeRoche. This isn't helping." She turned to the doctor and slowed her voice to a drawl, ultra-calm and composed. "Today we had the window of our hotel room open all day, and the hotel is under construction. They're pulling off tiles at the moment and we thought maybe this could disrupt snakes and send them into the hotel, through the open window. We're wondering if maybe you could just look at the marks and consider that as a possibility. I'm not saying it absolutely is a snakebite, and I realize it seems absurd to be bitten in bed by a snake at 4 a.m." She paused for a short self-deprecating laugh, to try to sell our sanity. "But to be extra-careful, we thought we would come here and have you take a look on the off-chance that it's something poisonous."

His head bobbled as he said, once again, "It's not a snakebite."

"Okay, so . . . "

"We have antivenin."

"But why would we need antivenin if it's definitely not a snakebite?"

"Calm down."

The interns had stopped scribbling in their notebooks. They stood there in a semi-circle, blinking at us. Under the bright glow of fluorescent lights, I felt embarrassingly Western.

Masha turned to me. "What is happening, Torre? Are we still asleep or something?"

"I've been wondering the same thing." I turned back to the doctor and tried one more time. "So if this isn't a snake, then what do you think it is?"

The doctor replied, "Ma'am, please go with your friend and sit in the waiting room for twenty minutes." He turned to me.

"Pay attention to your body and monitor your symptoms. If anything changes, then come back immediately." He pointed again to the unconscious pharmacist. "He has antivenin."

I looked at Masha and shrugged. She shrugged back. That was that. There was nothing else we could do, bite or no bite, so we walked out of the doctor's office and back into the dark space of the warehouse, where we sat in orange plastic seats among the sleeping mounds of coughing blankets.

I scanned my body for changes. There was something unusual happening: I was deeply, uncharacteristically calm. My mind was still. My pulse steady. As I waited for the deadly toxins to roll through my body—or not—I drifted into the state of flow I'd mastered during the pilgrimages.

We'd walked through dark woods, past wild boars and vipers, along single-lane roads with fast-moving traffic; we'd inhaled toxic fumes all day and walked headlong into rickety trucks, past lurking Russell's vipers, rabid dogs foaming at the mouth, men gaping with fascination. I'd survived all this without illness, injury, or even a blister, but then, in a four-star American-style hotel, a snakebite?

This was it. I was facing death, though not in a way I'd ever anticipated. That I had spent thirty-four years of my life mentally writing a survival guide for every imaginable scenario seemed not only absurd now, but also hilarious, because who could ever anticipate something like *this*?

I'd feared monsters and ghouls, carnivorous couches, and electric Jacuzzis. In cinemas I watched exits instead of films. On planes I watched engines for smoke. In bed I watched shadows for teeth, and in the woods I couldn't see the forest for all the possible murders.

But this?

This situation was hilarious, because I actually believed I could prevent disaster if only I just worried long and hard enough. Ha! Every day, no matter where we live in the world, we graze shoulders with unfathomable amounts of risk. Driving in cars. Disease. Killer robots. Catastrophic climate change. Nuclear war. Germ warfare. Corrupt politics. Genocide . . . Some people are born into the wrong country or race at the wrong time, and *bang, bang*: dead. Some people are born into an affluent country at a peaceful time, but then a dictator comes along and flips the script. Nobody is safe. Being born is dangerous. The unfolding of the future is always so uncertain, the variables so vastly huge. And given that the only thing we can ever truly control is how we feel inside ourselves, and given that living in a state of fear doesn't feel good, worry is useless.

What if, what if, what if . . .

What if I had wasted my whole entire life being afraid?

Peace seeped through me like warm chocolate. I felt so light and unburdened that I could float away.

"Are you okay?" Masha asked. "Any symptoms?"

I looked at her and smiled. In my orange hospital chair, my body started to convulse—with laughter.

✦

Twenty minutes later I was not dead. The hotel clerk walked us back to the hotel and gave us a new room key. In this room, we kept the window closed. The sun was coming up as we changed back into pajamas.

"Masha, what the hell just happened?"

"I think you just got bitten by a snake in India on Christmas Day."

"Did Santa just bring me a snakebite?"

"Torre, I have no idea about anything anymore. And honestly? I think I'm okay with that."

In our queen-sized bed, we crawled under the covers, and Masha wrapped her arms around my shoulders and pulled me into her spoon.

"I want to make sure you don't have a seizure," she said, gripping tight. "I'll be right here until you fall asleep."

"Thank you for taking care of me."

"Torre, I love you more than 99.9999999 percent of the population. I feel like our friendship was written in the cosmos a billion years ago. Of course I would take care of you, even if it means facing snakes. I couldn't have walked through India without you. I think I would've died. You saved my life by being here with me, and I won't let you die on my watch."

"We are very lucky to be alive, aren't we?"

"We are."

"A very Merry Christmas . . . "

" . . . very, very, Merry, Merry Christmas . . . "

" . . . to you."

Epilogue

Snakes Are the New Guests at Mumbai 5-Star Hotels

Midday.com

The Haffkine Institute in Parel has been receiving numerous requests from major hotels recently, for their premises to be made "snake-free." "In the last few years, there has been a steep rise in construction activity, forcing these reptiles out of their habitats. We suspect that the need for refuge and the availability of prey is forcing the snakes to seek shelter in the hotel premises. Also, there are huge quantities of garbage in the city's bigger hotels, an environment in which rodents thrive. And with rodents come snakes," said Dr. Abhay Chaudhary, director of Haffkine Institute. According to researchers in the Zoonosis department of the institute, three species of venomous snakes are common in the city: the Cobra, the Krait, and Russell's viper.

After finding this article online, I found a snake handler operating out of Mumbai and emailed him with my strange query:

> *Hi, Kedar,*
> *I found you via an Internet search about snakes in Mumbai.*
> *I'm contacting you because, when I was in Mumbai at the end*
> *of last year, I was bitten by something in a hotel room bed that I*

can only assume was a snake because of the shape and size of the mark left on my leg. We'd had the window open during the day and the hotel was under construction. No snake turned up in the hotel manager's search so we were unable to know for sure.

Obviously I am alive and uninjured, but for the sake of getting to the truth, I'm trying to explore this further. I'm wondering if you will take a look at the photo of my bite and give your expert advice on the situation?

Dear Torre,
Please send the image, will reply as per my ability. With all the description you have given, it may end up in Rat bite. Also give detail about Hotel as which part of town it's located, etc.

Dear Kedar,
Pictures attached. I don't think it was a rat because I felt something "stuck" to my leg and when I reached down to pry it off with my fingers, it felt like plastic. I used my finger to kind of wedge it off. I thought it was plastic, but then it started to burn a little bit and I looked down to see if it was a bite of some sort. Two clean holes were beading up with blood. The wound marks were very clean. I didn't take these photos until an hour or two later, after I'd gone over to the hospital. (The doctor didn't know what it was either.)
The hotel was [Omitted for privacy].
Thank you so much.

Hi, Torre,
With the distance between marks, the snake would need to be really huge to leave these marks, so I don't think it's snakebite. And as you did not experience any symptoms of pain and other things, I doubt about it. The only other thing I can think about is Centipede if not Rat.

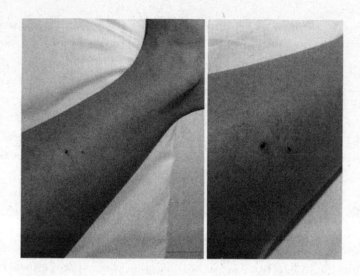

Hi, Kedar,
I don't think it was a rat or a centipede because of how it felt
under my fingers when I touched it. Hmm. Thanks. I appreciate
your opinion.

We still don't know what happened in that Mumbai hotel room, but the truth of it doesn't change anything. For as long as I can remember, I used to wake up every morning with my heart pounding, hands trembling from an omnipresent dread, worry jackhammering in my mind. I believed people were in danger, that the earth was in peril, and that running through all the possible What Ifs could keep me safe, but now I know that worry is the obnoxious, maniacal person in a burning house who is running around screaming, "We're all going to die!" when it's Calm that will fill buckets with water and call the fire brigade and remember to grab the family dog. Calm is my baseline these days, and it's much more peaceful without all that panicked screaming in the background.

Not long after I returned to Melbourne, the brick town-house right next door to my sister Summer's house became available for rent. At the inspection, I wandered around in the space and felt a familiar, irresistible coziness. I moved in. Summer loved her key ring. I haven't traveled since. Once, out of habit, I clicked on an advertisement for an airline sale and scanned through all the destinations before closing the browser window, knowing that there was nowhere on earth more appealing than where I've set my roots.

Ajit decided to pursue his dream of becoming a freelance photographer. He works as a photojournalist and activist who captures compelling human-focused stories through his art-work, shooting for organizations like the National Founda-tion for India, Indo-Global Social Service Society, Greenpeace, Oxfam, and CBM India. You can see his work at cargocollective .com/ajitbhadoriya. He says he misses walking—and us—but not enough to consider walking that route ever again. Masha and I agreed that we would never want to walk that route again either.

As for Masha: Well, that is her story to tell. At the time of this writing, a year and a half has passed since she finished her pil-grimages and, of course, she has much to share. She's a woman of incredible wisdom and unconditional love, and one day I look forward to reading her story. You can find her at unlikely pilgrim.com.

We've decided that one year we will spend Christmas together, where, in keeping with the new tradition, we will acquire a snake, put a little Santa hat on its head and a festive stocking on its tail, release it into our room, and see who gets lucky.

Acknowledgments

A BIG THANKS TO my wonderful editor Stephanie Knapp and the Seal Press team, as well as my agent Kari Stuart at ICM; I wanted to mix the theme of death with a touch of light comedy, and those two said: "Hey, great idea!" To Elizabeth Evans for nurturing this story in its development stages and for having the special power of getting me to believe in my ideas for long enough to get words on the page. To my early readers for their time and honesty: Pia Blair, Stephan Skov, Christian White, Karen Charlton, Moira Henrich, and the DeRoches: Monique, Tassy, Bree, Abra, and Summer. To my mother, Christina, for the many dinner-table therapy sessions over wine and the philosophical morning chats over coffees, and for always assuring me that it's a completely sane life choice to wear a robe for most of the day while disclosing the details of your personal life to complete strangers in the form of memoir. That woman has made a lot of things possible for a lot of people with her generosity, sense of humor, smarts, and unconditional love. To those always available to offer wisdom, warmth, wine, or all of the above: Jake Lawton, Rebecca Dalla Rosa, Stephan Skov, Jimmy Dau, Chris Khalil, the Kaponay family, Karen Charlton and Bruce Charlton, Moira Henrich, Phil Thompson, Dayna Warren, Candy Edwards, Mitty, Frida, and my family. To Jodi Ettenberg for her twin brain and her constant love and support. To Ajit, for embracing the unknown with us, for his insights and artistic vision, and for drinking all the tap water to save our bellies. And finally, to Chai Baby Masha Vapnitchnaia: There would be no story here without her profound love for the world and its people. Masha, you're an incredible inspiration, and I adore you as a friend, a writer, an unlikely pilgrim, and a human being.

About the Author

Torre DeRoche has been published in the Lonely Planet travel-writing anthologies *An Innocent Abroad* and *True Stories from the World's Best Writers*, alongside Cheryl Strayed, Dave Eggers, and many others. Her work has appeared in the *Atlantic*, the *Guardian Travel*, *Sydney Morning Herald*, and more. Her blog Fearful Adventurer (fearfuladventurer.com) has been profiled on the National Geographic Traveler website and hellogiggles.com as well as various other sites around the world. She lives in Melbourne, Australia.